Quiet Water
MAINE

Canoe & Kayak Guide
2nd Edition

Welcome to the AMC!

Founded in 1876, we are America's oldest conservation and recreation organization. We promote the protection, enjoyment, and wise use of the mountains, rivers, and trails of the Appalachian region. The Appalachian Mountain Club has twelve chapters from Maine to Washington, DC, comprised of 90,000 outdoor enthusiasts like you.

Just by purchasing this book you have contributed to our efforts to protect the Northeast outdoors. Proceeds from the sales of AMC Books and Maps support our land conservation efforts from the Maine Woods to the Mid-Atlantic Highlands and everywhere in between; trail building and maintenance; air- and water-quality research; and environmental education programs for school-age children, at-risk youth, and outdoor enthusiasts.

We encourage everyone to enjoy and appreciate the natural world because we believe that successful conservation depends on such experiences. So join us in the outdoors! Bring your friends and family. The AMC offers hiking, paddling, biking, skiing, and mountaineering activities for outdoor adventurers of every level and age. For more information about AMC membership, destinations, and conservation and education programs, turn to the back of this book or visit the AMC online at www.outdoors.org.

We're glad you're a part of our community, and we wish you fun and safe adventures, now and always.

Quiet Water
MAINE

Canoe & Kayak Guide
2nd Edition

Alex Wilson & John Hayes

APPALACHIAN MOUNTAIN CLUB BOOKS
BOSTON, MASSACHUSETTS

Front Cover Photograph: *Colorful Forest on the Shore of a Lake* © Corbis
Back Cover Photographs: *Still Kayaker* © Jerry & Marcy Monkman
                     Moose © Jerry & Marcy Monkman,www.EcoPhotography.com
                     Angler in Wooden Canoe © John McKeith
Cover Design: Mac & Dent
Interior Design: Amy Winchester
Map Design: Vanessa Gray; 1st Edition—Nadav Malin, John Sawers, and John Catlin
Illustrations: Marrin Robinson
All interior photographs by the authors unless otherwise noted.

Quiet Water Maine: Canoe & Kayak Guide, 2nd Edition © 1995, 2005 Alex Wilson &
John Hayes. All rights reserved.

Distributed by The Globe Pequot Press, Inc., Guilford, CT

Library of Congress Cataloging-in-Publication Data
Wilson, Alex.
Quiet water Maine : canoe and kayak guide / Alex Wilson and John Hayes.—2nd ed.
   p. cm.
Rev. ed. of: Quiet water canoe guide, Maine. c1995.
ISBN 1-929173-65-2 (alk. paper)
1. Canoes and canoeing—Maine—Guidebooks. 2. Lakes—Maine—Guidebooks.
3. Ponds—Maine—Guidebooks. 4. Maine—Guidebooks. I. Hayes, John. II. Wilson,
Alex. Quiet water canoe guide, Maine. III. Title.

GV776.M2W55 2005
797.122'09741—dc22

                                                2005005493

The paper used in this publication meets the minimum requirements of the American
National Standard for Information Science—Permanence of Paper for Printed
Library Materials, ANSI Z39.48—1984. ∞

**Due to changes in conditions, use of the
information in this book is at the sole risk of the user.**

Printed on recycled paper using soy-based inks.
Printed in the United States of America.

10 9 8 7 6 5 4 3 2 1   05 06 07 08 09

I want to go soon and live away by the pond, where I
shall hear only the wind whispering among the reeds.
It will be success if I shall have left myself behind.
But my friends ask what I shall do when I get there.
Will it not be employment enough to watch the
progress of the seasons?

—Henry David Thoreau

Locator Map

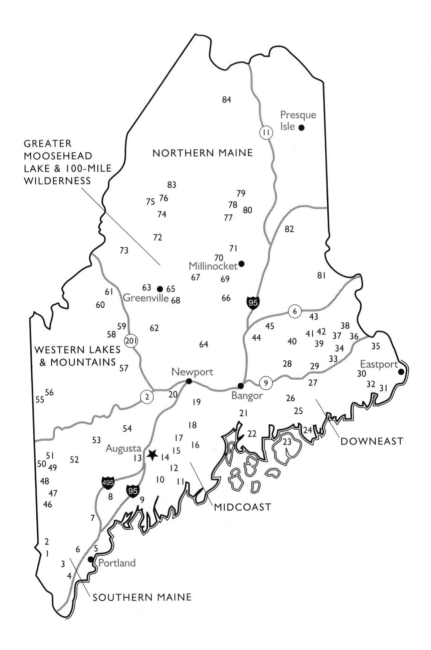

84

Presque
Isle ●

(11)

GREATER
MOOSEHEAD
LAKE & 100-MILE
WILDERNESS

NORTHERN MAINE

83
75 76
74
72
73

79
78 80
77

82

71
70
67   69

Millinocket ●

81

63 ● 65
61   Greenville 68
60

66

(95)

59
58   62
(201)

64

(6)   43
45   41 42   38
44   40   37 36
39   34
33   35
28   29   30   Eastport ●
32 31

WESTERN LAKES
& MOUNTAINS   57

Newport

26

27

DOWNEAST

56
55 56

(2)   20
19

(9)
Bangor ●

25

24

54

18
17
16

21

22

23

53

Augusta ★   15
13   14
12

51
50 49   52

10   11

48
47
46

(495)
8   (95)
9

MIDCOAST

7

2
1

6   5

3   ● Portland

4

SOUTHERN MAINE

Contents

Map Legend

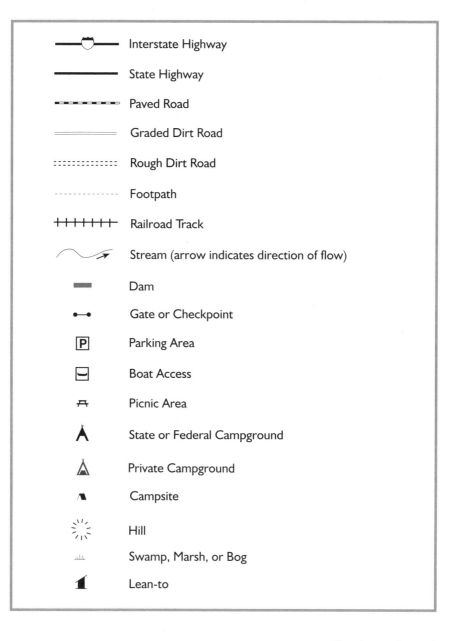

	Interstate Highway
	State Highway
	Paved Road
	Graded Dirt Road
	Rough Dirt Road
	Footpath
	Railroad Track
	Stream (arrow indicates direction of flow)
	Dam
	Gate or Checkpoint
P	Parking Area
	Boat Access
	Picnic Area
	State or Federal Campground
	Private Campground
	Campsite
	Hill
	Swamp, Marsh, or Bog
	Lean-to

Preface to the Second Edition

The first edition of the *Quiet Water Canoe Guide: Maine,* published in 1995, was the third in a series that now includes guides to New Hampshire and Vermont; Massachusetts, Connecticut, and Rhode Island; New York; and New Jersey.

The first edition enjoyed great success, but lake and pond descriptions inevitably go out of date. Also, we took this opportunity to add new material, including six new trips: Flagstaff Lake; Chesuncook Lake and West Branch Penobscot River; Josh Stream and Josh Pond; Big Musquash Stream; Big Lake, Clifford Stream, Little River, and Little Musquash Stream; and Long Pond on AMC's Katahdin Iron Works property in the 100-Mile Wilderness.

We rechecked the original bodies of water to ensure that new housing developments had not crowded the shores, and we revised directions to reflect new road names. When possible, we tried to avoid bodies of water with substantial development, but for the most part, we worried more about the effect of personal watercraft and high-speed boating on safety, the quiet-water experience, and the environment.

Through publication of this expanded guide, we hope to draw attention to the need to preserve these wonderful places. All quiet-water paddlers should work together at local and state levels to bring added protection to these precious resources.

Acknowledgments

For the second edition, we owe a great debt of gratitude to Leslie Turpin and Evan Griffith, who revisited many of these lakes, helping us to update information and to improve the access directions, and to cartographer Vanessa Gray, who drew the new maps and updated the existing maps. We also thank AMC Books Editor-in-Chief Sarah Jane Shangraw, Production Manager Belinda Thresher, and their associates Eric Edstam, Mike Burdon, and Athena Lakri for their contributions to improving the look and content of this edition.

Acknowledgments from the first edition: For the opportunity to paddle so many gorgeous spots, we are grateful to the Appalachian

Mountain Club and especially to its former editor, Gordon Hardy. While the authors alone accept responsibility for any incorrect information, we received assistance from many people, and to them we offer our sincerest thanks.

We thank our families for their understanding: Jerelyn, Lillian, and Frances Wilson; Joanne, Andrew, and Stefanie Hayes. Thanks to our close friends who joined us on research expeditions, put us up overnight, or offered tips on great paddling spots: Malcolm, Karen, Randy, and Kirsten George; Sally Andrews; Jet Thomas; Wyatt Wade; Joseph Kahn; John Nevins and Cherrie Corey; Bob Engel; Randy Knaggs; Malcolm Moore; Caleb Wilson; Nadav Malin; Allyn and Mary Copp; Russell Heath; and Philip Demay. Plus, a special thanks to Ted and Andy Crowley, who kept the Wilson research team warm and dry and entertained two young daughters on a cold, rainy day on Sysladobsis Lake, and to the Hatt family on Round Pond who did the same for the Hayes research team.

Thanks to the professional Maine Guides and recreation professionals who offered advice during the project: Don Kleiner of Maine Outdoors and the Maine Professional Guides Association, Martin Brown of Sunrise Country Canoe Expeditions, Garrett and Alexandra Conover of North Woods Ways, Eddie Raymond of Katahdin Outfitters, Darrell Whittaker of Whittaker Camps, Rick LeVasseur of Katahdin Shadows Campground and Penobscot River Outfitters, Kevin Harding of the Downeast Outdoor Recreation School, Larry McIntosh of Wildwater Outfitters, Craig Ten Broeck of the Maine Bureau of Public Lands, Howard Weymouth of Bowater–Great Northern Paper, and Al Cowperthwaite of North Maine Woods.

For information on Maine's wildlife, we thank Sally Stockwell of the Maine Audubon Society, Maury Mills of the Moosehorn National Wildlife Refuge, Molly Docherty of the State of Maine Natural Areas Program, and Karen Morris of the Maine Department of Inland Fisheries and Wildlife.

For assistance with our map research we thank Floyd Merritt of the Robert Frost Library at Amherst College and Dr. Klaus Bayer of Keene State College. For the meticulous work of drawing maps we thank Nadav Malin, John Sawers, and John Catlin. For skillful photographic printing we thank Sheila Roth. For the wildlife illustrations, we are deeply indebted to Marrin Robinson.

Introduction to Quietwater Paddling

Maine's quiet waters—its hidden treasures—receive much less attention than its famous rivers. Indeed, Maine offers some of the finest paddling in the eastern United States on the Allagash, St. John, Penobscot West Branch, Kennebec, Androscoggin, Machias, and Saco rivers. Many people overlook the superb paddling opportunities on hundreds of quiet lakes, ponds, and estuaries—the subject of this book.

The peaceful solitude of out-of-the-way lakes and ponds lures us to quietwater paddling. This guide will lead you to wood ducks and hooded mergansers swimming through early morning mists; the playful antics of a river otter in crystal-clear, pine tree–bounded lakes; the thrill of spotting moose—mouth full of pondweeds—as you round a bend in a winding inlet channel; the fascinating morphology of pitcher plants and the diminutive sundew; and the loon's plaintive wail wafting off the water as afternoon settles into dusk.

With quietwater paddling, you can focus on *being* there instead of *getting* there. You don't need a lot of fancy high-tech gear—though a light canoe or kayak makes portaging over beaver dams a lot easier. Binoculars and field guides to fauna and flora make up our most important gear.

This guide will not only lead you to a body of water but also describe why you might want to paddle it. Generally, we tried to include places that have abundant wildlife or extensive marshlands or beautiful scenery; most entries have all three. We hope that our research will allow you to spend your valuable time paddling, instead of driving around for hours trying to find elusive accesses. We designed the AMC Quiet Water Guides for paddlers of all experience levels, to help you better enjoy our wonderful water resources.

The Selection Process

This guide includes only a small percentage of Maine's lakes, ponds, estuaries, and slow-flowing rivers. In our selection process, we looked for great scenery; limited development; few motorboats; a varied shoreline with lots of coves and inlets to explore; and interesting plants, animals, and geological formations.

We include a variety of water types: big lakes and rivers for longer excursions, and small, protected ponds and marshes for when you have limited time or when weather conditions preclude paddling larger bodies of water. To make the book as useful as possible, we paid particular attention to lakes and ponds in the more populated regions of the state, even though many more locations in remote parts of eastern and northern Maine better fit our standards for what is an ideal paddling spot.

We found these spots by asking people about the best places to paddle; by consulting maps from DeLorme's *Maine Atlas and Gazetteer*, North Maine Woods, and Bowater–Great Northern Paper; and by systematically searching the 600-plus U.S. Geological Survey (USGS) 7.5-minute topographic maps of the state.

Though we tried to include the very best places to paddle, we doubtless have missed some really good locations. If you have suggestions of other lakes and ponds to include, please let us know (Alex Wilson or John Hayes, c/o AMC Books, 5 Joy Street, Boston, MA 02108).

Safety, Equipment, and Technique

We all long for the idyllic paddle on mist-filled, mirror-smooth surfaces of quiet ponds at daybreak. But if you spend any time at all paddling Maine's lakes and tidal rivers, you will also encounter quite dangerous conditions. Estuaries can have swift tides that, coupled with wind, can be very dangerous. On larger bodies of water, strong winds can arise quickly, whipping up two- to four-foot waves in no time— waves big enough to swamp an open boat. If you capsize in cold water far from shore, hypothermia—a cooling of the body's core that can lead to mental and physical collapse—can set in quickly. If you have just driven a long way to reach a particular lake and find it dangerously windy, choose a more protected body of water, or go hiking instead.

Safety First

All New England states require each boater to carry a U.S. Coast Guard–approved (Type I, II, or III) personal flotation device, or PFD. A good PFD keeps a person's face above water, even after losing consciousness. Children ten and under must wear their PFDs, and they must be the right size so that they will not slip off; adult PFDs are not acceptable for children so that if the boat capsizes you can help them better. Although the law does not require adults to wear PFDs, we strongly recommend that you do so, especially when paddling with children. A foam- or kapok-filled PFD will also keep you warmer in cold water. If you do not normally paddle wearing a PFD, at least don it in windy conditions, when crossing large lakes, or when you may encounter substantial motorboat wakes. It could save your life.

You should also bring along a waterproof first-aid kit. The best kit is one that you assemble yourself; make sure that it has bandages or moleskin for blisters, an antihistamine for allergic reactions, sunscreen, an extra hat, a pain reliever, and any special medications that you might require.

As for clothing, plan for the unexpected. Even with a sunny-day forecast, a shower can appear by afternoon. On trips of more than a few hours, we bring along rain gear and dry clothes in a waterproof stuff sack

On a rainy-day paddle, usually you see more wildlife and fewer boaters.

as a matter of course. Along with rain coming up unexpectedly, temperatures can drop quickly, especially in the spring or fall, making conditions ripe for hypothermia. Lightweight nylon or polypropylene clothing dries more quickly than cotton, and wool still retards heat loss when wet. Remember that heads lose heat faster than torsos—bring a hat.

Avoid shallow, marshy waters during waterfowl-hunting season. For hunting-season dates, check the Maine Department of Inland Fisheries and Wildlife website: www.state.me.us/ifw.

Other safety issues include:
- Getting off the water during lightning storms—lightning almost always strikes the highest object in the vicinity, which would be you in a boat out on a lake
- Knowing what to do and having experience doing it if you capsize
- Avoiding dehydration by drinking plenty of liquids
- Avoiding areas with a lot of high-speed boating
- Checking the weather forecast before going out

Paddling with Kids

When canoeing with kids, try to make it fun, and keep calm. Even though you may be plenty warm from paddling, children may get cold while sitting in the bottom of the boat. Remember that everyone should have PFDs on at all times, and PFDs will help keep children warm. They also need protection from sun and biting insects. Watch for signs of discomfort. Set up a cozy place where young children can sleep; after the initial excitement of paddling fades, a gently rolling canoe often puts children to sleep, especially near the end of a long day. Also, for those longer excursions, make sure to bring dry clothes for everyone in a waterproof stuff sack.

Equipment

For quietwater paddling, most any canoe or sea kayak will do, but avoid high-performance racing or tippy whitewater models. Borrow a boat before buying; selection will be easier with a little experience.

Whether canoe or kayak, look for a model with good initial and secondary stability. A boat with good initial stability and poor secondary stability will tip slowly, but once it starts it may keep going. The best canoes for lakes and ponds have a keel or shallow-V hull and fairly flat keel line to help track in a straight line, even in a breeze. Kayaks perform extremely well in rough water, particularly if equipped with a foot-operated rudder and a sprayskirt to keep from taking on water.

If you like out-of-the-way paddling requiring portages, get a Kevlar boat if you can afford it. Kevlar is a strong, lightweight carbon fiber. We paddle a rugged, high-capacity, 18' 4" Mad River Lamoille canoe that weighs just 60 pounds, a 15' 9" Mad River Independence solo canoe that weighs less than 40 pounds, a 14' Wenonah Wigeon kayak that weighs 38 pounds, and a 14' Wilderness Systems Chaika kayak that weighs 32 pounds. If you plan to go by yourself, consider a sea kayak or a solo canoe in which you sit (or kneel) close to the boat's center. You will find paddling a well-designed solo canoe far easier than a two-seater used solo. The touring or sea kayak—with its long, narrow design, low profile to the wind, and two-bladed paddling style—is faster and more efficient to paddle than canoes.

A padded portage yoke in place of the center thwart on a canoe is essential if you plan on much carrying. With unpadded yokes, wear a life vest with padded shoulders. Attach a rope—called a "painter"—to the bow so that you can secure the boat when you stop for lunch, line it up or down a stream, and—if the need ever arises—grab onto it in an emergency. We both have embarrassing stories about not using a painter to secure the boat—wind can cause Kevlar boats to disappear very quickly!

Choose light and comfortable paddles. For canoeing, we use a relatively short (50-inch), bent-shaft paddle. Laminated from various woods, the paddle has a special synthetic tip to protect the blade. Bent-shaft paddles allow more efficient paddling, because the downward force converts more directly into forward thrust. However, straight-shaft paddles also work well. Always carry at least one spare paddle per group, particularly on longer trips, in case a porcupine gets a hold of one.

Paddling Technique

On a quiet pond, does it matter if you use the proper J-stroke, the sweep stroke, or the draw? No. Learning some of these strokes, however, can make a day of paddling more relaxing and enjoyable. We watch lots of novices zigzagging along, frantically switching sides, shouting orders fore and aft. People have told us about marriage-counseling sessions devoted to paddling technique. . . .

If you are new to the sport and want to learn canoeing or kayaking techniques, buy a book or participate in a paddling workshop, such as those offered by the Appalachian Mountain Club, equipment retailers, and boat manufacturers. Books we recommend on canoeing are *Basic Essentials Canoeing*, 2nd ed., by Cliff Jacobson (Globe Pequot Press, 1999); and *Basic Essentials Canoe Paddling*, 2nd ed., by Harry Roberts and Steve Salins (Globe Pequot Press, 2000). For kayaking, good books include *The Essential Sea Kayaker*, 2nd ed., by David Seidman (International Marine Publishers, 2000); *Basic Book of Sea Kayaking* by Derek Hutchinson (Globe Pequot Press, 1999); and *Complete Book of Sea Kayaking*, 5th ed., by Derek Hutchinson (Falcon, 2004).

Start out on small ponds. Practice paddling into, with, and across the wind. On a warm day close to shore, with your PFD on and others to help you out of difficulties, you might want to practice capsizing. Intentionally tipping your canoe or kayak will give you an idea of how easily it can tip over. Try to get back into the boat when you are away from shore. Getting the water out of a kayak while treading water is impossible without a hand pump; you can mount one permanently on your boat or carry a portable one. You should be able to right a canoe with two people, getting most of the water out (keep a bailer *fastened* to a thwart). Getting back in is another story. . . . Good luck!

How to Use This Book

For each body of water, we have provided a short description, a map, some natural history, and other useful information.

Maps. If unfamiliar with your destination, you should use a good highway map or the DeLorme Mapping Company's *The Maine Atlas and Gazetteer*; www.delorme.com. We key each lake to the *Maine Atlas*, which divides the state into seventy 10" x 15" maps. These detailed, 1:125,000-scale maps include most—but not all—access locations, campsites, road names, campgrounds, parks, and other pertinent information. For more detail and information on topography, marsh areas, and so forth, refer to the 7.5-minute, 1:24,000-scale USGS topographic maps listed in each section.

Area and River Length. We include river lengths and areas of lakes and ponds to allow you to plan your trips better. Choose larger bodies of water and longer rivers when you have more time and a good weather forecast. Under windy conditions, paddle smaller bodies of water or rivers.

Camping. For many lakes and ponds, we show public campsite and campground locations. Refer to the introduction for information on camping and fire permits on private land, as well as for information on other lodging options. For information on private campgrounds, see the extensive list in the *Maine Atlas*.

Habitat Type. This section describes the type of environment that you will encounter. Most entries include substantial shallow-water marshlands.

Expect to See. Here we describe the predominant animals and the type of vegetation that you should see.

Take Note. This section describes any substantial development or hazards to avoid.

Getting There. We give directions from the nearest city or major highway to the access. We provide distances between points, with the cumulative distance given in parentheses. We assume that you will use a detailed highway map, such as DeLorme's *Maine Atlas*.

Stewardship and Conservation

Diverse wetlands—among the richest, readily accessible ecosystems—provide wonderful opportunities to learn about nature. You can visit saltwater tidal marshes; deep, crystal-clear mountain ponds; and unique bog habitats. You can observe hundreds of species of birds; dozens of mammal, insect, turtle, and snake species; and literally thousands of plants. Some quite rare species—such as a delicate bog orchid or a family of otters—provide a real treat when you observe them. But even ordinary plants and animals lead to exciting discoveries and can provide hours of enjoyable observation.

We have described a few interesting plants and animals that you might encounter. We interspersed these descriptions—and accompanying pen-and-ink illustrations by Marrin Robinson—throughout. By learning a little more about these species, we hope that you will find them more interesting to observe.

Do We Really Want to Tell People about the Best Places?

Many people have asked us how we could, in good conscience, tell others about the more remote, pristine places, still unspoiled by too many people—after all, increased visitation would make these places less idyllic. We spent many an hour grappling with this difficult issue as we paddled along. We believe that by getting more people out enjoying these places—people who value wild, remote areas—support will build for greater protection of these waters.

Maine's diverse wetlands—lakes, ponds, wooded swamps, bogs, fens, freshwater and salt marshes, brackish marshes, and floodplains—cover 25 percent, or more than 5 million acres, of its surface area, which is four times the wetland area of the other five New England states combined. Extremely important ecosystems, wetlands provide habitat for many rare and endangered species.

Even low-impact uses such as canoeing or kayaking can substantially affect fragile marsh habitat. An unaware paddler can disturb nesting loons and eagles, rare turtles, and fragile bog orchids. And even a canoe or kayak can carry invasive weeds and zebra mussels from one body of water to another—use care to clean off your boat before you visit other water bodies.

You can go even further than the old adage, "Take only photographs, leave only footprints." Carry along a trash bag and pick up the leavings of less thoughtful individuals. If each of us does the same, we will enjoy more attractive places to paddle. While motorboaters tend to have a bad reputation when it comes to leaving trash, paddlers should have the opposite reputation—which could come in handy when seeking restrictions on high-impact resource use.

For information on low-impact camping and other uses of fragile habitats, see *Soft Paths: How to Enjoy the Wilderness without Harming It*, 3rd ed., by Bruce Hampton and David Cole (Stackpole Books, 2003) or *Ultimate Guide to Backcountry Travel* by Michael Lanza (AMC Books, 1999). Also, visit Leave No Trace—an organization dedicated to teaching people how to have minimal impact on areas they visit—www.LNT.org.

Besides reducing our impact on the environment, we can actively work to protect it. Fragile bald eagle, osprey, otter, loon, and other wildlife populations need protection. If we care about preserving these species and their habitats for future generations, we will demand that elected and appointed officials make wildlife preservation and ecosystem protection a higher priority. We can also join conservation organizations—such as the AMC, Sierra Club, The Nature Conservancy, Maine Natural Resources Council, Maine Audubon, and many others—so that when those organizations speak about preserving the environment, their voices carry the weight of tens of thousands of like-minded members.

Public Access

Private land—mostly that of large paper companies—surrounds most of the wild lakes in eastern and northern Maine. Nearly all of these companies allow recreational use, for which we should be very thankful. In eastern and central Maine, access and camping are generally permitted at no cost. In some areas, you must obtain landowner permission to camp; never camp on land posted No Trespassing. You must also obtain a fire permit in most areas.

Since the first edition in 1995, Maine's forestlands have undergone tremendous change. After decades of stasis, punctuated by the sale of an occasional large parcel from one timber company to another, the announcement by SAPPI in 1998 that it would sell 905,000 acres of timberland triggered an unprecedented sell-off of northern forestlands. About 5.5 million acres, or nearly 30 percent, of northern Maine changed hands between 1998 and 2003; to put this into perspective, the 8,600 square miles sold is 2.5 times the size of Yellowstone National Park and equals the area of New Hampshire and of the Adirondack Forest Preserve. While some lands sold to The Nature Conservancy included conservation easements, the vastness of the sales from one timber company to another, to investment companies, or to land developers has galvanized the conservation community. In response to these changes in land ownership, the AMC in 2003 launched its Maine Woods Initiative, a land protection effort that balances outdoor recreation, education, conservation, and sustainable forestry in the 100-Mile Wilderness region. For more information, see "The Maine Woods" on page 246 of this book. In 3.5 million acres in northern Maine—roughly north of Moosehead Lake and west and north of Baxter State Park—North Maine Woods controls and charges fees for recreational access. Most of its 10 checkpoints open by 5:00 A.M., though some remain open 24 hours per day. For current operation hours and fees for camping and access, see www.northmainewoods.org, or call 207-435-6213. On these private roads, logging trucks have the right of way. We've seen tandem trucks barreling along these gravel roads, carrying mammoth log loads. Keep out of their way for safety reasons and out of courtesy to those who make their land available for our recreational use.

Fire Permits

Because Maine depends highly on forest products, the state takes great care to reduce fire risk. One does not need a fire permit in state parks and in private campgrounds; most other sites require permits. Designated campsites include two types: authorized campsites where you may carefully build a fire without a permit and fire-permit campsites where you must obtain a permit. Use of a camp stove does not require a permit.

To obtain a permit, contact the Maine Forest Service at the number listed in the trip write-up. *The Maine Atlas and Gazetteer* identifies authorized and permit campsites by closed and open tent symbols, respectively. Because the Maine Forest Service sometimes changes these designations, we recommend purchasing a new *Maine Atlas* periodically. We do not distinguish between the two types of campsites on the maps in this book.

Lodging Options

Along with camping on or near most bodies of water covered in this book, other lodging options often occur nearby. Information on inns is available from the Maine Innkeepers Association: www.maineinns.com.

In remote northern and eastern parts of the state, scattered sporting camps that hearken back to a bygone era offer comfort and protection from biting insects. Most sporting camps have five to twenty cabins and a central lodge for meals; some are set up for housekeeping. For information on sporting camps, refer to *Maine Sporting Camps: The Year-Round Guide to Vacationing at Traditional Hunting and Fishing Lodges*, 3rd ed. (Countryman, 2003), by Alice Arlen. A listing is also available from the Maine Sporting Camp Association: www.mainesportingcamps.com.

The Appalachian Mountain Club now runs one of the most spectacular and well-maintained Maine sporting camps: Little Lyford Pond Camps. Within 15 miles of Greenville and within 25 miles of Brownville, Maine, this camp features a dining lodge, a bunkhouse, and seven individual cabins, each with beds, a woodstove, and a porch overlooking the property. The Club maintains a boathouse with free use of canoes and kayaks on the Lyford Ponds. As part of its Maine Woods Initiative, the AMC maintains trails throughout the area, connecting its property to mountains of the 100-Mile Wilderness and nearby Gulf Hagas, a National Natural Landmark featuring miles of gorges and waterfalls. For more information and reservations, see www.outdoors.org/lodging, or call 603-466-2727.

Southern Maine

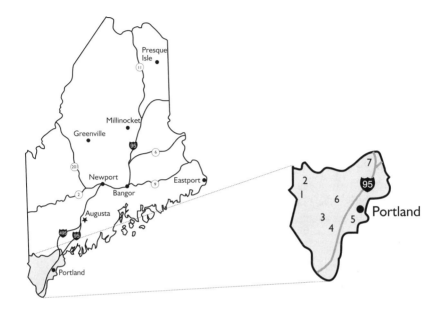

The most accessible region of Maine for out-of-staters, this area includes Portland and adjacent Casco Bay. Thirty miles of beautiful coastline extend from Kittery to South Orchard Beach, and lakes abound inland. Myriad activities await explorers in this well-traveled area. You can visit historical sites in the Yorks and climb Mount Agamenticus for a landscape-level view; Old Orchard Beach stretches for 7 miles and has whale-watching opportunities; Kennebunk has a working waterfront harbor; and Biddeford-Saco boasts the pristine Saco River, which offers unlimited, multiday paddling opportunities. Featured trips include little-traveled Mousam River (Trip 4), which meanders through a surprisingly undeveloped landscape; and Scarborough Marsh (Trip 5), with 31,000 acres of marshland, including 15 percent of Maine's salt marsh.

Salmon Falls River
Acton

> **MAPS:** Maine Atlas, Map 2
> USGS Quadrangle, Great East Lake
> **RIVER LENGTH:** 2 miles
> **HABITAT TYPE:** shallow weedy river, forested shores
> **FISH:** smallmouth bass
> **EXPECT TO SEE:** acres of pickerelweed, other aquatic vegetation,
> kingfisher, ducks, beaver in evening
> **TAKE NOTE:** barely submerged boulders near the dam

GETTING THERE

From Milton Mills, New Hampshire, with the U.S. Post Office on your right, go straight uphill (north) for 0.3 mile (0.3 mile), turn right onto Hopper Road, and go 0.5 mile (0.8 mile) to the access, just over the bridge on the left. Go 0.5 mile (1.3 miles) to a second access that avoids the backyards and submerged boulders.

From Sanford, Maine, go northwest on Routes 11 and 109. Where Routes 11 and 109 split, go west on Route 109 for 3.6 miles (3.6 miles), and take a shallow left onto Sam Page Road. Go 0.2 mile (3.8 miles), and turn left onto Hopper Road. Go 3.1 miles (6.9 miles) to the access on the right. The boulder- and backyard-free access is 0.5 mile back (6.4 miles).

The Salmon Falls River forms the boundary between lower Maine and New Hampshire. Though a small stream for most of its considerable length, in Milton Mills a dam widens it to paddleable proportions.

Although this section of the river runs for only about two miles, if you paddle here it will seem much longer. The channel meanders aimlessly through endless acres of aquatic vegetation, with some beautiful patches of floating heart, with its diminutive waterlily-like leaves. The huge amount of underwater structure supports healthy fish populations, with some huge smallmouth bass lurking under the lily pads.

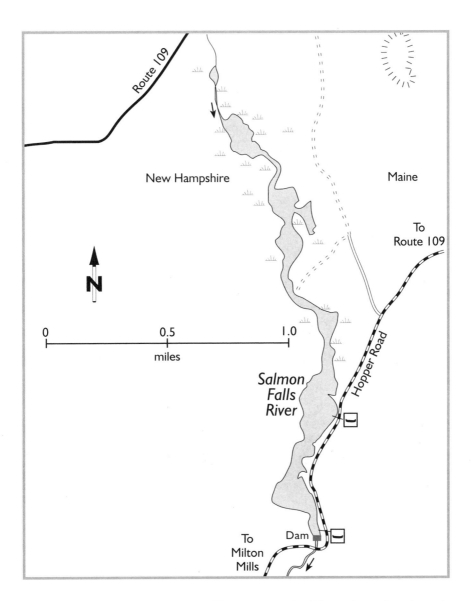

If you enjoy exploring pond life among the lily pads, pickerelweed, arrowhead, sedges and rushes, paddle here. In places, vegetation masks the main channel; while what looks like widened channel dead-ends, the real channel snakes through a dense stand of pickerelweed.

The last time that we paddled here, we had to carry over a new beaver dam about a mile from the access point. In addition to seeing a new beaver lodge, we saw a muskrat, many ducks, kingfisher, hundreds of red-winged blackbirds, and many dragonflies and damselflies. In the upper reaches, lots of tamaracks grow out of sphagnum hummocks.

The dam access has more parking, but if you put in at the upper site, you will avoid paddling through the backyards of two houses. Once past these, the evidence of human civilization recedes until you reach the upper stretch of this small reservoir. Putting in up above allows you to avoid the barely submerged rocks that choke the lower section. Go slowly there.

Look for the diminutive leaves of round-leaved sundews (Drosera rotundifolia) *on the sphagnum hummocks.*

～2～

Shapleigh, Smarts, and Hansen Ponds
Acton, Newfield, and Shapleigh

MAPS: Maine Atlas, Map 2
  USGS Quadrangle, Great East Lake

AREA AND MAXIMUM DEPTH: Hansen Pond, 30 acres, 8 feet;
  Smarts Pond, 20 acres, 5 feet; Shapleigh Pond, 80 acres,
  10 feet

HABITAT TYPE: shallow, weedy ponds; shallow stream with overgrown banks

FISH: Hansen and Shapleigh Ponds, largemouth bass, chain pickerel; Smarts Pond, chain pickerel; smallmouth bass in stream

EXPECT TO SEE: aquatic vegetation, deer, ducks, beaver in evening

TAKE NOTE: river gets shallow during dry periods

GETTING THERE

From Sanford, go north on Routes 11 and 109, and turn right onto Route 11
when they split. From the Shapleigh Corner Store at the flashing yellow
light, take a hard left on Route 11; go 4.8 miles (4.8 miles), and turn left onto
an unmarked road (Mann Road goes right). Go 0.2 mile (5.0 miles), and turn
left by the Post Office. In half a block, turn right, and go about one more
block to the access (5.1 miles), next to the iron bridge.

Small, shallow, and with a tiny, rustic boat access, Shapleigh Pond sees
few visitors. Several houses cluster near the boat access, but the rest of
the area is fairly free of development. If you ascend the Little Ossipee
River into Hansen and Smarts Ponds, you likely will paddle alone in
this little patch of wilderness.

Paddling up the right-hand side of Shapleigh Pond, we encountered fresh beaver cuttings. As we rounded a bend, sure enough, a
beaver swam in front of the boat. It let us get quite close before slapping the water with its broad tail and diving into the underwater
entrance to its lodge. A little farther along, up in the northwest arm, we
surprised a white-tailed buck who, after flagging us with the underside

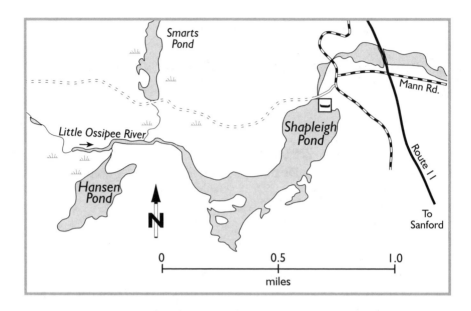

of his tail, stood a few feet back in the alders and snorted with indignation for several minutes at being interrupted while taking his evening drink. The beautiful flutelike notes of hermit thrushes serenaded us from the dense understory.

Continue paddling up the right side into the Little Ossipee River, with its barely perceptible current. Stick to the main channel, especially during drier times of the year. We wound our way through acres of aquatic vegetation, loaded with feeding black ducks. The river channel narrows, then opens up a bit with a lot of aquatic vegetation on the right side. At this point, if you search carefully on the right, you will find the outlet from Smarts Pond. Beaver have dammed the narrow, shallow, outlet stream. Although we did not travel past the first beaver dam, we suspect that you would have to get wet several times before making it to Smarts Pond, which lies a few hundred yards off through the brush.

We confess that we did not check out Smarts Pond because it was one of those warm, humid evenings in June when you would be drenched if you wore a long-sleeved shirt. With no wind to keep the bugs down, the mosquitoes whined about our ears, and the thought of dragging a boat through a brush-filled passageway for a couple hundred yards did not seem very appealing.

Travel up the river a little farther, keeping your eye out for the channel choked with pickerelweed leading to shallow, plant-choked

Hansen Pond on the left. Because of its small size and encroaching tree canopy, Hansen Pond exudes a real wilderness feel, though it does have one cabin on it. Large white pines line the eastern shore, while short red maples, alders, and other scrub vegetation dominate the marshy western shore.

Except during high water in the spring, you won't be able to travel upriver more than about a quarter mile past the outlet from Hansen Pond. The river here actually has a little current to it; more importantly, it gets narrow and quite shallow.

3

Estes Lake
Alfred and Sanford

> **MAPS:** Maine Atlas, Map 2
>   USGS Quadrangle, Alfred
> **AREA AND MAXIMUM DEPTH:** 387 acres, 30 feet
> **HABITAT TYPE:** reservoir with narrow arms
> **FISH:** smallmouth bass, largemouth bass, chain pickerel
> **EXPECT TO SEE:** loon, Eastern kingbird, great blue heron, mallard, double-crested cormorant
> **TAKE NOTE:** section south of campground has some development

GETTING THERE

From Sanford, go east on Route 202. Just after leaving Sanford, at the light just past the hospital, turn right onto Grammar Road. Cross Route 4, after which Grammar Road becomes New Dam Road, and turn left onto Bernier Road. Go 1.4 miles, passing Apache Campground, to the short iron bridge that spans Hay Brook.

Estes Lake, a long, widened section of river, backs up behind a small hydroelectric dam on the Mousam River. Actually, the Middle Branch of the Mousam River forms the northern three-quarters of Estes Lake, as the main river enters the lake near the south end.

Paddling from the access on Hay Brook, you pass through cattails, horsetails, and many other marsh plants. Wood duck nesting boxes dot the shoreline, though we only saw a tree swallow peer out from one of the holes. Eastern kingbirds darted out from exposed perches to snatch insects from the air, and hermit thrushes sang from the understory, along with rufous-sided towhees and common yellowthroats. Aquatic vegetation chokes the shallow water everywhere on Hay Brook.

As you enter the main lake, off to the right you will see Apache Campground and a few houses on the opposite shore. Paddle around to the left, heading north. Besides the many marshy coves to explore, you

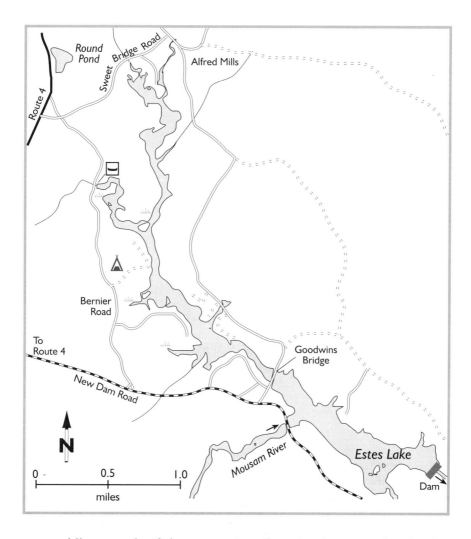

can paddle up each of the two main tributaries for a couple of miles before they become impassable. The varied vegetation here, ranging from scrubby marsh plants to tall deciduous trees and pine plantations, enhances the scenic character of upper Estes Lake.

You should not see many power boats here. No access exists for large boats; the Estes Lake Association tries to limit motors to 10 HP, and the large number of barely submerged rocks and stumps make speedboating dangerous. We paddled here on a warm Saturday in late June and saw no other boat—human- or motor-powered.

~4~

Mousam River
Kennebunk

> **MAPS:** Maine Atlas, Maps 2 and 3
> USGS Quadrangles, Alfred and Kennebunk
> **RIVER LENGTH:** 3 miles
> **HABITAT TYPE:** meandering river backed up behind a dam
> **FISH:** brook, brown, and rainbow trout
> **EXPECT TO SEE:** great blue heron, kingfisher, double-crested cormorant, beaver in the evening
> **TAKE NOTE:** shoreline is private but with limited development

GETTING THERE

From I-95, Exit 3, go northwest on Alfred Road for 0.8 mile (0.8 mile), and turn left onto Mill Road (Thompson Road goes right). Go 0.5 mile (1.3 miles) to the access at the bridge on the upstream side (easier access on the eastern [approach] side).

The Mousam River provides an outstanding paddling resource for much of its length, from Mousam Lake down to Kennebunk Beach. The section included here runs upstream from a dam just west of I-95, Exit 3. The river meanders so much that you rarely see much of it at once. Side passages abound, and the main channel has no perceptible current, at least at times of low water.

Throughout this section, standing dead trees seem to

Irises growing along the bank of the Mousam River

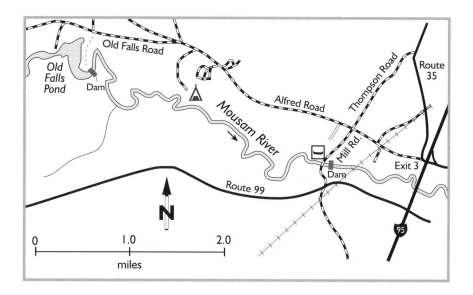

sprout from the water, and the typical assortment of aquatic plants and shoreline shrubs adorn the many marshy areas. Rhodora blooms in early June, followed by sheep laurel and a viburnum, probably arrowwood. Extensive patches of iris bloom in marshy areas, wherever the canopy is open. If you get as far as the high-tension wires crossing overhead, look for the black locusts hanging out over the water. These trees belong to the pea family and sport large clusters of white flowers in June.

Great blue herons stalk fish and amphibians along the shoreline, double-crested cormorants dive for fish, and herring gulls patrol the air, hunting for dead things floating in the water, always ready to snatch food away from other birds that venture near. Beaver cuttings and lodges occur all along the shore, and this should be a good place to look for river otters.

The privately owned shoreline has very few No Trespassing signs. In the more secluded reaches, you probably could picnic on the flat grassy spots; please treat the land with respect so that it does not get posted off-limits to others who follow. An occasional house or camp punctuates the shoreline, but in places you can paddle for a mile without seeing any evidence of civilization. This wild river's presence within a few miles of Kennebunk, I-95, and thousands of summer vacationers is remarkable. Boating here on a warm Saturday in June, we saw nary another human being.

Scarborough Marsh
Scarborough

> **MAPS:** Maine Atlas, Map 3
>   USGS Quadrangles, Prouts Neck and Old Orchard Beach
> **AREA:** 3,100 acres
> **INFORMATION:** Scarborough Marsh Nature Center, Maine
>   Audubon Society, Route 9/Pine Point Road, Scarborough,
>   ME 04074; 207-883-5100; www.maineaudubon.org; Friends
>   of Scarborough Marsh, www.scarboroughmaine.com/marsh
> **TIDE TABLES:** www.maineharbors.com
> **HABITAT TYPE:** salt marsh
> **EXPECT TO SEE:** muskrat, snowy egret, great blue heron, salt-
>   marsh sharp-tailed and Nelson's sharp-tailed sparrows
> **TAKE NOTE:** wind can make paddling difficult; novice paddlers
>   should avoid this area; wear PFD

GETTING THERE

From Portland, go south on Route 1, and turn left onto Route 9/Pine Point Road. Go 0.8 mile to the nature center on the left. You will see a raft of rental canoes out front.

Preserved by the Wetlands Protection Act of 1972, Scarborough Marsh is a 3,100-acre estuary of fresh, brackish, and salt water filled with birds, mammals, insects, and crustaceans and represents 15 percent of Maine's salt-marsh area. Native Americans called marshes *owascoag*, which means "land of many grasses," and indeed, endless acres of cord-grass, cattails, rushes, and sedges, along with many other aquatic plants, stretch into the distance.

We have much to learn about the ecology of estuaries and their value as producers of huge quantities of biomass, with more production per acre than farm fields, pine plantations, or even tropical rain forests. The Friends of Scarborough Marsh, a coalition of citizens and organizations, works to protect and to restore the marsh. The Maine Depart-

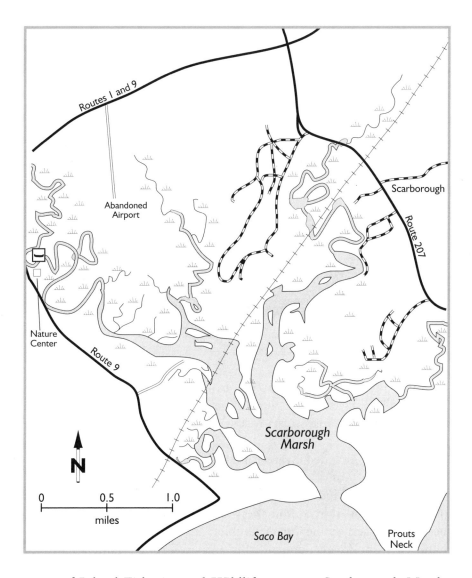

Routes 1 and 9

Scarborough

Route 207

Abandoned
Airport

Nature
Center

Route 9

N

0   0.5   1.0

miles

Scarborough
Marsh

Saco Bay

Prouts
Neck

ment of Inland Fisheries and Wildlife oversees Scarborough Marsh, and through a cooperative agreement allows the Maine Audubon Society to operate a nature center here. The center operates education programs—including canoe and walking tours—nature trails, canoe rentals, and a boat-launch site.

The nature center maintains a list of recent sightings in this bird-watcher's paradise. One bird of interest that occurs in relatively large numbers, the glossy ibis, looks black at a distance but iridescent purple at close range. About two feet long with a three-foot wingspan, it uses

Areas of cordgrass, cattails, rushes, and sedges greet paddlers as they venture out onto the serpentine rivers of Scarborough Marsh.

its long, downcurved bill to poke around marshy areas, hunting up crustaceans or whatever else it can find. Formerly, it ranged only as far north as the mid-Atlantic states but has recently expanded its range into Canada.

We have included Scarborough Marsh with some reservations because of ten-foot tides and wind. The wind blows almost constantly, with no trees to block it. Paddling against both tide and wind can be quite tiring, and this combination will confront you on windy days, because the serpentine rivers double back on themselves every few hundred feet. We recommend this area to strong paddlers and that paddlers wear PFDs at all times in Scarborough Marsh.

The Audubon Society recommends that you paddle out against the tide while fresh and then allow the tide to help carry you back in— very wise advice, indeed. With a little planning, you could ride both out and back in on the tide as it turns. Contact the nature center just before your trip to find out the local tide times. The staff also told us horror stories of people who paddle up narrow creeks and get stranded as the tide runs out, leaving them in hip-deep mud. We recommend that you stick to the miles of main river channels, which do not go dry at low tide.

～6～

Hollis Center Arm of the Saco River

Buxton, Dayton, and Hollis

MAPS: Maine Atlas, Map 3
  USGS Quadrangle, Bar Mills
AREA: 428 acres; river length, 3.5 miles
HABITAT TYPE: wooded reservoir
FISH: smallmouth bass
EXPECT TO SEE: deciduous tree–covered hillsides
TAKE NOTE: wind from the northwest can make paddling diffi-
  cult; novice paddlers should avoid this area under windy con-
  ditions; wear PFD

GETTING THERE

From Hollis Center, go east on Routes 4, 117, and 202 to Salmon Falls. Cross the Saco River bridge, and turn right, following Route 117 (Routes 202 and 4 go straight). Go 0.4 mile (0.4 mile), and turn right onto Simpson Road. Go 0.3 mile (0.7 mile), and turn right between the stone pillars onto the access road. Do not drive down to the water unless you have four-wheel drive; park on the flat areas up above, as far off the road as possible.

The Saco River drains the White Mountains of Maine and New Hampshire, meandering southeast until it dumps into the Gulf of Maine at Saco. Whitewater dominates the upper reaches, but once it crosses from New Hampshire into Maine the Saco becomes a quiet-water paddler's dream. From Swans Falls in Fryeburg it meanders slowly for miles down to Hiram and seems to be bank-to-bank with canoeists for most of the summer, inducing anyone who wants a modicum of solitude to seek less-traveled ways. The Hollis Center Arm described here, just south of Salmon Falls and southeast of Hollis Center, backed up behind a dam, sees far fewer paddlers.

The Buxton Town Park access gate remains open from sunrise to sunset. If you wish to paddle in the cooler evening hours, check on the

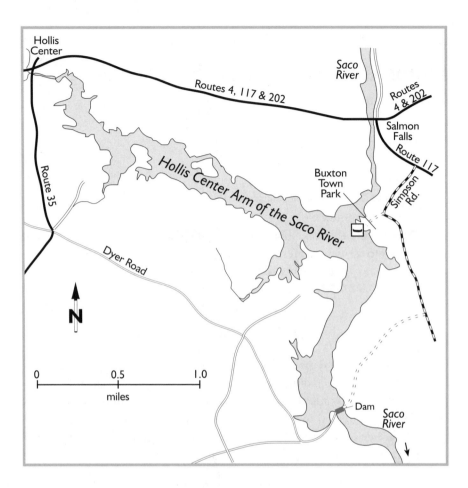

gate-closing hour with the caretaker, who often sits in his truck near the park entrance.

Large deciduous trees line the shore and the hillsides around this wide lake, with a smattering of lofty conifers, mainly white pine, interspersed. Huge granite boulders poke up here and there along the shoreline. Numerous coves, some of them quite deep and with jagged shorelines, beg to be explored. With all of the maples, oaks, and other deciduous trees lining the banks and covering the hillsides, this should be a beautiful spot to paddle in the fall when the leaves are turning. We would avoid this popular recreation spot on midsummer weekends. When we paddled here, we passed several canoes out on the water, but we saw only one small motorboat.

~7~

Lower Range Pond
Poland

MAPS: Maine Atlas, Map 5
   USGS Quadrangles, Minot and Mechanic Falls
AREA AND MAXIMUM DEPTH: 290 acres, 41 feet
HABITAT TYPE: deep, clear, wooded, kettle pond with some
   marshy areas
FISH: smallmouth bass, largemouth bass, chain pickerel
EXPECT TO SEE: loon, osprey, ducks, great blue heron
TAKE NOTE: 10-HP limit; some development; popular swimming
   area includes handicapped access across beach into water;
   entrance charge $3.50; park hours: 9:00 AM to 8:00 PM

GETTING THERE

From the south, from I-495, Exit 11, turn right, followed by the first two lefts (onto Route 202 north, then onto Route 26 north). Go 9.8 miles (9.8 miles), and turn right (east) onto Route 122 (Poland Springs Road). Go 1.4 miles (11.2 miles), and turn left onto Empire Road at the Range Pond State Park sign. Go 0.8 mile (12.0 miles), and turn left into the park.

From the north, from I-495, Exit 12, go south on Route 202, and turn right (west) on Route 122. Go 3.8 miles, turn right onto Empire Road, and follow as above.

On the right day, with the weather just threatening enough to keep most people away, Lower Range Pond offers a real treat. A 10-HP limit keeps the place fairly quiet. The pond boasts crystal-clear water with sandy shores—superb for swimming—and the marshy coves teem with wildlife. We visited on a late afternoon midweek in August and had the place to ourselves. But you won't find much solitude here on a nice summer weekend, though, as the state park receives 70,000 visitors per year.

Some development intrudes on the pond's north end, including a campground and a YMCA camp. The houses along here, with their

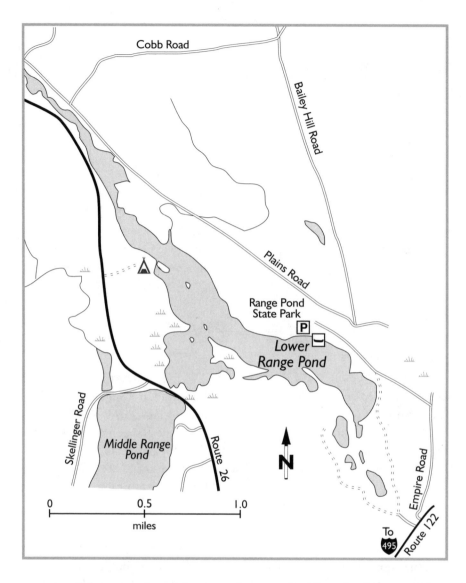

associated boats and activity, can detract significantly from a quiet-water experience. We prefer paddling the south end—and the marshy extension off to the southwest toward Route 26 and Middle Range Pond (if you carry over the road into Middle Range Pond, be very careful of traffic). By midsummer, this marshy cove may be too shallow and weed choked for paddling, except for a deep, winding channel.

During our visit, we saw a variety of wildlife: a loon pair with well-developed chick, osprey, great blue heron, black duck, kingfisher, kingbird, spotted sandpiper, numerous fish, freshwater mussels, and a fascinating invertebrate—bryozoa. In its own phylum (birds, mammals, and reptiles are other phyla), the bryozoan we saw here is in the genus *Pectinatella*. Individual units, or zooids, of the underwater colonies use tiny hairs or cilia to sweep the water for microscopic algae, diatoms, and protozoa. *Pectinatella* colonies grow as large as watermelons, though here they range considerably smaller. The slimy, gelatinous colonies look somewhat like translucent pineapples growing on underwater branches or rocks. Though we see bryozoa only rarely in Maine, we appreciate their presence, as they require extremely pure water and thus serve as indicators of pollution-free lakes and ponds.

Close proximity to Maine's most famous springwater bottling plant, Poland Spring, also tells of the water's purity. Paddling around the pond's southern edge, you can hear the hum of pumping machinery coming from the plant. (Poland Spring pumps from a huge underground aquifer, not from the pond.)

Trees around Lower Range Pond include white pine, a few red pine, hemlock, gray birch, red maple, and pitch pine, some unusually large. Extensive areas of pickerelweed, water-shield, pondweed, bulrushes, and grasses grow along the shallower shores. In places you will

The sand beach and swimming area of Range Pond State Park

see patches of cattail, fragrant waterlily, yellow pondlily, and a waterlily-like member of the gentian family: floating heart (with small heart-shaped leaves and small white flowers).

Kettle ponds, such as Lower Range Pond and its larger neighbors to the south (Middle and Upper Range Ponds), formed when the last glacier receded about 10,000 years ago, leaving behind huge chunks of ice buried in glacial till. As the ice gradually melted, the deep depressions filled with water. You can often recognize kettle ponds by their sandy shores and bottoms.

Midcoast

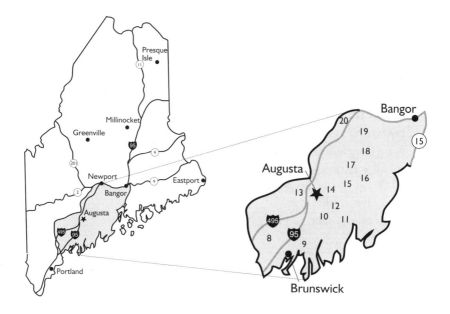

The Midcoast Region's diverse landscape—with bustling towns of Augusta, Bangor, Brunswick, and Bath; rolling farmland; coastal harbors; and rocky shoreline—gives way to pockets of inland wilderness with surprising paddling opportunities. Featured trips include secluded Dresden Bog (Trip 10), just a short distance from the state capital, in the Earle R. Kelley Wildlife Management Area; Lower Togus Pond (Trip 14), actually within Augusta's city limits, but which remains undeveloped and boasts an abundance of unique bog vegetation; and Carlton Pond and Carlton Bog (Trip 19), close to Bangor, in the middle of a state waterfowl production area, where you have a great chance to see wildlife such as waterfowl including black terns.

8

Runaround Pond
Durham

MAPS: Maine Atlas, Map 5
  USGS Quadrangle, North Pownal
AREA AND MAXIMUM DEPTH: 91 acres, 18 feet
HABITAT TYPE: shallow, weedy, dammed-up stream
FISH: largemouth bass, chain pickerel
EXPECT TO SEE: great blue heron, kingfisher, ducks, painted turtle, muskrat, beaver in the evening, osprey and great horned owl possible
TAKE NOTE: slow paddling because of aquatic vegetation

GETTING THERE

From Auburn, go south on Route 136. Route 9 enters from left. Where Routes 9 and 136 split in Durham, go right on Route 9 for 2.2 miles (2.2 miles), and turn right onto Runaround Pond Road (Rabbit Road goes left). Go 1.0 mile (3.2 miles) to the access on the right.

Runaround Pond—really two shallow, weedy streams—teems with wildlife and aquatic vegetation. It takes several hours to paddle back to the farthest navigable reaches of each stream, but it's well worth the effort. You should see wood duck, mallard, great blue heron, muskrat, turtles, fish, and myriad other wildlife. When we paddled here on a beautiful Sunday morning in July, we met only one other canoe. Aquatic vegetation severely limits access for motorboats.

Several large, flat boulders at the boat access, overhung by red pines, provide perfect spots for a picnic. From the access, you can paddle into a beautiful little cove by going through one of the two large culverts under the road. The creek emerges in a walled canyon with large white pines above.

As you return to the boat access and head upstream, huge rafts of beautiful, bright blue–flowered pickerelweed greet you, abuzz with the

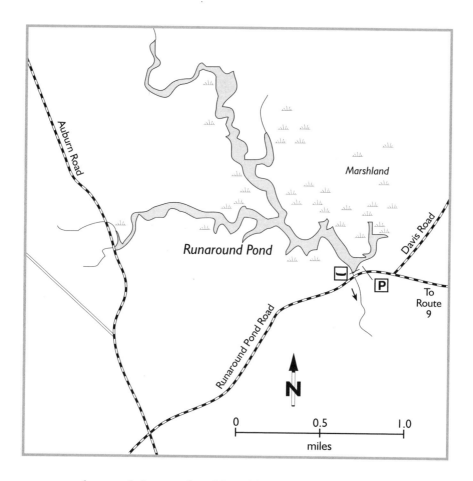

Marshland

Auburn Road

Davis Road

Runaround Pond

Runaround Pond Road

P

To
Route
9

N

0   0.5   1.0
miles

constant drone of thousands of bumblebee pollinators. Water-shield, fragrant waterlily, yellow pondlily, and yellow-flowered bladderwort are your constant companions. Tannic acids released during plant degradation color the water a yellow-brown.

When the stream channel forks, go left, weaving your way back up the meandering channel. Shrubs and aquatic vegetation choke the wide valley, leaving open only a narrow channel. Back on higher ground, maples dominate the shoreline, along with scattered pines, pointed balsam fir, and red oak. You can paddle all the way to Auburn Road—more than two miles—where the stream becomes impassable.

A great horned owl took off from one of the many side coves as we approached. Kingfishers scolded us all the way up the stream. Several great blue herons took off as we approached, and wood ducks and mallards exploded from the surface as we rounded several of the numerous stream bends. We did not expect to see a cormorant on this shallow, weedy stream, but there it was as we rounded a bend. You should see muskrats and turtles, and in the evening look for the numerous beaver whose presence is evident everywhere.

The right-hand fork, not quite as long, has thicker aquatic vegetation, a less open channel, and lots of duckweed obscuring visibility into the water. Nonetheless, it offers much of the same beauty as the left fork and is well worth paddling.

Nequasset Lake
Woolwich

MAPS: Maine Atlas, Map 6
  USGS Quadrangle, Bath

AREA AND MAXIMUM DEPTH: 392 acres, 63 feet; stream length,
  1 mile

HABITAT TYPE: wooded reservoir and inlet stream

FISH: brown trout, smallmouth bass, largemouth bass, white
  perch, chain pickerel

EXPECT TO SEE: loon, great blue heron, ducks on inlet stream,
  woodland bird species on reservoir and stream

TAKE NOTE: strong winds from north or south can cause dangerous conditions; novice paddlers should paddle the stream during windy conditions; wear PFD; 10-HP limit

---

GETTING THERE

From Bath, go north on Route 1 across the Kennebec River bridge to Woolwich. In Woolwich, go left (north) on Routes 127 and 128. When they split,
go right on Route 127 for 2.0 miles (2.0 miles), and turn right onto Old Stage
Road. Go 0.5 mile (2.5 miles) to the access on the right just before the
Nequasset Brook bridge. A trailer access is on the left just after the bridge.

An alternate access exists at the lake outlet (not shown) near the George
Wright Road bridge.

From the Nequasset Lake access, one can paddle in both directions.
We first paddled north up the inlet, Nequasset Brook. The wide channel starts out lined with pickerelweed but soon takes an abrupt left turn
into a heavily forested area where the stream narrows a bit. Hemlocks
and maples form a beautiful canopy over the water for most of this
heavily wooded stream.

The 30-to-40-foot–wide stream has plenty of water, with no
noticeable current. Marshy areas abound with swamp rose, pickerelweed, waterlilies, ferns, and bladderwort. A variety of trees extends

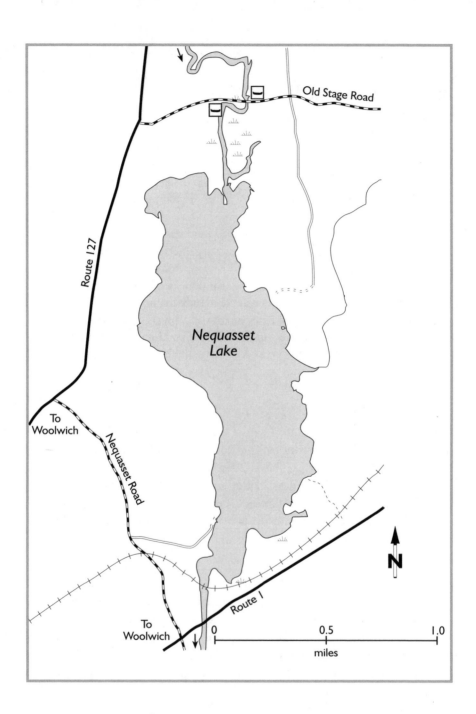

Old Stage Road

Route 127

To
Woolwich

Nequasset Road

Nequasset
Lake

Route 1

N

To
Woolwich

0   0.5   1.0
miles

along the wooded shore. Some spots look good for camping, back under the hemlocks and pines. The stream meanders around, heading alternately north, west, south, and west, and then starts over again.

After paddling back about a mile, we came to some fields on the left and a two-foot waterfall. It looked like one could portage up over the falls and continue paddling. We turned around here. We loved paddling up this quiet, beautiful little stream. Great blue heron and many ducks burst from the water as we rounded the sharp turns, and songbirds called constantly from the woods. Perhaps most numerous were the flutelike notes of hermit thrushes, announcing their territories.

The access stream, every bit as beautiful as the upstream portion, widens from the boat landing down into Nequasset Lake. Lily pads choke the several side channels, and at high water levels, you can check out the extensive wetland on the left on the way down. The lake's north end contains a fair amount of water-shield, a member of the waterlily family whose stalk attaches at the center of a floating oval leaf. A slimy, gelatinous film coats the underside of the leaves and stems.

Mixed hardwoods and evergreens, with many large white pines, line the heavily forested shore of Nequasset Lake, with little development in evidence. Large rocks protrude from the shore and the lake, inviting swimming. Birds appear everywhere, from great blue heron, hermit thrush, mallard, and wood duck on the stream to loon, great crested flycatcher, Eastern kingbird, kingfisher, yellowthroat, and many more along the lake shore.

Fishermen use this lake regularly, though we only saw a few boats on a July weekend, most of them fishing quietly. On weekends, you will find more solitude paddling up Nequasset Brook. Though this lake lies close to vacation heaven, you should have to contend with only a modest amount of boating activity during the week.

10

Dresden Bog
Alna and Dresden

MAPS: Maine Atlas, Map 13
　　USGS Quadrangle, Wiscasset
AREA: 341 acres; 730 acres in Wildlife Management Area
HABITAT TYPE: shallow, weedy pond
FISH: largemouth bass, white perch, chain pickerel
EXPECT TO SEE: beaver in evening, wood ducks
TAKE NOTE: no access for motors

GETTING THERE

From Augusta, go south on Routes 201 and 27 through Hallowell. When they split, turn left on Route 27. Just after Routes 197 and 127 go right, turn left onto Blinn Hill Road, go 1.3 miles (1.3 miles), and turn right onto Bog Road. Go 2.3 miles (3.6 miles) to the access on the right. Portage over a few beaver dams to get to the pond.

Because access to Dresden Bog requires portaging over a few beaver dams, this beautiful, peaceful area surrounded by the Earle R. Kelley Wildlife Management Area, just a short distance from the state capital, receives few visitors.

Paddle down the beautiful little inlet creek, past the beaver dams that bar most people as surely as a gate. Emerging from the marshy entrance, you will be struck by the varied beauty of this place, with many islands dotting the surface, emergent vegetation covering the pond, and mature trees lining the shore.

Many wood duck nesting boxes perch along the shore and out in the water. One hundred years ago massive cutting of forests in the East and Midwest and unregulated hunting decimated wood duck populations. Concerned birdwatchers, sportsmen, and wildlife-management officials began erecting nesting boxes around swamps and rivers, resulting in a dramatic comeback for this beautiful duck. The wood duck

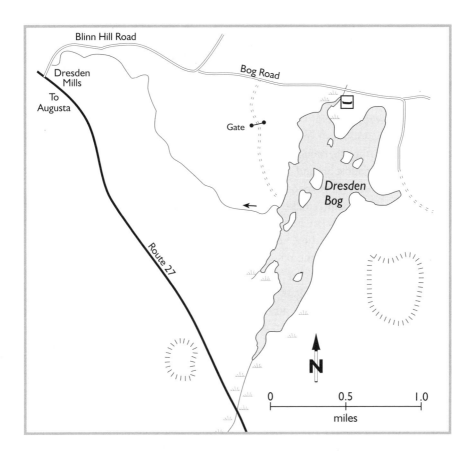

exhibits unusual arboreal behavior. When paddling wooded swamps and rivers, you sometimes see wood ducks perched in trees.

Most ducks and geese nest on the ground; in this area, only wood ducks and common and hooded mergansers nest in cavities. Because common and hooded mergansers prefer wooded swamps and some-what deeper water for diving for fish, we suspect these boxes see mostly wood ducks.

We saw several flocks of black ducks and wood ducks feeding in the south end of this very shallow marsh. After a cursory, unsuccessful look for a passageway to Gardiner Pond, we retreated from the south end to let the ducks feed undisturbed.

Tall trees surround the pond, with mostly deciduous trees on the west shore and many very tall white pines along the east shore. Dense undergrowth grows down to the water and on the heavily vegetated islands. Pickerelweed and water celery, whose long leaves protrude up through and then lie flat on the water surface, cover the water's surface.

The Spectacular Wood Duck

Of all our ducks—and perhaps of all our bird species—few approach the wood duck for sheer beauty, with its distinctive multicolored breeding plumage, iridescent in sunlight. Getting a close look at these extremely wary ducks, though, requires very quiet paddling. Look for them in marshy areas as you paddle around grassy islands and meandering inlet channels.

Along with its gorgeous plumage, the wood duck, *Aix sponsa,* has an unusual nesting habit. Unlike most ducks, wood ducks nest in trees, using abandoned woodpecker holes, cavities hollowed out by decay, and—more recently—artificial nesting boxes. Sharp down-curved claws on the toes help the bird cling to tree trunks. The duck can also walk or run overland far better than most other ducks. We remember paddling on Umbagog Lake and being quite surprised to see a female wood duck with a string of chicks swim to the shore and then run into the protective vegetation. When danger threatens, wood ducks can dive and swim underwater for a fair distance.

Wood ducks pair up in the Southeast, where they overwinter. During spring migration, the male follows the female usually to the same pond where she was raised. The female selects a suitable nesting cavity from 4 to 50 feet up in the air and up to a mile from water.

The hen lays ten to fifteen eggs, and when the young hatch—all within a few hours of each other—they remain in the nest for only a day. After checking carefully for signs of danger, the mother flies down to the water or ground below and calls. The chicks use their toe claws to climb up to the nest entrance and, without hesitation, jump out. Their short, stubby wings and downy feathers slow the chicks' descent, and remarkably, even when jumping from a nest 50 feet above ground, they seldom get hurt.

Chicks can swim right away, but predators take many before they reach water. In the water, large fish (bass, northern pike, chain pickerel) and snapping turtles prey on the young. Wood duck chicks grow quickly during the summer and can fly when eight to ten weeks old.

Wood ducks molt in the summer, the male losing his beautiful breeding plumage until fall. In the nonbreeding, or eclipse, plumage, the male resembles the female (the male retains his red eyes and bill, and the female has distinct white eye rings). For a two- to three-week period during molting, the male cannot fly. The female also goes through a molt a little later than the male, but her plumage does not change significantly in appearance.

In the fall, wood ducks congregate in large numbers, especially in the evening. Sometimes hundreds or even thousands of wood ducks fly to the same roosting pond each evening and leave at daybreak to feed on nearby ponds and streams. By midautumn, most wood ducks have migrated south, traveling in small, loosely aggregated flocks.

While wood duck populations remain relatively strong today, un-regulated hunting nearly drove the species to extinction around 1900. Efforts began to protect it through state legislation after the U.S. Biological Survey reported in 1901 that wood ducks faced possible extinction. At that time the newly formed National Audubon Society and a few other organizations began a long effort to get federal legislation enacted—considered necessary to assure survival.

The first national legislation protecting waterfowl passed in 1913 (the Weeks-McLean bill). The Migratory Bird Treaty Act, signed into law in 1918, extended protection of wood ducks and other migrating birds to Canada, gave the federal government greater authority to regulate hunting, and prohibited the sale of wildfowl. The hunting season on wood ducks closed completely in the United States and Canada until 1941, when the species had recovered enough to open a limited fall season.

The 1938 hurricane, which blew down many old trees with nesting cavities, set back wood duck recovery in the Northeast. To provide more sites, biologists erected the first artificial nesting boxes in Great Meadows National Wildlife Refuge in Massachusetts, and the idea soon spread around the country. Today, tens of thousands of wood duck nesting boxes appear throughout the East.

Loss of suitable nesting habitat threatens wood ducks and other cavity-nesting birds. Wood ducks need remote ponds and marshes to raise their young, and development increasingly threatens these areas. Keep your distance in the presence of ducks with young.

~ 11 ~

Duckpuddle Pond
Nobleboro and Waldoboro

Maps: Maine Atlas, Maps 7 and 13
  USGS Quadrangle, Wiscasset

Area and Maximum Depth: 293 acres, 23 feet; stream length, 2 miles

Habitat Type: shallow, marshy pond and long connecting stream with shrubby shores

Fish: smallmouth bass, white perch, chain pickerel

Expect to See: seas of aquatic vegetation, swamp rose, loon, great blue heron, ducks, beaver in the evening, bald eagle and osprey a possibility

Take Note: substantial boat traffic on Pemaquid Lake; the marsh breeds mosquitoes

---

GETTING THERE

From Waldoboro, go west on Route 1 for 3.6 miles (3.6 miles) past the Route 32 junction, and turn left onto Winslow Hill Road (loop road; returns to Route 1) at the sign for Duck Puddle Campground. Go 0.4 mile (4.0 miles), and turn left onto Duck Puddle Road. Go 1.3 miles (5.3 miles), and turn left onto Bremen Road. Go 0.3 mile (5.6 miles) to the access on the left, just after the bridge.

As you paddle the narrow passageway from the access toward Duck-puddle Pond, a sea of waterlilies, alders, pickerelweed, rushes, grasses . . . and mosquitoes . . . greets you. When we visited in mid-July, a huge pondwide algae bloom clouded the water; given the pond's scattered development, we could not understand what nutrient influx might cause such a bloom. The state reports that algae blooms occur frequently on Duckpuddle, though none was reported during the four years 2000–2003.

Trees around this shallow pond include white pine, hemlock, birch, sugar and red maples, and red oak, with oak predominating along the

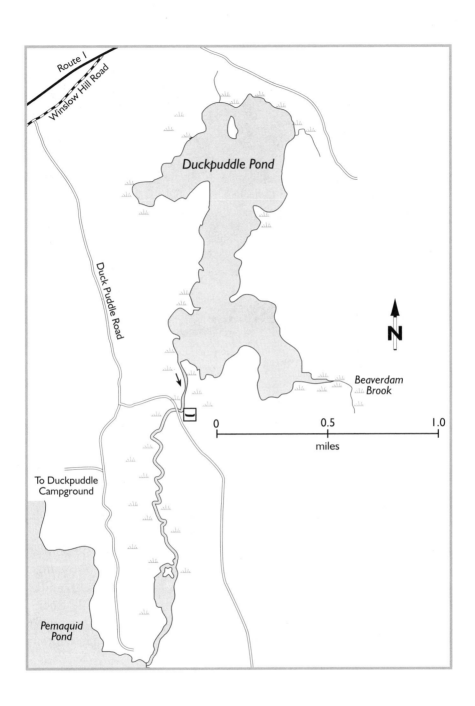

Route 1

Winslow Hill Road

Duck Puddle Road

Duckpuddle Pond

Beaverdam
Brook

N

0   0.5   1.0

miles

To Duckpuddle
Campground

Pemaquid
Pond

The two-mile-long marshy connecting stream between Duckpuddle and Pemaquid Ponds contains a large variety of marsh plants, providing outstanding habitat for beaver, deer, and other wildlife.

north shore. Several marshy coves beg to be explored, but save time to paddle down the beautiful outlet stream—about a four-mile round trip.

Start east from the access and stay to the right around the peninsula, covered with large white pines, that separates the two lower bays. In the marshy eastern bay, pickerelweed hides an inlet. Paddle right through the center of the pickerelweed, back into Beaverdam Brook, threading your way through the sweetgale and other marsh plants. Though a narrow passage, you can paddle back in quite far, especially if you portage over the beaver dams of this appropriately named stream.

Portaging not your cup of tea? Paddle back to the access, go under the large culvert, and down the two miles to Pemaquid Pond. The connecting stream usually does not require portages, and the vegetation and channel width change several times, making this a very quiet, interesting place to paddle.

In places, pickerelweed, yellow pondlily, and fragrant waterlily cover the wide channel, while in other areas, alders, sweetgale, buttonbush, and other shrubs line the narrower waterway. Beautiful pink swamp rose blooms everywhere, and a variety of songbirds calls from the undergrowth. Monster beaver lodges poke up here and there, some with tons of cuttings protruding up through the water surface just in front of the lodge. The beavers seem just barely able to keep the alders from closing the channel.

The channel winds around the valley, drifting past many wood duck nesting boxes. Note in the quieter stretches the patches of yellow-flowered bladderwort, a fully aquatic carnivorous plant whose bladders ingest microscopic organisms. The largest patch seems to be near Pemaquid Pond, just before a large grove of tamarack.

The outlet stream, with its great blue herons, ducks, and loads of other wildlife, provides a genuinely wild place to paddle right in the middle of one of the most heavily used recreational areas on the eastern seaboard.

Waterlilies

12

Dyer Long Pond and Musquash Pond

Jefferson

> **MAPS:** Maine Atlas, Map 13
> USGS Quadrangle, North Whitefield
> **AREA AND MAXIMUM DEPTH:** 423 acres, 16 feet
> **HABITAT TYPE:** long, narrow, wooded pond
> **FISH:** largemouth bass
> **EXPECT TO SEE:** towering white pine, loon, tree swallow, osprey,
> beaver in evening
> **TAKE NOTE:** development but little boat traffic; the marshy south
> end breeds mosquitoes

GETTING THERE

From Augusta, go east on Routes 17 and 32. Where they split, go south on Route 32, and turn right onto Route 215 south. Go 2.1 miles (2.1 miles), and turn left onto Old Mill Road (Atkins Road goes right). Go 0.8 mile (2.9 miles; stay straight [right] at the fork) to the access on the right just before the bridge. Do not block the easily missed road that heads back into the woods.

True to its name, long and narrow Dyer Long Pond extends in a northeast-southwest orientation. From the access at the southern tip, paddling around to the right, we could find no way to reach Musquash Pond, which has access reachable by four-wheel-drive trail. The marshy south and north ends and the coves provide interesting areas to explore; towering white pines that hide several cottages dominate the shoreline around the rest of the pond. Although the pond sees little boat traffic, paddling here is not a wilderness experience.

Granite boulders, deposited by glaciers 10,000 years ago as they gouged out the lake bed, cover much of the shoreline. Those just under the water's surface scrape the boat bottoms of unwary paddlers. Go slowly near the shoreline, especially where boulders jut out to form a point.

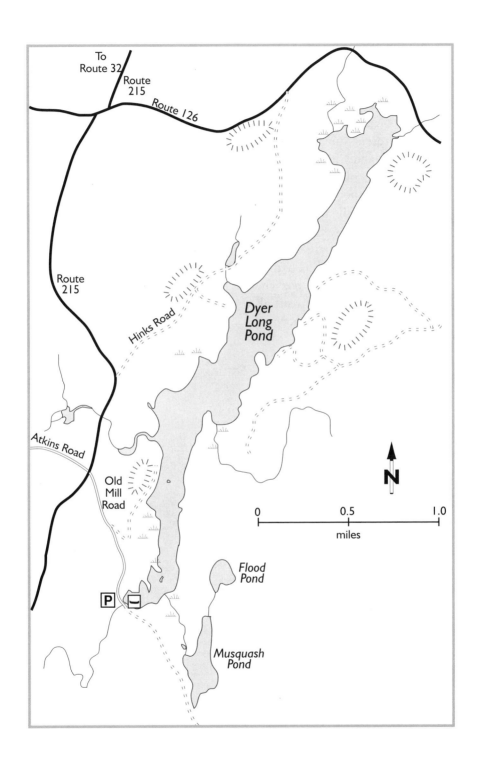

To
Route 32

Route
215

Route 126

Route
215

Hinks Road

Dyer
Long
Pond

Atkins Road

Old
Mill
Road

N

0   0.5   1.0
miles

P ⊟

Flood
Pond

Musquash
Pond

We saw an osprey, loons, and several beaver when we paddled here in the early evening. At the marshy southern end, the adjacent landowner had erected 30 songbird nesting boxes on poles out in the water. After a few minutes, we understood why. Obviously, the owners try to encourage tree swallows to feed their ever-hungry young with the ever-present hordes of mosquitoes. Our boat launch occurred in record time, and within minutes we were insect free out on the water.

Unlike purple martins, tree swallows normally do not nest colonially. Instead, they chase other tree swallows away. To encourage bluebird nesting, people often put nesting boxes up in pairs. Tree swallows occupy the first box, leaving the other box free for bluebirds, which the swallows ignore. Apparently, these tree swallows have not heard of this theory, because every box had nesting tree swallows. Perhaps the sheer volume of pesky insects overwhelmed the swallows' aggressive territorial tendencies (if they spend all their time chasing insects, they have less time to chase each other).

13

Hutchinson Pond and Jimmie Pond
Farmingdale and Manchester

MAPS: Maine Atlas, Map 12
USGS Quadrangles, Augusta and Winthrop
AREA AND MAXIMUM DEPTH: Hutchinson Pond, 100 acres, 24
feet; Jimmie Pond, 107 acres, 75 feet
HABITAT TYPE: Hutchinson—shallow, marshy pond with long
connecting stream; Jimmie—southern end shallow, marshy;
northern end deep with wooded shores
FISH: Hutchinson—largemouth bass, chain pickerel; Jimmie—
brook trout, smallmouth bass, largemouth bass, chain pickerel
EXPECT TO SEE: loon, osprey, great blue heron, ducks, beaver
TAKE NOTE: no development on Hutchinson, a little on Jimmie

GETTING THERE

From Augusta, go south on Route 201 to Hallowell. Turn right onto
Winthrop or Central Street. Go sharply uphill for two or three blocks, turn
left onto Middle Street, and turn right onto Litchfield Road at the T. Go 0.7
mile (0.7 mile), and turn right onto Bog Farm Road (Smith Road). Go 1.4
miles (2.1 miles), and turn left with the main road. Go 0.9 mile (3.0 miles),
and turn left onto Collins Road (Bog Farm Road). Go 1.4 miles (4.4 miles) to
the access on the right just before the bridge. Be careful; people speed around
the blind curves on both sides of the bridge.

Jimmie Pond alternate access: From the Collins Road access, go back 1.4
miles toward Hallowell, and turn left onto Jamies Pond Road (Meadow Hill
Road). Turn left into the pumping station in less than a mile.

From the access on Bog Farm Road, one can paddle upstream into Jimmie Pond with comparative ease or downstream into Hutchinson Pond
with comparative difficulty. These two quite different ponds both supply water for the town of Hallowell. With the exception of the small
southern arm, Jimmie Pond lacks marshy areas and supports a cold-water

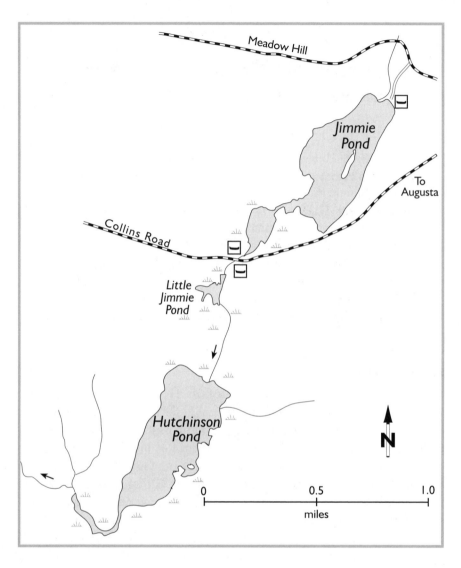

fishery. In contrast, shallow, marshy Hutchinson Pond supports a warm-water fishery. The question becomes: How hard do you want to work in order to see the beautiful, seldom visited, wild Hutchinson Pond?

Jimmie Pond

Resist the temptation to rush on through the small, southern arm to the larger, less interesting main pond. Immediately after getting in your boat, note the dead tree with an osprey nest on the far side, and check the boggy areas for sundews and pitcher plants. Diverse species of bog plants inhabit this area, and shrubs dominate the shoreline, with large deciduous trees and a few scattered pines farther back. A beaver announced the displeasure of our company with a tail slap as we paddled by, and a loon swam before us in the channel between the two sections of Jimmie Pond.

The deeper main pond, in contrast, has almost no boggy areas. A tall mixed canopy marches down to the shoreline on all sides and, aside from one island, provides little to explore. It is still a picturesque little pond, well worth your visit, especially if you fish.

Hutchinson Pond

On the other hand, Hutchinson Pond attracts very little attention because of difficult access. First, before going to Hutchinson (notice we did not say *paddling*), ask permission at the house by the access to launch your boat from their grass on the downstream side of the bridge. The sign out front when we paddled here said Ed Rowe, Coleman Repair. They were very friendly and actively encouraged us to paddle down to Hutchinson Pond.

As you look down the narrow channel leading to Hutchinson, note the first of several beaver dams. It seemed as though all we did was portage over these amazing little engineering wonders when, in truth, we had to go over only six in a half-mile. Of course, the same six dams impeded our progress on the way back.

Vegetation crowds the beautiful channel after the last dam, and you have to thread your way through. Along the way, note the several lodges of the perhaps overly diligent waterway engineers. Extensive marshy areas occur on all sides of Hutchinson Pond, providing a lot to explore. On the northeast shore look for the only bog-free area. A huge, beautiful granite boulder creeps up the shoreline to a great little campsite. One gets the impression that you could spend a few days here and not see another soul.

Beware of leeches. We found three in the bottom of the boat, having dropped off our legs. At a gas station a half-hour later, we removed one tenacious little leech that escaped detection under a sandal strap.

14

Lower Togus Pond
Augusta

> **MAPS:** Maine Atlas, Map 13
>   USGS Quadrangle, Togus Pond
> **AREA:** 230 acres
> **HABITAT TYPE:** shallow, marshy pond
> **FISH:** largemouth bass, smallmouth bass, white perch,
>   chain pickerel
> **EXPECT TO SEE:** acres of fragrant waterlily, sundew, pitcher plant,
>   beaver, great blue heron, wood duck
> **TAKE NOTE:** little boat traffic

GETTING THERE

From Augusta, east of the Kennebec River on the rotary where Routes 202 and 105 divide, go east on Route 105 for 5.8 miles to the unmarked access along the roadway that separates Togus Pond from Lower Togus Pond.

Quite a surprise waits for you on Route 105: first, the contrast between the development on Togus Pond and the lack of it across the road on Lower Togus Pond; second, and perhaps more surprising, that such a wild and beautiful place as Lower Togus Pond exists within the corporate limits of Maine's capital city.

Long, narrow Lower Togus Pond has no development until you get to the very lowest section. Few boats ply these shallow and weedy waters. Several islands and lots of coves beg to be explored, but hundreds of acres of fragrant waterlily, especially in the extensive coves along the western shore, really draw one's attention. Some patches extend unbroken for 100 yards and more. Sundews and pitcher plants occur everywhere on the hummocks, and every native variety of bog vegetation certainly must be present.

In the spring, try to stay clear of the many wood duck nesting boxes as you thread your way back into the recesses of these coves. Big fish and beaver both slap the water as you glide by, and two cormorants

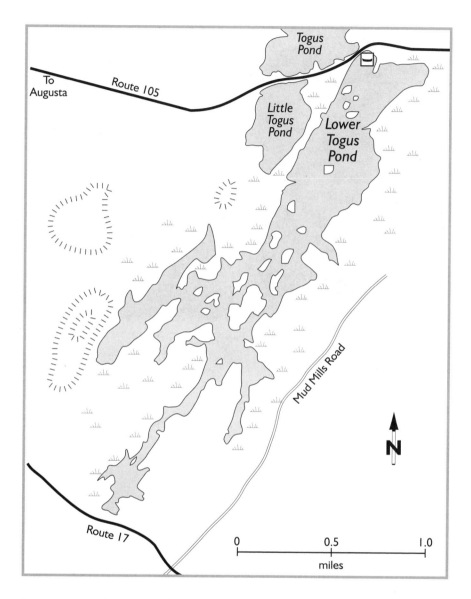

let us cruise close enough to catch the gleam in their eyes. We also saw several great blue heron fishing the shoreline and turtles sunning on nearly every log. Some beaver lodges extend six feet or more above the water line.

It would take the better part of a day to explore fully this extraordinarily beautiful spot, a place that you can paddle on windy days because acres of waterlilies damp the swells and numerous islands block the wind.

Acres of fragrant waterlily welcome paddlers to the protected coves of Lower Togus Pond. The aromatic white flowers appear midsummer and last into fall.

15

Turner Pond
Palermo and Somerville

MAPS: Maine Atlas, Map 13
USGS Quadrangle, Razorville
AREA AND MAXIMUM DEPTH: 193 acres, 7 feet
HABITAT TYPE: shallow, weedy pond
FISH: largemouth bass, chain pickerel
EXPECT TO SEE: loon, osprey, ducks
TAKE NOTE: no development; motors limited by access and shallow water

GETTING THERE

From Augusta, go east on Route 3. After passing out of Kennebec and into Waldo County, watch for a Fish Culture Station on the right at the top of a rise. Just after the station, turn right onto Turner Ridge Road. Go 4.8 miles

This large granite boulder in Turner Pond is a great place from which to swim.

(4.8 miles), turn right onto Colby Road, and go 0.6 mile (5.4 miles) to the access on the right.

Alternate access: Go east on Route 105 through Windsor. Turn left on Turner Ridge Road in Somerville, then left on Colby Road, and follow directions as above (use the *Maine Atlas*).

When we paddled here in the early 1990s, we found a rare, undeveloped gem with few visitors. More recently, the mill dam has begun to fail, exposing a few feet of muddy banks. Islands of all sizes dot the surface of this long, narrow pond, making it seem much larger than its 193

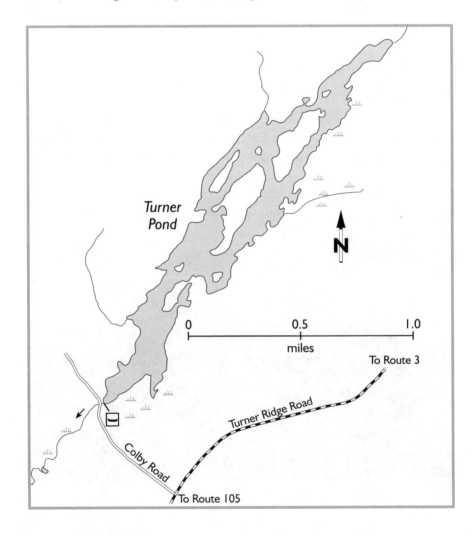

acres. One very smooth, gigantic boulder out in the middle just invites you to climb on it. Flat spots tucked up under the pines on both the mainland and islands appear perfect for picnicking. We like two locations in particular: From the access, travel up the right shore, just past the first peninsula, to the right-hand shore opposite the large island. The second: Go farther up the pond on the left-hand side, to a beautiful little spot on an island.

We saw a fuzzy, newborn, black baby loon swimming with its parents. The attentive parents called frequently as we tried to give them a wide berth, and they herded the little one between them. In contrast to the total chaos that erupts when one comes suddenly upon a mother merganser with a dozen babies in tow, the loons beat a much more dignified retreat. We had hoped to see one of the parents give the young loon a piggyback ride. They probably have the fishing pretty much to themselves here.

Explore the numerous coves for wildlife, and enjoy the waterlily-filled passages between islands. Marshy areas fill much of the shallow pond with typical bog vegetation. Many different tree species occur here, enhancing the pond's scenic quality. Because of numerous coves and islands, it takes quite a bit of time to explore all of Turner Pond. Just when you think you have gotten to the end, you pass around yet another large island and emerge out onto another stretch of open water.

Back at the boat access, rusting machinery abounds at the old dam and Turner Mill site. Please stay off the private property immediately on the left side as you walk down the access road to the water.

Mergansers

16

Stevens Pond
Liberty

MAPS: Maine Atlas, Map 14
   USGS Quadrangles, Washington and Liberty
AREA AND MAXIMUM DEPTH: 336 acres, 43 feet
HABITAT TYPE: shallow, marshy pond with many tree-covered
   islands
FISH: smallmouth bass, largemouth bass, chain pickerel (brown
   trout introduced recently)
EXPECT TO SEE: acres of fragrant waterlily, sundew, pitcher plant,
   beaver, great blue heron, wood duck
TAKE NOTE: town park with swimming and some development;
   10-HP limit

GETTING THERE

From Augusta, go east on Route 3, and turn right (south) onto Route 220. Go
1.1 miles (1.1 miles), and turn left (south) onto Route 173. Go 1.3 miles (2.4
miles) to the access on the right.

The town of Liberty maintains a park on Stevens Pond, so on warm
summer days, especially on weekends, bathers crowd the access near
the outlet dam. Stevens Pond serves as a major tributary to the St.
George River, and with the popular Lake St. George just upstream, the
motorboat traffic pretty much stays busy elsewhere. Most fishermen
here use canoes or rowboats; occasionally a small outboard will risk
continual fouling from the ubiquitous aquatic vegetation. Even though
others may intrude on your solitude occasionally, Stevens Pond provides a wonderful place to paddle, especially midweek.

Heading out from the access, stay left to explore the extensive
marshes and to avoid the development screened by the first large
island. Beautiful granite boulders extend down into the water from
the island.

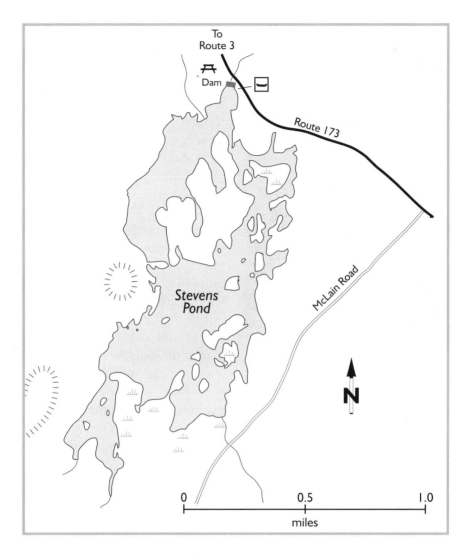

Very tall white pines that thrive on the thin soil above the hard granite outcroppings dominate the shorelines of both the mainland and the large island. In contrast, hardwoods need more soil for their tap-roots, which generally go straight down. This explains, at least in part, the dearth of very large hardwoods along most of these granite-laden shorelines, while at the same time the white pines and other conifers can grow to great size there. One wonders, however, how such a thin layer of soil can support such towering trees. Perhaps they wedge their roots into the fissures in the underlying rocks.

Swamp pink, *Arethusa bulbosa*

Curving around to the left, you come to a boggy island with a sizable population of a rare pink orchid, rose pogonia. Borne on ten-inch stalks, the delicate pink flowers bloom in late June. Please be very careful not to injure these gorgeous flowers or any other orchids that you might encounter. You will see an unusually large number of pitcher plants in flower if you paddle here in the early summer. Each tuft of sphagnum along here also seems to harbor a patch of tiny sundews, their sticky leaves waiting to latch on to unwary insects. Like the pitcher plant and other carnivorous plants, the sundew absorbs nitrogen and other nutrients from captured insects it dissolves with enzymes.

Have you ever noticed the huge eyes on deerflies before you swatted them? They are sight predators, which explains their pesky daytime presence. More than a few of them buzzed around our heads in the marsh's narrow passages. At times, we wished that some of those people around the boat access had paddled out to help share the burden, but we explored completely alone on a warm, sunny weekend in June.

17

Branch Pond
China and Palermo

MAPS: Maine Atlas, Map 13
  USGS Quadrangle, Palermo
AREA AND MAXIMUM DEPTH: 322 acres, 38 feet
HABITAT TYPE: reservoir with several islands
FISH: brown trout, largemouth bass, white perch, chain pickerel
EXPECT TO SEE: loon, osprey, ducks
TAKE NOTE: little development; motors limited by Dinsmore
  Grain Company

GETTING THERE

From Augusta, go east on Routes 3, 9, and 202. When Routes 9 and 202 split off, stay on Route 3. Go 4.3 miles (4.3 miles), and turn left to Palermo. Go 0.7 mile (5.0 miles) to the access on the left. Do not block the fire-company hydrant. The Dinsmore Grain Company owns the gristmill and access; to paddle here, you must ask permission at the General Store, just across the street.

Branch Pond is a small shallow pond, dotted with islands and festooned with marshy channels and coves. Retaining access to this delightful spot hinges on our willingness to treat others' property with respect. We should clean up after ourselves and after the thoughtless litterbugs who unfortunately frequent these sites.

The Dinsmore dam and millsite until relatively recently still milled grain, although the lumber mill was shut down some time ago. The owners have kept the property in good shape, and we hope that the mill can be restored.

From the access, travel up the right side of the pond because it offers much more to explore, and a few cottages intrude on the left side. You can weave in and among the numerous islands, exploring coves and small streams. We saw a loon pair with a small black chick in tow, as well as many feeding ducks.

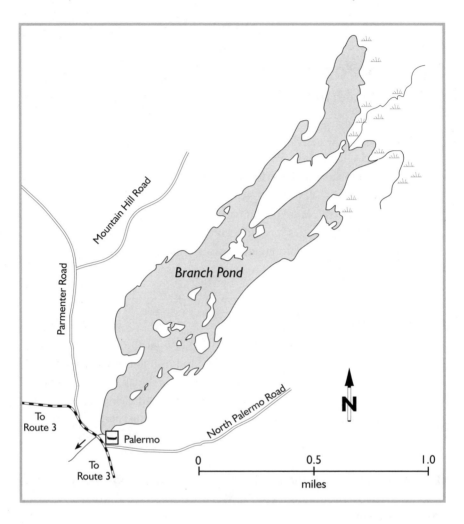

We paddled here during a warm rain not heavy enough to keep either a fishing osprey or us off the pond. Because it lacks a state-maintained public access, Branch Pond does not suffer from overuse. We hope the owners of the Dinsmore Grain Company will generously continue to allow quietwater paddlers access to this beautiful spot.

18

Sandy Pond
Freedom

> **MAPS:** Maine Atlas, Map 22
>   USGS Quadrangle, Unity
> **AREA AND MAXIMUM DEPTH:** 430 acres, 11 feet
> **HABITAT TYPE:** shallow lake with some marshy areas and lots of coves
> **FISH:** largemouth bass, white perch, chain pickerel
> **EXPECT TO SEE:** osprey, tree-clad hillsides
> **TAKE NOTE:** little development

GETTING THERE

From Waterville, go east on Route 139 through Unity. Where Route 139 goes left, continue south on Route 220, and turn right onto Route 137. Go 1.2 miles (1.2 miles), and as you come downhill into Freedom, turn diagonally left onto High Street. Go 0.3 mile (1.5 miles) to the stop sign, and turn left. Go 0.3 mile (1.8 miles), and turn right at the access sign.

Fishermen in small boats and canoes use this nice little pond located right in the town of Freedom, but you should have it pretty much to yourself during the week. As you leave the access in the northeast cove, curve to the right into the extensive marshy area along the pond's northcentral section. The floating islands extend well out into the pond and will take a long time to explore fully. The rest of the shoreline lacks marshy areas, although aquatic vegetation occurs everywhere in this very shallow pond.

Acres of cattails, marsh grasses, and boggy islands provide extensive exploration opportunities. Protruding logs in various stages of decay drip with sphagnum, sundews, and basking turtles. Yellow pondlilies and pickerelweed fill the channels. When we paddled here, an osprey with a fish in its talons had better luck than the rod-and-reel set.

Some beautiful little islands appear just where the pond widens, about a half-mile from the access, and the first one looks like a great spot

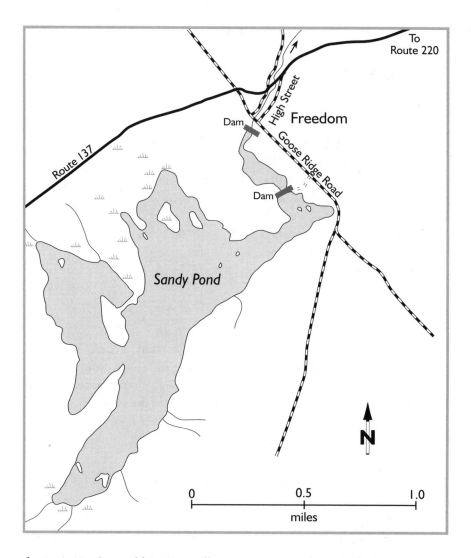

for a picnic. Several herring gulls were ensconced on its shores, trying to keep out of the wind. We had much less success and had to use the islands and the marshy areas to shelter us from wind-driven swells.

Beautiful layered hillsides surrounding the pond fade into the distance, and large trees dot the shoreline and cover the hills, making this a picturesque spot and a pleasurable place to paddle. The far, southwest end of the pond has some development, and we worry about the pond's ultimate fate. As we paddled, we listened to the ominous sound of chain saws on the surrounding hills. Paddle here now while this little gem remains relatively untrammeled.

19

Carlton Pond and Carlton Bog

Troy

> **MAPS:** Maine Atlas, Map 22
>   USGS Quadrangle, Unity Pond
> **AREA AND MAXIMUM DEPTH:** 430 acres, 8 feet; 1,055 acres in
>   wildlife management area
> **HABITAT TYPE:** shallow marsh
> **FISH:** largemouth bass, chain pickerel
> **EXPECT TO SEE:** black tern, osprey, ducks, snapping turtle,
>   muskrat, acres of marsh vegetation, moose possible
> **TAKE NOTE:** no development

GETTING THERE

From Waterville, go east on Route 139 to Unity, and turn left onto Routes 202 and 220. Just past Unity, at Greens Corner, turn left onto Route 220 (easy to miss). Go 1.2 miles (1.2 miles), and turn right at Smarts Corner. Go 0.6 mile (1.8 miles), and turn left at Cooks Corner. Go 1.2 miles (3.0 miles), and turn right onto Bog Road. Go 0.3 mile (3.3 miles) to the access on the left; park on the right.

From I-95, Exit 39, turn southwest onto Routes 11 and 100 south. Go about 2 miles, and turn left onto Route 220. When Routes 220 and 69 east divide, continue south on Route 220 for 7.7 miles, turn left onto Bog Road, and continue as above.

The state of Maine maintains Carlton Pond and Carlton Bog as a waterfowl-production area. We found it suitable not only for waterfowl but also for paddlers and for the rare black terns that nest here. Indeed, Carlton Pond remains one of our favorite places to explore. Because development has not intruded on the vast marshes here and to the immediate north, this is an excellent place to look for moose, though in four times that we paddled here we did not see any. In the spring and at other times of high water, one can paddle almost the entire bog area,

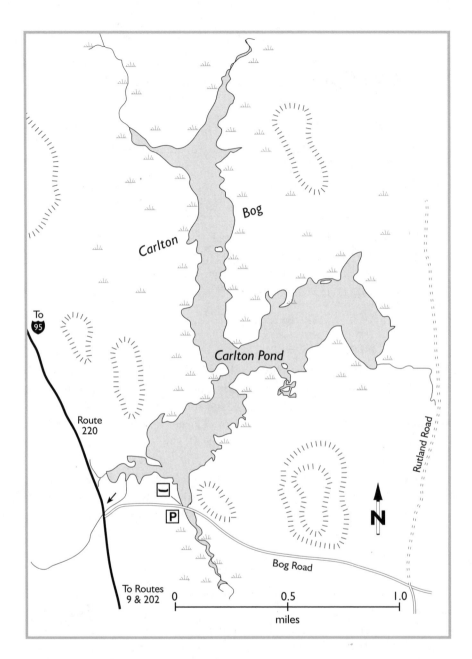

Bog

Carlton

To
95

Route
220

Carlton Pond

Rutland Road

P

N

To Routes
9 & 202

Bog Road

0   0.5   1.0

miles

including on the sinewy channel on the other side of the road, and it would take most of a day to explore every nook and cranny. With a maximum depth of only eight feet, nearly every species of aquatic vegetation found in this area—including slender blue flag *(Iris prismatica),* a threatened species in Maine—covers the pond's surface, except for a few narrow channels.

Typical bog vegetation covers the higher ground in and around this gigantic marsh. Hummocks seem to float everywhere, covered with sweetgale, rhodora, blueberries, sheep laurel, and lots more. Pitcher plants, sundews, and sphagnum abound. The sphagnum provides habitat for rose pogonia, an orchid that bloomed in large numbers in late June.

Sphagnum provides more than a soft, mossy pad for sundews, pitcher plants, and orchids. It exchanges some of its hydrogen ions for waterborne metal ions, thereby acidifying its immediate vicinity. This process makes the habitat unsuitable for most other plants that might crowd it out, except those that can tolerate an acid environment. When many layers of sphagnum accumulate, the bottom layers become devoid of oxygen and cannot decay much; as a result, peat develops.

When we paddled here, we saw hundreds of waterfowl but no loons, cormorants, or diving ducks, probably because of the shallow water, but dozens of dabbling ducks bobbed on the surface, occasionally dipping for a mouthful of aquatic vegetation. We tried not to get too close, but when we did, the ducks would leap into the air with a single wingbeat, helicopter style. This takeoff contrasts with the way heavier loons and cormorants run across the water's surface to get up enough speed to become airborne.

When you see a duck on land, note its horizontal profile, in contrast to the vertical profile of a perching cormorant. Cormorants and loons have their feet set well back on their bodies to enhance their underwater swimming capabilities as they chase fish. Their resulting streamlined horizontal profile in the water, along with their heavy bodies, makes it difficult for them to get vertical for liftoff. On the other hand, puddle ducks, which only bob their heads and necks underwater to gobble up plants, have their legs set at midbody. Consequently, they just stretch their necks upward to get vertical.

You might have to share this bog with a few mosquitoes. Fortunately, few make it out onto the water. Back on land, though, we must have set a record for getting the boat loaded up.

20

Douglas Pond
Palmyra and Pittsfield

> **MAPS:** Maine Atlas, Map 21
> USGS Quadrangle, Pittsfield
> **AREA:** 566 acres
> **HABITAT TYPE:** shallow, weedy pond; slow-flowing river
> **FISH:** smallmouth bass, chain pickerel, white perch
> **EXPECT TO SEE:** acres of marsh vegetation, ducks, great blue heron, muskrat
> **TAKE NOTE:** no development; motors

GETTING THERE

From I-95, Exit 38, go 0.9 mile (0.9 mile) east to Pittsfield, and turn left onto Route 152. Go 0.6 mile (1.5 miles), and turn right onto Waverly Avenue. Go 0.2 mile (1.7 miles) to the access on the left.

Douglas Pond, a natural body of water enhanced by a small dam on the Sebasticook River, forms part of the Madawaska Marsh Game Management Area, set aside primarily as duck-breeding and fish-breeding habitat. Because of its popularity with fishermen, you may not paddle alone here, but few people travel back into the marsh itself, where you will find acres of solitude.

From the access, paddle left, going under the interstate. Large deciduous trees, including red and sugar maples, elm, red oak, and mature paper birch, line the banks of this narrow section of river. Look for the drooping branches of a hemlock grove hanging out over the water on the left. As the channel widens, an alder swamp appears on both sides. Notice the large beaver lodges just past the interstate.

Acres and acres of cattails, rushes, and pickerelweed greet you as the channel broadens out into the shallow pond. Except perhaps in late summer, you should be able to paddle way back into the marsh, where you should see wood duck, muskrat, pickerelweed, arrowhead, great blue heron, and red-winged blackbird—to mention only a few.

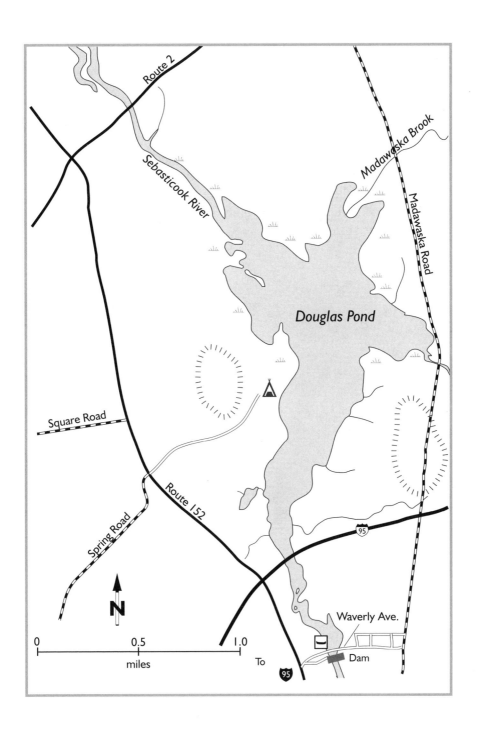

Route 2

Sebasticook River

Madawaska Brook

Madawaska Road

Douglas Pond

Square Road

Route 152

Spring Road

I-95

N

0   0.5   1.0
miles

Waverly Ave.

To

95

Dam

As you enter the marsh, interstate noise gradually fades into the distance as your focus turns to the sounds of birds, insects, and frogs, while your eyes feast on the vast beauty of Madawaska Marsh. It is hard to believe that such a wonderful place, teeming with fish and wildlife, exists right under the road that whisks the trailered boats to more exotic destinations.

If you crave exercise, paddle up the Sebasticook River. Except during flood stages, the river flows with modest to nearly undetectable current. We paddled about a mile above the Route 2 bridge and saw Canada goose, kingfisher, great blue heron, green heron, two loons, and many other birds.

Downeast

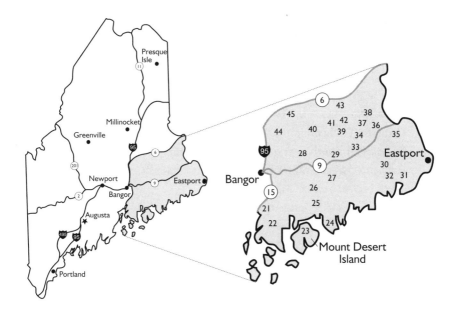

A maritime term, "Downeast" refers to sailing downwind in an easterly direction. From southern New England, where in summer the wind blows roughly south to north along the coast, sailing downeast takes you to the northeastern Maine coast. Here, ocean meets land along scenic rocky shores and cliffs, but the region's inland landscape and waters can be just as dramatic. Acadia, one of the most popular and spectacular national parks, covers large portions of Mt. Desert Island along the Downeast Coast. This rocky and mountainous island boasts 100 miles of hiking trails through thriving forests; freshwater streams, ponds, and lakes; and 17 mountains, including Cadillac Mountain, at 1,530 feet the highest point on the East Coast north of Rio de Janeiro. This guide includes Acadia's Long, Seal Cove, and Jordan Ponds and Eagle Lake (Trip 23), so paddlers may explore its inland waters. (For more outdoor adventures, including hiking, biking, and paddling in Acadia National Park, see *Discover Acadia National Park, Second Edition*, published by AMC Books in 2005.) Other featured trips include Scammon Pond (Trip 26), which lies in the center of Lyle Frost Wildlife Management Area; and Bog Brook Flowage (Trip 27), which takes you through an undeveloped, seldom-visited wetland, bursting with wildlife.

21

Silver Lake

Bucksport

> **Maps:** Maine Atlas, Map 23
>   USGS Quadrangle, Bucksport
> **Area and Maximum Depth:** 630 acres, 33 feet
> **Habitat Type:** pond dotted with islands
> **Fish:** smallmouth bass, chain pickerel, white perch
> **Expect to See:** loon, osprey, bald eagle, ducks, muskrat
> **Take Note:** no development; motors

Getting There

From Bangor, from where Route 15 crosses under I-395, go south on Route 15 for 12.8 miles (12.8 miles), and turn left onto Town Farm Road. Go 2.1 miles (14.9 miles), and turn right onto Silver Lake Road. Go 1.7 miles (16.6 miles) to the access on the left.

From Bucksport, from the Routes 1 and 3 bridge across the Penobscot River, go west on Route 15 for 0.5 mile (0.5 mile), turn right, and go steeply uphill on McDonald Street, which turns into Silver Lake Road. Go 1.6 miles (2.1 miles) to the access on the right.

Even though Silver Lake lies in close proximity both to Bangor and to the vacation meccas of Acadia, Blue Hill, and Camden, it remains relatively untrammeled and, as far as we could tell, seldom visited. When we paddled here on a warm, sunny Sunday in August, we saw only one other canoe, which is surprising, given the natural wonders we found.

We saw at least three and probably four bald eagles at close range: two immatures, which superficially resemble golden eagles, and one or two different adults with their characteristic white heads and tails. A group of seven loons swam together, and the far eastern cove harbored dozens of feeding wood ducks. Right at high noon, when you would least expect it, a doe and her spotted fawn came down to the shore of the northern arm to take a lengthy drink, seemingly oblivious to our

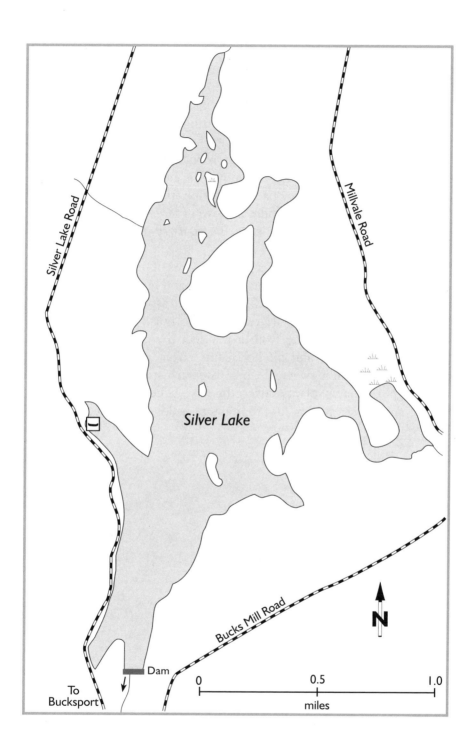

Silver Lake

Silver Lake Road

Millvale Road

Bucks Mill Road

Dam

To
Bucksport

N

0   0.5   1.0
miles

presence, while two adult and one juvenile osprey took serious exception to our presence within fifty yards of their nest on a utility pole.

We saw muskrats swimming out to harvest aquatic plants, young ungainly great blue heron learning to fish the shallows, and several beaver lodges with masses of fresh cuttings. Most grassy areas near shore harbored large numbers of frogs, and we found piles of mussel shells where raccoons frequent the shoreline on nightly feeding forays.

A power line cuts diagonally along the northwestern shore, providing aeries for two osprey pairs. Look for an excellent camping spot along the northwest shore, under a grove of large conifers. An elegant hand-carved sign contains the plea: Please carry in, carry out. Cut no live trees.

The marshy coves sport luxuriant growths of pickerelweed, cattail, bulrush, arrowhead, horsetail, bladderwort, and bur-reed. Shrubs grow densely along the shoreline, while white pine, aspen, birch, red maple, and red spruce dominate the canopy. The northern reaches harbor dozens of islands, ranging from a few feet to a half-mile in length. Sphagnum, sundews, and pitcher plants cover a few of the smaller, floating islands, while sweetgale, bog rosemary, stands of tamarack, and other typical marsh plants cover the rest. The intricate pattern of islands and waterways can lead to hours of paddling in quiet seclusion.

Bald Eagle
Our National Bird Back from the Brink

The bald eagle—with its unmistakable white head and tail—flies over the nation's waterways on powerful wings. In flight, its large size stands out—it soars on wings that span up to 8 feet. From beak to tip of tail, eagles measure from 34 to 43 inches; males weigh 8 to 9 pounds, while the larger females weigh 10 to 14 pounds. Bringing new meaning to "light as a feather," the feathers can contribute up to 15 percent of the bird's body weight.

A bald eagle attains its distinctive plumage only after attaining an age of four or five years. Until then, it resembles the dark brown golden eagle, except with some white mottling on the underside and tail. As it matures, the head and tail become progressively whiter. At close range, the adult's large yellow beak and piercing yellow eyes convey a fierce strength. Our country's founders evidently felt this image symbolized what our young nation stood for, selecting *Haliaeetus leucocephalus* as our national symbol. Appropriately, this is the only eagle found exclusively in North America.

The bald eagle ranges throughout Maine. Eagles generally locate their nests in trees at the water's edge. Pairs return to the same nest for years, adding to it annually. An old eagle nest can easily measure 6 feet in diameter,

8 feet deep, and weigh more than a ton. The largest nest ever found measured 9.5 feet in diameter and 20 feet deep. Because eagles often build nests in dead trees, the huge mass of the nest eventually topples the tree.

Bald eagles usually lay two eggs several days apart. Incubation lasts 30 to 36 days, during which the male and female share nesting duties. The young hatch several days apart, a strategy that improves the chances of fledging at least one chick. If food is scarce, the earlier-born chick may outcompete its younger sibling for food, and the younger chick will die. Because eagles live long lives—as long as 30 years in captivity but usually much less in the wild—they really only need to fledge a few chicks to replace themselves, thus maintaining a stable population.

After 10 to 12 weeks of a diet consisting mostly of fish, chicks fledge and begin to fly. For the next 7 or 8 weeks, they increasingly gain independence, eventually leaving the nest to migrate to coastal areas and to outfalls below dams where the water does not freeze. In years past, they congregated in great numbers off both coasts and in the Mississippi drainage each fall. Eagles still congregate by the thousands in mid-November along a ten-mile stretch of the Chilkat River in Alaska to feed on hordes of dead and dying salmon.

While bald eagles occur frequently in Maine today, just a few years ago only a few remained. Maine's population of eagles plummeted to a low of 21 breeding pairs in 1967, producing just six chicks. In the late 1960s and early 1970s, long-lasting chlorinated hydrocarbons—such as DDT and its breakdown product DDE, left over from mosquito-control projects—reached high concentrations in eagles, peregrine falcons, and other species at the top of the food chain and caused eggshells to break during incubation.

Eagle populations have rebounded to about 7,000 nesting pairs (up from 4,000 in 1993) in the United States outside Alaska, 309 of them in Maine in 2003 (150 in 1993)—with the greatest concentration around remote lakes in the eastern and northern regions. Despite the gains, however, Maine's annual nesting success rate remains below 1 fledged chick per nest. Some pairs fledge two chicks, which means that many fail to produce a single surviving chick.

The Maine Department of Inland Fisheries and Wildlife blames the low nesting success rate on various toxins in the eagle's food chain: mercury, mostly from coal-burning power plants in the Midwest, deposited in Maine by rain; DDE, a breakdown product from DDT that still remains in Maine's environment more than 30 years after the DDT ban; dioxins, released by the paper industry; and PCBs, released from various industrial operations and found in older electrical transformers.

Because eagle populations rose over the 23 years after DDT's ban, aided by reintroductions in many areas in the country, the U.S. Fish and Wildlife Service removed the bald eagle from the Endangered Species List in 1995, placing it on the Threatened List.

We feel privileged to paddle on lakes with bald eagles. Some accuse them of being opportunists, and indeed we have watched a few chase smaller osprey, laboring with heavy fish, circling to gain altitude before flying off to their aeries. In one case, after the osprey dropped its hard-won catch, a bald eagle snatched it and flew off. This is not a case of good and evil; instead, it represents the triumph of bald eagle adaptation, ensuring its survival.

Humans still shoot eagles on occasion and build high-voltage lines that electrocute them—although designs and devices exist that reduce eagle mortality—and many eagles die from flying into human-made structures (power lines, towers, smokestacks, and buildings). But the biggest threat to the eagle's continued survival comes from an expanding human population, one that spews forth toxic chemicals into the environment and continues to develop shorelines. If we wish to continue to enjoy this majestic creature as it patrols America's waterways—and keep it from returning to the Endangered Species List—we must take steps to keep some of its habitat undeveloped and unadulterated by the toxic wastes of a consumer society. The eagle represents an enduring wildness that we must protect for future generations to enjoy.

～22～

Wight Pond
Blue Hill and Penobscot

> **MAPS:** Maine Atlas, Map 15
>   USGS Quadrangle, Penobscot
> **AREA AND MAXIMUM DEPTH:** 135 acres, 21 feet
> **HABITAT TYPE:** long, narrow pond rimmed with boulders; marshy
>   stream
> **FISH:** largemouth bass, chain pickerel, white perch
> **EXPECT TO SEE:** kingfisher, mallard, osprey
> **TAKE NOTE:** no development

GETTING THERE

From Blue Hill, from the point where Routes 15, 172, and 176 turn off, go north on Route 177 for 5.8 miles to the easy-to-miss access on the right (just past an S-curve warning sign).

Amazingly, given its close proximity to Penobscot Bay and millions of tourists, Wight Pond has no development along its shoreline. The long, narrow pond has much to offer. If you paddle here in late summer, check out the outlet stream for cardinal flower, a brilliant-red member of the lobelia family. We visited here with a New England Wildflower Society naturalist who said that this was the largest and most spectacular concentration of cardinal flowers she had seen.

Paddling out from the access, you pass through acres of aquatic vegetation, including pickerelweed, arrowhead, yellow pondlily, fragrant waterlily, bulrush, bur-reed, and purple bladderwort. We managed to paddle right up to a painted turtle that was out sunning on a log. It never moved as we floated on by.

Passing out into the main part of the lake, the aquatic vegetation disappears as large rocks take over the shoreline. Seemingly everywhere we found piles of empty mussel shells, indicating the dining locations of otters or raccoons. Look for a great picnic spot for humans at the north end on the left.

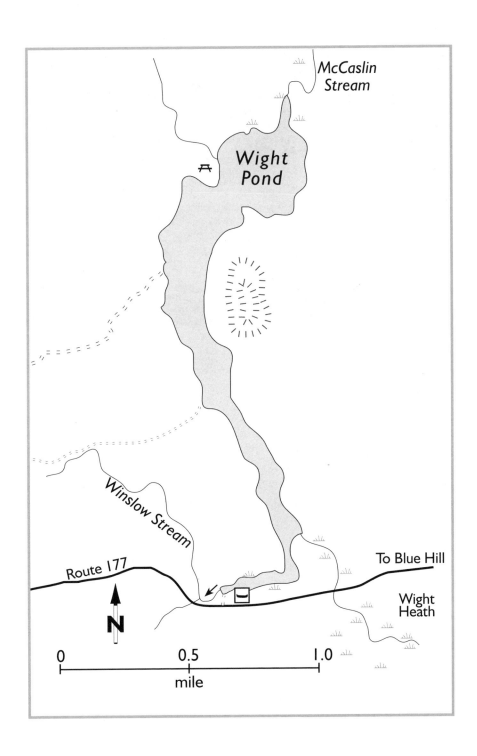

McCaslin
Stream

Wight
Pond

Winslow Stream

Route 177

To Blue Hill

Wight
Heath

N

0　　　　　0.5　　　　　1.0
mile

Alex glides by a painted turtle perched on a log. Turtles bask in the sun's warmth to raise body temperature and boost metabolism.

A large variety of trees, shrubs, and ferns line the shore; predominant tree species include white pine, red oak, red spruce, red maple, and balsam fir.

On the lake's northeast corner, an inlet weaves back through the marsh for about a half-mile. We scared out black ducks and a bittern from the reeds. Besides the wildlife and two fishermen, we had this pond to ourselves on a beautiful Saturday in mid-August.

~ 23 ~

Mount Desert Island:
Long Pond, Seal Cove Pond, Eagle Lake, and Jordan Pond

Bar Harbor, Mount Desert, Southwest Harbor, and Tremont

MAPS: Maine Atlas, Map 16; see also the AMC's *Hiking, Biking, and Paddling Map to Acadia National Park*, available on Tyvek for $7.95 at www.outdoors.org/amcstore.
USGS Quadrangles, Long Pond: Southwest Harbor and Bartlett Island; Seal Cove Pond: Bartlett Island; Eagle Lake: Southwest Harbor, Seal Harbor, Salsbury Cove, and Bar Harbor; Jordan Pond: Southwest Harbor

AREA AND MAXIMUM DEPTH: Long Pond: 897 acres, 113 feet; Seal Cove Pond: 283 acres, 44 feet; Eagle Lake: 436 acres, 110 feet; Jordan Pond: 187 acres, 150 feet

HABITAT TYPE: long, narrow, deep lakes

FISH: Long Pond: salmon, smallmouth bass, chain pickerel; Seal Cove Pond: brook and brown trout, smallmouth bass, perch; Eagle Lake and Jordan Pond: salmon, lake trout, brook trout

CAMPING: Acadia National Park, 800-365-2267 or www.nps.gov/acad/camping.htm; reservations essential

CANOE AND KAYAK RENTALS: Long Pond, 207-288-3338 or www.acadia.net/canoe

EXPECT TO SEE: scenic hillsides, osprey, bald eagle, loon, ducks

TAKE NOTE: no personal watercraft on Long Pond; 10-HP limit on Eagle Lake, Seal Cove, and Jordan Ponds; wind can make paddling on the southern half of Long Pond dangerous

---

GETTING THERE

Long Pond: From the causeway leading to the island, go south on Routes 102 and 198 to Somesville, staying on Route 102 as Route 198 goes left. Go 0.8 mile (0.8 mile), and turn right onto Pretty Marsh Road. Go 1.4 miles (2.2 miles) to

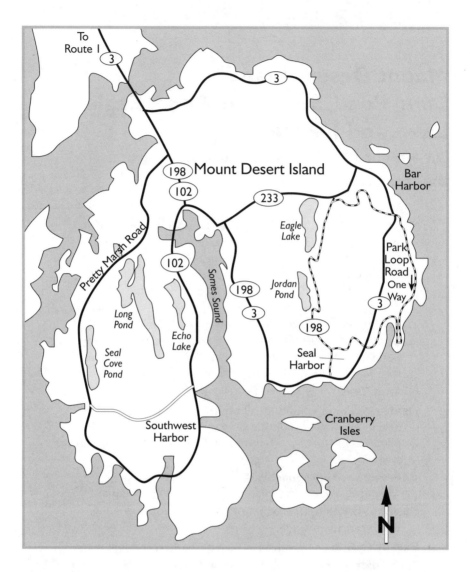

To Route 1

3

3

Mount Desert Island

198

102

233

Bar Harbor

Pretty Marsh Road

Eagle Lake

Park Loop Road One Way

102

Somes Sound

198

Jordan Pond

3

3

Long Pond

198

Echo Lake

Seal Cove Pond

Seal Harbor

Southwest Harbor

Cranberry Isles

N

the access on the left (boat-rental facility on the right). Southern access: From Somesville, go south on Route 102 for 4.9 miles (4.9 miles), and turn right onto Seal Cove Road. Go 0.5 mile (5.4 miles), turn right onto Long Pond Road, and go 1.1 miles (6.5 miles) to the access.

Seal Cove Pond: From Long Pond's north end, continue on Pretty Marsh Road for about 6 miles, and turn left onto Seal Cove Road 0.2 mile after crossing a small bridge over the Seal Cove Pond outlet. Go 0.5 mile (0.5 mile), turn left, and go 0.8 mile (1.3 miles), passing a road to the left leading to Bald Mountain. Turn left onto Western Mountain Road, and go 0.7 mile (2.0 miles) to the access.

Eagle Lake: From Somesville, go east on Route 198 for 1.3 miles (1.3 miles), and turn left onto Route 233. Go 3.6 miles (4.9 miles) to the access on the right. From Bar Harbor, at the junction with Route 3, go west on Route 233 for 2.1 miles to the access on the left.

Jordan Pond: Go south on the western (two-way) Park Loop Road, getting on at the north end near the Visitors Center or from Route 233 near the north end of Eagle Lake. Go 5.1 miles south of Route 233 to the exit for Jordan Pond. From Seal Harbor, go north on Jordan Pond Road for 0.8 mile (0.8 mile), and turn onto Park Loop Road. Go 0.7 mile (1.5 miles) to the access on the left.

Known primarily for its craggy shorelines, deep harbors, sailboats, tide pools, lobsters, and coastal vacationing, Mount Desert Island also offers some surprisingly pleasant freshwater lake and pond paddling. The island, Maine's most popular vacation spot, extends roughly 15

Jordan Pond on Mount Desert Island offers a civilized paddle in Acadia National Park, one of America's most popular parks.

miles north to south and 12 miles east to west. Acadia National Park—the oldest national park east of the Mississippi and the second most visited, with more than four million visitors per year—comprises about half of this rocky island. Four freshwater lakes and ponds that we highly recommend nestle among the island's majestic granite peaks.

One can paddle on at least five lakes and ponds on Mount Desert Island. We've paddled four of these: Eagle Lake and Long, Seal Cove, and Jordan Ponds. We didn't paddle on Echo Lake because busy Route 102 runs along the eastern shore.

Long Pond

The largest freshwater lake on the island, Long Pond stretches for about 4.5 miles. Quite a bit of development exists at the north end, so on a nice summer weekend you will share the pond with motorboats, water-skiers, and the like. Lots of people paddle here, as well. Across the road from the access, a concessionaire rents canoes and kayaks. Acadia National Park covers nearly the entire western shore of the lake, as well as the eastern shore near the southern tip.

Long Pond runs generally north-south, with the north end divided into eastern and western sections by Northern Neck. The pond's eastern arm suffers from more development than the western arm, which has some surprisingly isolated and wild coves where you can get away from most activity. We passed a few northern fens here, with sphagnum, pitcher plant, sundew, tamarack, cranberry, leatherleaf, and other species one sees much more commonly farther north.

The long, narrow, southern half of Long Pond suffers from winds that commonly blow from south to north, and the water can get quite rough. The south end provides dramatic views, with mountains rising on either side, tall rock cliffs overlooking the water, and jagged, wind-sculpted pines perched here and there. Numerous trails radiate out from the pond's southern end.

Seal Cove Pond

Seal Cove Pond, much smaller and more remote than Long Pond, also differs ecologically. Most of the shallow pond grows thick with fragrant waterlily, bulrush, horsetail, and pickerelweed, providing superb wildlife habitat. We saw wood duck, cormorant, loon, great blue heron, and a mature bald eagle. You can see a few houses along Route 102, but the entire eastern shore lies within the park.

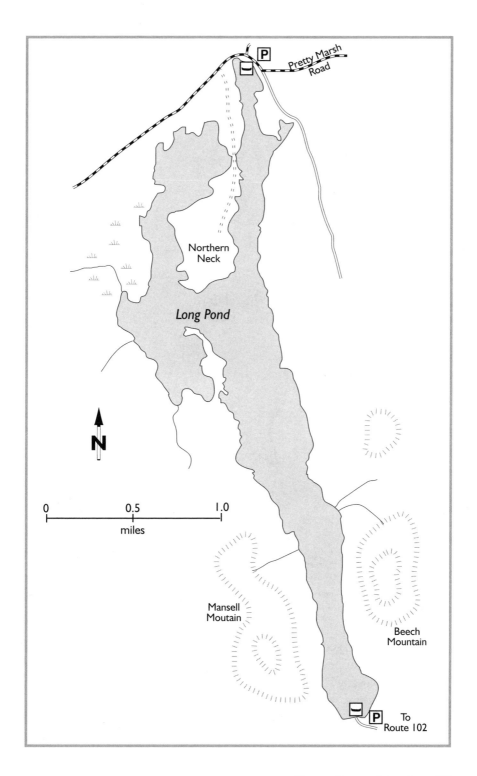

Pretty Marsh
Road

P

Northern
Neck

Long Pond

N

0   0.5   1.0
         miles

Mansell
Moutain

Beech
Mountain

P

To
Route 102

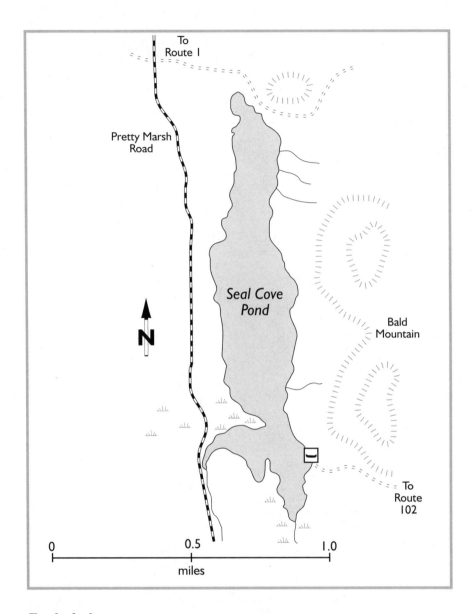

To
Route 1

Pretty Marsh
Road

*Seal Cove
Pond*

N

Bald
Mountain

To
Route
102

0		0.5		1.0

miles

Eagle Lake

Eagle Lake, the second largest freshwater body on Mount Desert Island, remains undeveloped and very attractive. It serves as a water supply for the island, with the northeastern tip off-limits and no swimming. Spectacular vistas of 1,248-foot Pemetic Mountain to the south and 1,530-foot Cadillac Mountain to the east await you as you paddle Eagle

Lake. Carriage roads and trails extend around the lake and connect to Jordan Pond, the West Face Trail up Cadillac Mountain, and a beautiful area between Eagle Lake and Jordan Pond known as The Bubbles.

In places, massive slabs of the characteristic pink granite extend down into the water. Along other sections, coarse, chunky gravel—stuff that could cut deep scratches in your boat—populates the shoreline. A

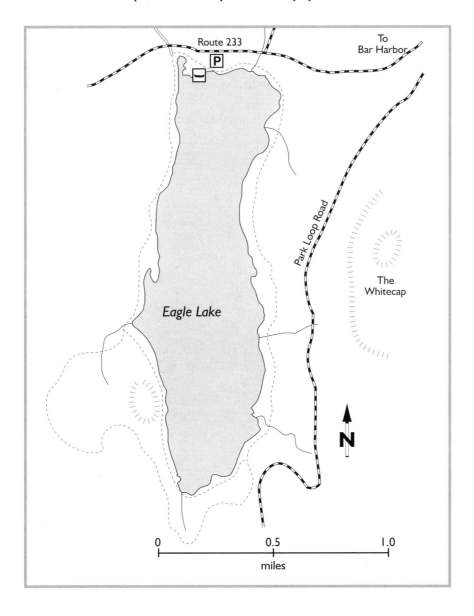

few marshy areas occur along the western shore where you'll see pickerelweed, bulrush, and a few other wetland plants, but mostly this is an unproductive (oligotrophic) lake. Where they have succeeded in gaining a foothold in the rocky soil, you'll see white and red pines, cedar, spruce, and fir.

Jordan Pond

Despite its small size, Jordan Pond is probably the best-known pond on Mount Desert Island. The dramatic scenery around the pond, the trail and carriage-road network, and—probably most significantly—the Jordan Pond House restaurant at the southern end all contribute to its

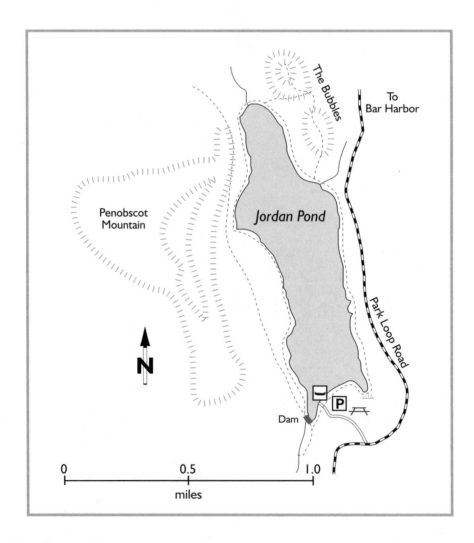

reputation. The original house dated to 1847, when the Jordan family of Seal Harbor built near a mill close to the pond's outlet. The house became a restaurant in the early 1870s, operated by Mr. and Mrs. McIntire for more than fifty years starting in 1895. John D. Rockefeller, Jr., purchased the property and gave it to the National Park Service to ensure its continuation. In June 1979, the original house burned but was rebuilt. From the restaurant you can enjoy elegant dining in view of the spectacular pond.

Because the pond serves as a public water supply, the park restricts boats at the south end to a narrow strip up the pond's center. Paddling along the shore provides beautiful views but no coves or marshy areas to explore. On the plus side, the park restricts motors to 10 HP here.

Jordan Pond's bottom drops off to more than 100 feet just a few yards from shore, with a maximum depth of 150 feet. The cold, well-oxygenated waters provide fairly good habitat for coldwater fish. A picnic area near the access, as well as the easy half-mile Jordan Pond Nature Trail, provide extra enticements for a visit.

Geologic History of Mount Desert Island

Several important geologic events shaped Mount Desert Island. Volcanic activity deep underground 350 to 400 million years ago extruded molten rock into the thick layers of rock that had originally formed as sea-bottom sediment. This magma bubble did not erupt as a volcano but instead cooled underground. Because the rock (technically a "pluton") cooled slowly, it formed distinctive, coarse, pink granite crystals. Then the entire region uplifted as North America collided with Europe and Africa.

Over the next few hundred million years, the overlying rock gradually eroded away, exposing the pink granite below. Finally, during the last million years, glaciation scoured the granite, rounding off mountain peaks and gouging the deep valleys and cliffs so characteristic of the island. The last glacier melted off Mount Desert Island only 13,000 years ago—a mere wink of an eye in geologic time. The deep glacier-carved troughs of Somes Sound connects with the ocean, making it a fiord—the only true fjord in the United States outside of Alaska. Its steep rock faces extend deep into the salt water. Several other glacial troughs, sealed off from the sea, form freshwater lakes and ponds.

24

Jones Pond

Gouldsboro

> **MAPS:** Maine Atlas, Maps 16 and 17
>   USGS Quadrangle, Winter Harbor
> **AREA AND MAXIMUM DEPTH:** 467 acres, 48 feet
> **HABITAT TYPE:** pond with several islands
> **FISH:** smallmouth bass, chain pickerel, brown trout
> **EXPECT TO SEE:** loon, cormorant, gulls, kingfisher, beaver in
>   evening
> **TAKE NOTE:** some development

GETTING THERE

From Ellsworth, go east on Route 1, and turn right onto Route 195 in West Gouldsboro. Go 0.4 mile (0.4 mile), turn right into Gouldsboro Town Park, and go 0.3 mile (0.7 mile) to the access.

Just a few miles, as the gull flies, from Mount Desert Island lies much less well-known Jones Pond. Gouldsboro maintains a heavily used recreation area on the pond. On a nice summer weekend, expect to see a lot of people. In addition, scattered houses intrude on the shoreline. Though paddling here will not be a wilderness experience, you can enjoy wildlife in the early morning or before or after the main summer season. The nesting loons we saw here suggest that it never gets too crowded, because repeated human disturbance drives loons away.

Several attractive islands add scenic character, and beautiful mosses and lichens festoon the huge granite boulders on the far shore. A mature mixed canopy with a well-developed understory surrounds the pond. Though the understory exhibits good diversity, sweetgale, with its pungent leaves, dominates the shoreline.

According to local fishermen, some huge brown trout lurk in Jones Pond depths, as well as a healthy population of smallmouth bass. Because of the pond's close proximity to salt water, large numbers of

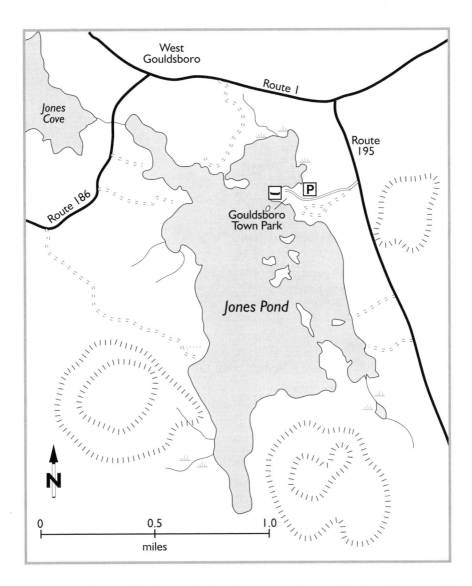

herring and great black-backed gulls appear, along with double-crested cormorant, great blue heron, and belted kingfisher. We saw yellow and chestnut-sided warblers, American redstart, and song sparrow. Look for beaver at the base of the southeast arm.

The town park has several picnic tables, grills, and a small building with bathrooms, screens, and a woodstove. Spring wildflowers bloom in profusion in the vicinity.

25

Donnell Pond
Franklin and T9 SD

> **MAPS:** Maine Atlas, Map 24
>   USGS Quadrangle, Sullivan
> **AREA AND MAXIMUM DEPTH:** 1,120 acres, 119 feet
> **HABITAT TYPE:** deep, oligotrophic lake
> **FISH:** salmon, lake trout, white perch
> **EXPECT TO SEE:** loon, raven, osprey, bald eagle possible, scenic
>   mountains
> **TAKE NOTE:** no personal watercraft; 15 authorized campsites (no
>   fire permit required)

GETTING THERE

From Ellsworth, go east on Route 1, and turn left onto Route 182. Go 7.5 miles (7.5 miles), and turn right onto Donnell Pond Road. Go 0.2 mile (7.7 miles), and turn right. Go 1.2 miles (8.9 miles), turn left, and go 0.2 mile (9.1 miles) to the access.

Don't be too discouraged by the development along the western arm. Past Little Island, largely undeveloped Donnell Pond offers superb paddling on all but the busiest summer weekends—when motorboats and water-skiers can be oppressive. To enjoy the pond's full beauty, paddle here on weekdays or after Labor Day—when the bugs and most of the people have departed.

This deep, rocky pond has low biological productivity, which keeps the water exceptionally clear. Granite boulders, bedrock, and sand beaches define much of the shoreline, with thick woodland extending back from the water. The pond nestles beneath several mountains that rise up a thousand feet from the water's surface. About a mile east of the access you will come to a cluster of islands. Great slabs of exposed granite bedrock extend down into the water, dominating the largest of these—appropriately named Mile Island—a superb picnic spot.

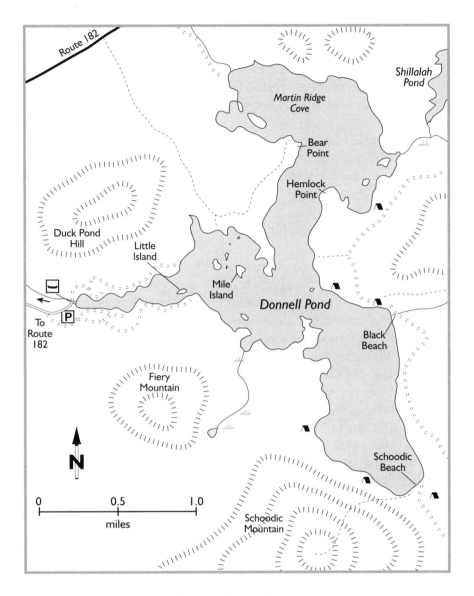

Geologically, Donnell Pond lies in the center of a massive granitic intrusion extending over 70 square miles. The granite, rich in quartz and feldspar, weathers into a coarse, well-drained, acidic soil, leading to generally dry conditions and fire-prone vegetation. Researchers believe that fires contributed to the exposed "balds" on Schoodic and Black mountains. A number of plant species reach the northern limit of their ranges here, including bayberry, common juniper, golden heather, and highbush blueberry. The Schoodic and Black mountain balds support a number of rare plant species.

Several loon pairs nest here, and osprey have nested in a dead spruce along the pond in recent years. We frequently see bald eagles. For anglers, Donnell Pond's deep, clear waters offer coldwater fishing opportunities.

Schoodic Bay and the day-use area—with picnic tables, outhouses, and camping area—lie at the south end, roughly three miles from the access. Coarse, pebbly granite sand comprises this broad natural beach. Schoodic Mountain (1,069 feet) rises from the pond's south end; a trail extends up the mountain from the day-use area. Black Beach, an equally nice beach and camping area, perches along the east side where Redman Brook flows in.

The pond has an interesting recent history. A land speculator, Patten Corporation, purchased much of the surrounding land in the late 1980s and planned to develop it with hundreds (or thousands) of vacation homes. Fortunately, conservation groups and the state of Maine got wind of the impending loss, and in 1988 the state acquired approximately 7,000 acres around the pond, including roughly two-thirds of the shoreline and land to the east and south, through a complex five-way land swap (the state now owns more than 14,000 acres in the area). This land transaction helped catalyze the formation of the Northern Forest campaign by several environmental/outdoors organizations in the Northeast, including the Appalachian Mountain Club.

While Donnell Pond narrowly escaped large-scale development that would have ruined its beauty and tranquillity, any warm, sunny, summer weekend will remind paddlers that the pond still sees heavy use by motorboaters. To remain relatively pristine, Donnell Pond needs an initiative to restrict motorboat access. The state banned personal watercraft, but we would love to see a local group petition the state to restrict access to carry-in boats only, though a 10-HP restriction would be a great step forward.

Hiking opportunities abound at Donnell Pond. As noted previously, a trail to Schoodic Mountain begins at Schoodic Beach at the pond's south end, and a network of trails from Black Beach on the east shore leads to Black Mountain and Wizard Pond, which harbors a 21-acre stand of old-growth red spruce. In addition to these maintained trails, many old logging roads crisscross the public lands to the east.

～26～

Scammon Pond
Eastbrook

Maps: Maine Atlas, Map 24
  USGS Quadrangles, Eastbrook and Molasses Pond
Area: 396 acres (658 acre wetland)
Habitat Type: shallow, weed-choked pond
Fish: chain pickerel
Expect to See: loon, osprey, raven, ducks, aquatic vegetation, muskrat, beaver in evening
Take Note: watch for stumps and boulders; no development; motors limited by shallow water and obstacles

---

Getting There

From Ellsworth, go east on Route 1, and turn left onto Route 182. Go 5.0 miles (5.0 miles), turn left onto Route 200 north, and go 6.5 miles (11.5 miles) to Eastbrook. At the fork in town, turn right onto Molasses Pond Road, and go 0.3 mile (11.8 miles) to the access on the right.

Scammon Pond, a beautiful place to paddle and well worth exploring, lies in the center of the Lyle Frost Wildlife Management Area. Some huge granite boulders line the shore, and you should expect to run into an occasional submerged stump or granite boulder. We recommend that you go slowly and enjoy the birds, plants, and animals of this quiet and scenic spot.

A few enormous, flat-topped boulders protruding from the water make great picnic spots. On hot, sunny days, a better picnic spot would be under the pines on either shore where the pond narrows, about a mile from the access.

Many tree species and a dense understory line the shore. Along with acres of fragrant waterlily, we found lots of sundews growing on exposed stumps and hummocks. This boggy area provides ideal habitat for carnivorous plants, including many pitcher plants.

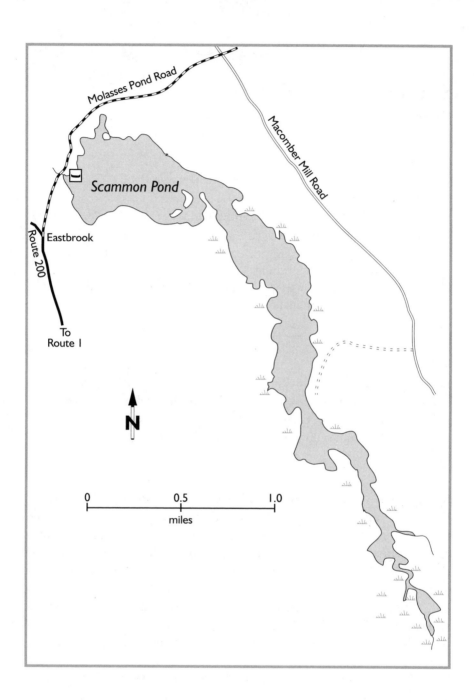

Molasses Pond Road

Macomber Mill Road

Scammon Pond

Route 200

Eastbrook

To
Route 1

N

| 0 | 0.5 | 1.0 |
miles

Although pitcher plants digest unlucky insects that enter the water-filled tubular leaves, for some mysterious reason they do not digest the larvae of one species of mosquito. Why does this mosquito lay its eggs in pitcher plants when every conceivable location in Maine harbors stagnant or slow-moving water? Probably because no dragonfly or other predacious insect larvae or small fish or bladderworts inhabit the pitchers. In the competition for space, this mosquito seems to have done well.

We found ducks everywhere, feeding among the aquatic plants, and we saw several osprey fishing. Ravens, cedar waxwings, and swallows cavorted over the water, while several great blue herons fished the shoreline. We thought we heard young birds calling from a great blue heron rookery, but we could not locate the nests among the dense rows of trees lining the shore.

Several mammoth beaver lodges perch along the pond's upper end. Keep an eye out for muskrats harvesting grasses in the shallows. As you pass into the pond's upper reaches, it narrows considerably, and you have to wend your way through meandering channels filled with pickerelweed and dense patches of waterlily. After paddling about three-quarters of the way to the end of the pond, you will have to portage over a beaver dam to gain access to the rest.

Aquatic vegetation, stumps, and granite boulders keep motorboats out of Scammon Pond.

Carnivorous Plants
The Table Is Turned

Carnivorous plants are fascinating—and a common sight as you paddle through the bogs and marshes of Maine's lakes and ponds. Specialized adaptations make them one of nature's true wonders and make us wonder how their meat-eating habit evolved.

Carnivory in plants apparently resulted from convergent evolution: the taking on of similar traits among unrelated species. Many different, completely unrelated plant families on nearly every continent have some carnivorous species. These plants have two characteristics in common: Almost all live in mineral-poor soils and supplement meager soil nutrients with those from animals, and they use modified leaves to trap food.

Two main capture strategies have evolved: active and passive. Most people recognize the active capture strategy of the Venus-flytrap, a plant that grows in sandy soils in a narrow band along the coastal border between North Carolina and South Carolina. A few other carnivorous plants have adopted active capture strategies, and one of them grows abundantly— sometimes forming dense mats—in the quiet, shallow marshes and bogs of Maine: bladderworts of the genus *Utricularia*. Bladderwort leaves consist of minute bladders that, upon stimulation, inflate and ingest insect larvae and other organisms, to be digested by the plant's enzymes.

Passive capture strategies have taken two main paths among the remaining carnivorous plants. Pitcher plants—*Sarracenia purpurea*—collect rainwater in their funnel-shaped modified leaves. Insects, attracted to nectar secreted around the top of the pitcher, fall in. The plant's stiff, downward-pointing hairs keep most insects from climbing back out. Eventually the insects drown, and a combination of plant and bacterial enzymes reduces the insects to absorbable nutrients.

Another passive-capture plant uses sticky surfaces to ensnare insects. Sundews (genus *Drosera*) form tiny rosettes that protrude from a central root. Stalked glands of two types cover the modified-leaf surface. One type secretes a sticky substance that glistens like dew in the sun, giving the plant its name. Entrapped insects, drawn initially by the nectarlike secretions, are digested by enzymes secreted by the second set of glands.

Each of the plants described above—bladderworts, pitcher plants, and sundews—captures its intended victims in a different way, but they all do so because, in nutrient-poor marshes and bogs, absorbing nitrogen and other minerals from insects and other prey gives them a selective advantage over other plants.

Do not be fooled by black, fertile-looking soils of marshes and swamps. Black dirt like this in Iowa means fertile soil, but in bogs it means carbon from undecomposed plants. The tea-colored water, laden with organic acids from decaying vegetation and supplemented by acid rain, effectively washes out minerals. Although carbon dioxide and water remain plentiful, nitrogen, phosphorus, potassium, and other important elements get leached out or bound up in underlying layers of sphagnum and peat. Carnivorous plants, with their diet of insects and other organisms, supplement the lost nutrients, making them effective competitors in the bog ecosystem.

Bladderworts. Bladderworts grow in quiet, shallow waters or in shoreline muck. Look for small yellow or purple snapdragonlike flowers, leading on short stalks to their carnivorous underwater bladders. The vast majority of the plant lives underwater in dense, feathery mats, bearing hundreds of tiny (0.02 to 0.1 inch long), bulbous traps that are the plant's leaves. The bladders have two concave sides and a trap door. When an insect larva or other small organism bumps into the door's guard hairs, the bladder's sides pop out, creating suction, the door swings open, and water along with and the hapless critter get sucked in. All of this occurs in about 1/500 of a second, followed by slow digestion by plant enzymes.

In most ponds, mosquito larvae form the bulk of the plant's diet, but it also ingests other larvae, rotifers, protozoans, small crustaceans, and even tiny tadpoles. Plant tissues digest and absorb animal remains, causing the trap's sides to go concave again. With large prey, such as a tiny tadpole, the door closes around the organism, and part gets digested. The next time the hairs get triggered, the plant ingests more of the organism, eventually sucking it all in.

Several species of bladderwort grow in our area, including two with purple flowers, one aquatic and one terrestrial, and as many as ten species with yellow flowers, mostly aquatic but including at least two terrestrials. We usually notice the presence of these plants when we see their snapdragonlike flowers protruding a few inches above the water's surface. Their dense underwater mats attest to their successful adaptation to nutrient-poor waters.

Pitcher Plants. Although several other species of *Sarracenia* pitcher plants exist in North America, the northern pitcher plant, *Sarracenia purpurea,* has the widest distribution, growing from British Columbia to Nova

Scotia, southward through the Great Lakes region, down the eastern coastal plain, crossing the Florida panhandle to the Mississippi River.

Initially green in the spring, the pitcher plant's funnel-shaped leaves turn progressively more purple, becoming deep maroon in the fall, and return to green again in the spring. Flowering occurs in June and July in Maine, and single reddish flowers, borne on stout stalks, tower a foot or more above the cluster of pitchers.

In contrast to most other species, the northern pitcher plant does not have a hood to keep rain out. The curved pitchers recline, allowing rain to fall freely into the open hood. Because of dilution of the pitcher's contents, insects drown well before digestion

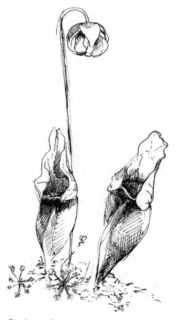

Pitcher plant

occurs. The stiff, downward-pointing hairs in the plant's throat keep insects from climbing back out, and the relatively narrow funnel leaves little room for airborne escape. The upper pitcher walls sport a waxy coating, making for slippery footing. A combination of plant and bacterial enzymes degrades the unlucky insects, and their nutrients pass easily through the unwaxed surface of the lower pitcher.

Amazingly, several different types of organisms can live in the pitchers, unharmed by digestive juices. One genus of mosquito harmless to humans, *Wyeomyia,* lives the aquatic part of its lifecycle in the pitcher, and other insects can escape by walking up the waxy cuticle and out over the downward-pointing hairs.

Sundews. To find sundews, look for tiny glistening drops at the ends of their traps. The smallest plants may measure only an inch across, making it easy to overlook them. Four species occur in our area, and we describe the most common species here: roundleaf sundew *(Drosera rotundifolia).*

This remarkable plant grows mainly in sphagnum bogs, from Alaska to northern California, across the Canadian Rockies and plains, through the Great Lakes, north throughout Labrador, south to Chesapeake Bay, and down through the Appalachians. The same plant grows in Europe as well;

Darwin devoted much of his book *Insectivorous Plants* to this one species. It averages about three inches across and about an inch high, with all of its leaves modified into sticky traps. A short leaf stalk ends in a flattened oval pad covered with red, stalked glands. The longer glands secrete a sticky fluid, while the shorter glands secrete digestive enzymes. Insects, attracted to the nectarlike secretions, become trapped. Slowly, imperceptibly, the pad edges roll over slightly, placing the insect in contact with digestive juices.

The usually white but sometimes pink flowers hover well above the plant's leaves, borne on a slender stalk. Although easy to miss, a little careful looking on sphagnum mats will reveal many of these reddish rosettes. You should also see several small insects in various stages of digestion. And you, too, can wonder about how these plants developed the incredible ability to supplement the meager amount of nutrients available from the soil with those from insect prey.

~ 27 ~

Bog Brook Flowage
Beddington and Deblois

MAPS: Maine Atlas, Map 25
USGS Quadrangles, Northeast Bluff and Lead Mountain
AREA: 565 acres (924 acres in the Wildlife Management Area)
HABITAT TYPE: shallow pond and marshland
FISH: chain pickerel
EXPECT TO SEE: loon, osprey, bald eagle, ducks, snapping turtle
TAKE NOTE: steer clear of osprey nests

GETTING THERE

From Bangor, go east on Route 9. From the junction with Route 193, go east on Route 9 for 1.2 miles (1.2 miles), and turn right just after crossing the Narraguagus River. Go 2.0 miles (3.2 miles), and stay right. Go 3.7 miles (6.9 miles), and turn left, just after crossing a bridge. Go about 100 feet, park,

John breaks in a new sea kayak while paddling over this beaver dam between Flynn Pond and Bog Brook Flowage.

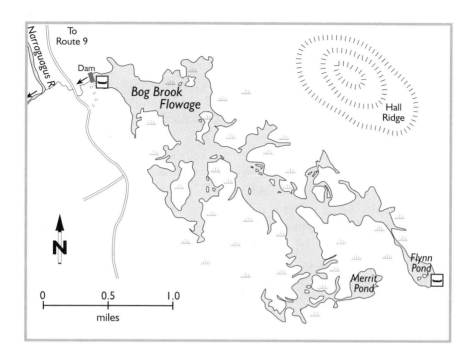

walk up a short, steep hill, and fork left down to the water.

The Flynn Pond access is exceedingly difficult to find and requires driving through miles of blueberry fields.

Bog Brook Flowage can only be described with superlatives. Completely undeveloped, seldom visited, and maintained as a Maine Wildlife Management Area, it would take an entire day to explore every nook and cranny of this small, three-mile-long lake. Numerous side channels and coves extend, seemingly in every direction, away from the open water in the main channel.

True to the area's name, bog shrubbery dominates the shoreline, including bog rosemary, sweetgale, rhodora, cranberry, leatherleaf, and Labrador tea. While exploring the coves, you will have to thread your way through numerous small islands covered with these plants. Large patches of yellow pondlilies and other aquatic vegetation poke up through the shallow water. Keep an eye out for small yellow, snapdragonlike bladderwort flowers, leading on short stalks to carnivorous underwater bladders that suck in and digest (all too few) mosquito larvae (see p. 128 for more on their feeding habits).

As you paddle up the left side, look for osprey nests next to the water. A great blue heron rookery occupies another extensive patch of dead trees. If you paddle here in the spring or early summer, enjoy these wonders with binoculars, as paddling too close may interfere with nesting or interrupt feeding the young. Large numbers of black ducks and wood ducks feed in the shallows. A couple of loon pairs nest here, as well.

As you paddle through boggy areas, keep an eye out for bobolinks, one of the few birds that is black underneath and brightly colored on the back, in this case yellow and white. The black tern, another rare marsh bird also black underneath, inhabits these wetlands as well. We also saw upland sandpipers, increasingly rare in the East, strolling about the blueberry fields. Northern harriers cruise these same fields, tilting back and forth, patiently waiting to pounce on rodents that do not have the good sense to be under cover in the middle of the day.

28

Great Pond

Great Pond

> **MAPS:** Maine Atlas, Map 34
>   USGS Quadrangle, Great Pond
> **AREA AND MAXIMUM DEPTH:** 679 acres, 34 feet
> **HABITAT TYPE:** scenic lake; meandering, marshy stream
> **FISH:** brown trout, smallmouth bass, yellow perch, chain pickerel; brook trout in streams
> **EXPECT TO SEE:** beaver in Dead Stream
> **TAKE NOTE:** camping allowed when not in use by military personnel; 10-HP limit

GETTING THERE

From Bangor, go east on Route 9 for about 26 miles to the junction with Route 179. Continue on Route 9 for 1.6 miles (1.6 miles), turn left, then immediately right onto Great Pond Road. Go 7.1 miles (8.7 miles) to the access.

Though the site of the Navy's Outdoor Adventure Center, we saw few other visitors the two times that we paddled here; we paddled mostly alone here on the Saturday of Labor Day weekend and later in September. We saw a couple of other boats, but most of the time we paddled in complete solitude. Great Pond also marks the beginning of the West Branch of the Union River trip. The West Branch starts just around a bend to the left from the access. If you paddle down this stream, you will not be able to paddle back up against the substantial current at the pond's outlet. Supposedly, the river turns to flat water shortly after leaving the pond, but we did not explore this.

Deciduous vegetation covers the hillsides and islands here, with only a few scattered pines, making us wonder about the recreation area's former name, Dow Pines. It is a scenic spot, with two nice tree-covered islands. Unless you get caught up watching the antics of the resident beaver population, it should not take more than a few hours to explore all of Great Pond.

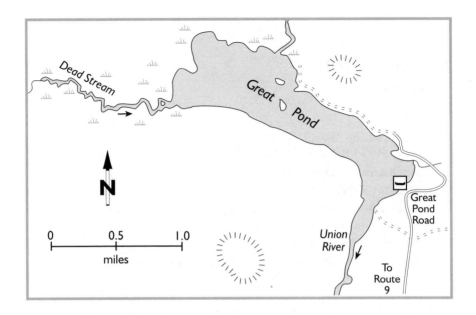

We recommend paddling here in the evening or very early morning, especially up the Dead Stream inlet at the lake's west end. At nearly every bend in the meandering stream we came across beaver that protested our presence with loud tail slaps. Several waited until we got right up to them before sounding the alarm and diving for cover, splashing us with water. We had such a good time that we waited until well after sunset to paddle back, our way lighted by alpenglow on the hillsides.

29

Mopang Lakes
Deveraux Twp and T30 MD BPP

MAPS: Maine Atlas, Maps 25 and 35
USGS Quadrangles, Peaked Mountain and Quillpig Mountain

AREA AND MAXIMUM DEPTH: Mopang Lake, 1,487 acres, 76 feet;
Second Mopang Lake, 145 acres, 20 feet

HABITAT TYPE: large lake with islands, coves, and marshy
entrance stream

FISH: brook trout (in stream), splake, salmon, white perch, chain
pickerel

EXPECT TO SEE: loon, osprey, common and black terns

TAKE NOTE: owned by International Paper; for designated campsites, 207-827-3700; high clearance required to reach Second
Mopang Lake access; fire permits required, Maine Forest Service, 207-827-1800

GETTING THERE

Mopang Lake: From Bangor, go east on Route 9 to the junction with Route
193. Continue on Route 9 for 6.5 miles (6.5 miles), and turn left. Go 1.3 miles
(7.8 miles), and go left. Go 1.2 miles (9.0 miles), and go left. Go 0.1 mile (9.1
miles) through a hemlock corridor to the access on the right.

Second Mopang Lake: As above, except go right at 7.8 miles. Go 1.7 miles
(9.5 miles), and turn left onto an unmaintained, high-clearance road (if you
reach a major road to the left, you have gone about 0.2 mile too far). Go 0.3
mile (9.8 miles) to the access (stay right at the fork).

Mopang Lake and Second Mopang Lake are among the many great
paddling lakes in Washington County, also known as Sunrise County,
as it feels the sun's morning rays before anywhere else in the United
States. The larger, somewhat bell-shaped lake harbors a sizable peninsula near the south end and numerous islands and large boulders near
the north end. Typical Maine trees populate the shore: red spruce,
northern white cedar, white pine, hemlock, some red pine, paper birch,

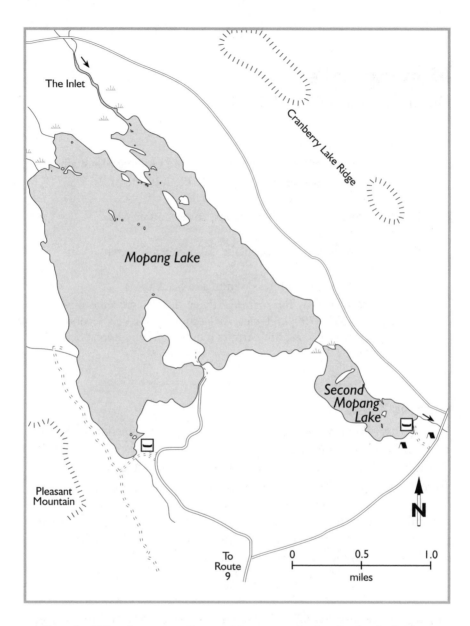

The Inlet

Cranberry Lake Ridge

Mopang Lake

Second Mopang Lake

Pleasant Mountain

To Route 9

N

| 0 | 0.5 | 1.0 |

miles

and maple. The shore overflows with sweetgale, leatherleaf, rhodora (a beautiful pink wild azalea that blooms in May), alder, and highbush blueberry. Second Mopang Lake resembles its larger neighbor but has a more remote feel to it.

In spring, one can paddle a small boat upstream from Second Mopang into Mopang, especially in smaller boats. Pick your way carefully among the rocks as you paddle up the briskly flowing, small connecting creek. We only paddled in one direction; going downstream, the current would carry you into rocks. Alternatively, carry your boat either through the water or through the brush and trees. Several very nice campsites hide along the southeastern end of Second Mopang Lake.

Common tern

We watched two species of terns here: the more prevalent common tern (but no longer very common over most of its range) and the distinctive black tern, nearly solid black with a white undertail patch and dark, silvery wings. The common tern nests in small colonies on some of the large protruding boulders on the lake's northern half. During nesting season, keep your distance from nesting terns. At the north end in the marshy inlet, you may see wood ducks, mergansers, and other waterfowl. We noticed at least three loon pairs on the two lakes.

A coarse pegmatite granite—mostly black-and-white with large crystals of biotite mica, feldspar, and quartz—dominates the rocky shoreline. The large crystal size indicates that the granite formed deep underground where molten magma cooled very slowly.

For camping, we prefer the neck connecting the large peninsula near the southern end. Sandy coves occur on both sides of this neck, with pleasant tenting sites under the tall conifers and several trails for exploring the area and observing the numerous wildflowers, including painted trillium, pink lady's slipper, wild sarsaparilla, and bunchberry.

30

Rocky and Second Lakes
T18 ED BPP and T19 ED BPP

> **MAPS:** Maine Atlas, Map 26
> USGS Quadrangles, Long Lake and Whiting
> **AREA AND MAXIMUM DEPTH:** Rocky Lake, 1,555 acres, 37 feet
> **HABITAT TYPE:** large lake with many coves and inlets
> **FISH:** smallmouth bass, white perch, chain pickerel; a few salmon in winter; small brook trout in southern inlet
> **EXPECT TO SEE:** loon, bald eagle, moose
> **TAKE NOTE:** under windy conditions, Rocky Lake can be treacherous; do not take novice paddlers here; several authorized campsites (no fire permits required); no fires allowed elsewhere

---

GETTING THERE

Rocky Lake, South Bay, and Second Lake: From East Machias, at the junction of Routes 1 and 191, go north on Route 191 for 7.3 miles (7.3 miles), and turn left at the blue Rocky Lake sign. Go 1.6 miles (8.9 miles; right at the fork at 1.4 miles) to a campsite and access. This Diamond Match Road continues on to Second Lake, ending in a small parking area with a several-hundred-foot portage down to the lake.

Rocky Lake, Mud Landing: From East Machias, go north on Route 191 for 8.7 miles (8.7 miles) to the next blue sign, turn left, and go 0.7 mile (9.4 miles) to the access and campsite.

Which one of these lakes you choose to paddle depends on what type of trip you have in mind and on the weather. Rocky Lake and its inlet and outlet streams include lots of interesting water to paddle. Although we did not paddle Second Lake, we include a short description here because it is four-fifths owned by the state and has no development.

Rocky Lake

The state owns the southern two-thirds of this 4.5-mile-long lake. Several access points allow flexibility in planning a trip—an important

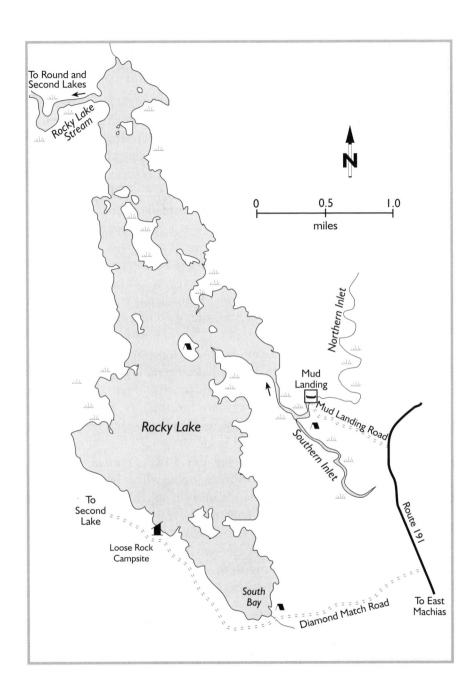

To Round and
Second Lakes

Rocky Lake
Stream

N

0   0.5   1.0
miles

Northern Inlet

Mud
Landing

Mud Landing Road

Rocky Lake

Southern Inlet

Route 191

To
Second
Lake

Loose Rock
Campsite

South
Bay

Diamond Match Road

To East
Machias

point when north or south winds roll deep swells and whitecaps up or down this north-south oriented lake. In calm or modest wind conditions, by all means paddle Rocky Lake.

We prefer the main access at Mud Landing. As you leave the inlet, the left (southeast) shore sports an extensive stand of white cedar that provides an important wintering yard for deer. Quite shallow, the lake remains true to its name, with rocks everywhere: lining the shore, protruding from the water, lurking just beneath the surface, effectively keeping down the number of high-speed boats. Generally, you will see only other paddlers and a few fishermen with small outboards. One can still have a true wilderness experience here in a great location for looking at plants and wildlife.

You can camp at both access points: Mud Landing and South Bay. Along the southwestern shore at Loose Rock, you will find a third official campsite with picnic table, outhouse, and lean-to. In addition to official campsites, several informal campsites exist on islands and at various points along the shore.

If you have enough time, explore Rocky Lake Stream at the lake's northwest end. Paddling down Rocky Lake Stream, you will come to Northern Stream entering from the right (north). Take a side trip up Northern Stream, or continue downstream to the East Machias River, where you can turn left and paddle downstream to Second Lake or turn right and paddle upstream to Round Lake.

We paddled on Rocky Lake in May, July, and September. In May, a severe wind and driving rain kept us from leaving the inlet at the end of the Mud Landing. In July, the wind barely rippled the water, but in September the whitecaps broke over the bow as we dipped through two-foot swells that almost—and should have—kept us off the lake. If the wind keeps you off the main lake or if you want solitude, by all means paddle from Mud Landing to the right up Northern Inlet or to the left up the southern inlet, taking you into remote, marshy areas, filled with plants and wildlife.

In the southern inlet, you will have to portage over a beaver dam almost immediately. After we crossed the dam, we had smooth sailing up the meandering stream—though, as you know, other dams may appear. This quite boggy area, mainly filled with shrubs, also contains occasional stands of dwarfed red maple and some good-size tamarack. Alder, birch, aspen, and red maple dominate the shoreline farther back, and white pine, spruce, and many other tree species appear back in the woods. We paddled more than a mile into the marsh until a second beaver dam blocked our way; you certainly could go farther.

We also paddled up Northern Inlet some distance, until we reached the first beaver dam. We leave it to you to explore this area more fully.

If the wind blows from the south, as it often does during the summer, you could launch from South Bay and stick to that area. Alternatively, you could paddle Second Lake or put in at Round Lake (see *Maine Atlas* for directions) on the East Machias River and paddle to Rocky Lake or Second Lake on streams generally unaffected by wind.

Second Lake

You can paddle from Rocky Lake to Second Lake, a distance of about nine miles from Mud Landing. Not having paddled all the way to Second Lake, we can't comment about water conditions, especially at Munson Rips; paddling back upstream may be difficult. However, if you leave a car at Second Lake, you can make this a one-way trip. Bald eagles have nested over the years just above Second Lake. You can also reach Second Lake by the Diamond Match Road.

A tiger swallowtail (Papilio glaucus) *sips nectar from a streamside shrub.*

31

Rocky Lake II
Edmunds Twp, Marion Twp, and Whiting

MAPS: Maine Atlas, Map 26
   USGS Quadrangles, Long Lake and Whiting
AREA AND MAXIMUM DEPTH: 1,126 acres, 33 feet
HABITAT TYPE: large, shallow lake; marshy, weed-choked coves
FISH: brown and brook trout, yellow perch
EXPECT TO SEE: loon, osprey, Canada goose, beaver, moose
   possible
TAKE NOTE: in 2004, a substantial portion of the northern part of
   Rocky Lake was for sale; development a real threat

GETTING THERE

From East Machias at the junction of Routes 1 and 191, go east on Route 1 for 7.4 miles (7.4 miles), and turn left onto Halls Mills Road. Go 1.5 miles (8.9 miles), turn left about 100 feet before the bridge onto Rocky Lake Shore Road, and go 0.1 mile (9.0 miles) to the access.

Why would two large lakes within eight miles of each other both carry the name Rocky Lake? To keep them separate, we affectionately call them Rocky I and Rocky II. Perhaps affection does not really describe our feeling toward these lakes, given the large number of submerged rocks and the generally shallow character of both. This lake—Rocky II—lies east of Machias, while Rocky I lies north of Machias (see preceding section).

As we paddled up the southern arm from the access (albeit during a dry summer), almost every single paddle stroke struck the mud bottom of this heavily vegetated, marshy lake. We tried to paddle up the northwestern arm to Sunken Lake but had to turn back at about the halfway point because of shallow water. With repairs to the dams and resultant deeper water, it would be well worth the trip up this most interesting arm of the lake.

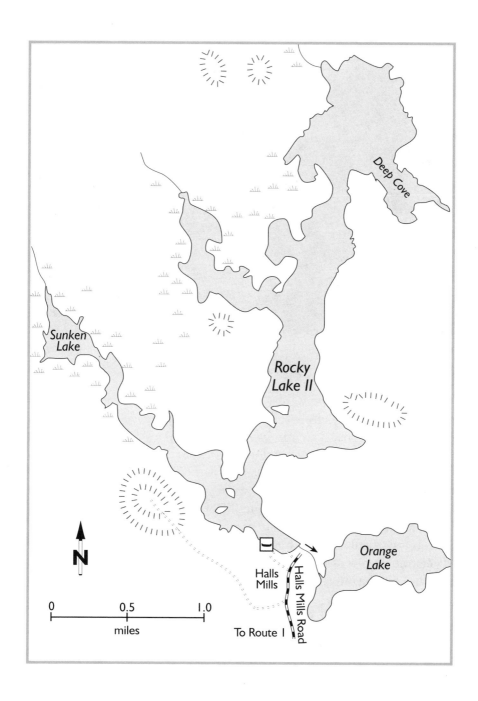

Deep Cove

Sunken
Lake

Rocky
Lake II

Orange
Lake

N

Halls
Mills

Halls Mills Road

To Route 1

0   0.5   1.0
miles

*Bunchberry (*Cornus canadensis*), a member of the dogwood family, is a low-growing spring wildflower that blooms in profusion in the woods around Rocky Lake.*

As you look up the waterway with binoculars you will see among the lily pads and pickerelweed a series of evenly spaced beaver lodges and evidence of beaver cuttings everywhere. Back up in this remote area would be a good place to look for moose. We saw osprey fishing here, one with a fish in its talons, and a pair of Canada geese with a raft of downy goslings.

As you go up the main section of Rocky II, the much deeper water accommodates at least one pair of nesting loons. The shallow coves, however, particularly the large one on the left, grow thick with aquatic vegetation. A few scattered cottages occur along this part of the lake, but one gets the impression that Rocky II does not see much traffic. We hope it stays that way!

32

Josh Pond and Josh Stream
Marion Twp and Whiting

MAPS: Maine Atlas, Map 26
   USGS Quadrangles, Long Lake
AREA: 140 acres; stream length, 1.5 miles
HABITAT TYPE: marshy stream, pristine lake
FISH: smallmouth bass, white perch, chain pickerel
EXPECT TO SEE: loon, osprey, Canada geese, ducks, beaver
TAKE NOTE: entire lake for sale in 2004; development a real
   threat; paddle here when the wind blows on large lakes

GETTING THERE

From Machias at the junction of Routes 1 and 1A, go east on Route 1 for 3.8 miles (3.8 miles), turn left onto Gardners Lake Road, and go 3.9 miles (7.7 miles) to the access on Josh Stream on the right (stay straight at the fork).

We enjoyed paddling here, especially when wind made paddling the area's larger lakes treacherous. Unfortunately, when we visited in 2004, the entire shoreline was for sale as one large 1,565-acre parcel. As we paddled up narrow Josh Stream as it meandered through a vast, shrubby marsh, listening to the ever-present yellowthroats and white-throated sparrows calling from the undergrowth, we wondered about the fate of this pristine lake.

A kingfisher fled before us and an osprey wheeled overhead as we portaged over a beaver dam to reach the pond. Along the way, we spotted lots of Canada geese, wood ducks, and ring-necked ducks, as well as the usual array of marsh birds, including a bittern.

Lots of very large tamaracks and some balsam firs, along with black spruce, scrubby red maples, and a few aspen, have encroached on the boggy substrate of this broad marsh. In late May, huge patches of rhodora in electric bloom put on quite a display, in contrast with the more subdued flowers of bog rosemary and leatherleaf, which also bloomed in profusion.

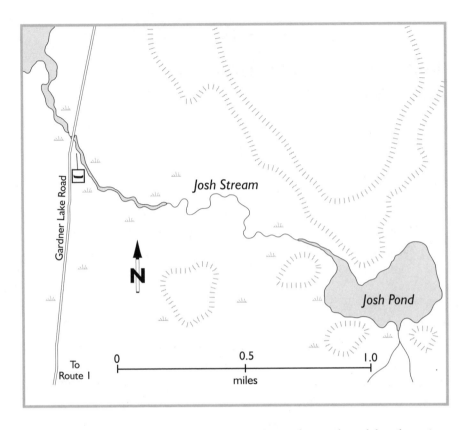

The water, deeply stained by tannic acids produced by decaying vegetation, flows down a sinewy channel from the pond. Paddling the shoreline of this small pond does not take long, and though we enjoyed the pond's solitude—for now—we spent most of our time exploring the more interesting stream where you can find a couple of flycatchers with distinctive calls in the breeding season: olive-sided flycatcher (*quick-three-beers*) and alder flycatcher (*fee-bee-o*). We prefer paddling here in May before blackflies and mosquitoes take to the air.

33

First, Second, and Third Chain Lakes
Wesley, T26 ED BPP, T31 MD BPP, and T37 MD BPP

MAPS: Maine Atlas, Map 35
   USGS Quadrangles, Wesley and Clifford Lake

AREA AND MAXIMUM DEPTH: First Chain Lake, 336 acres, 35 feet; Second Chain Lake, 589 acres, 30 feet; Third Chain Lake, 157 acres, 33 feet

HABITAT TYPE: long narrow lakes

FISH: white perch, yellow perch, chain pickerel

EXPECT TO SEE: loon, great blue heron, ducks, beaver in evening, moose is possibile

TAKE NOTE: some development, particularly on First Chain Lake; fire permits, Maine Forest Service, 207-827-1800

GETTING THERE

From Bangor, go east on Route 9 to the junction with Route 193. Continue on Route 9 for about 22 miles, and turn left, just after the town maintenance garage. Go 0.5 mile (0.5 mile), and bear right at the fork; go 1.3 miles (1.8 miles), and bear right; go 0.1 mile (1.9 miles), and bear right again. Go 0.3 mile (2.2 miles), passing a small pond on the left, and bear left around the pond, aiming for the water.

From Calais or Machias, from the junction of Routes 9 and 192, go west on Route 9 for 3.1 miles, turn right, and follow as above.

First, Second, and Third Chain Lakes provide very good paddling, particularly the northern sections between Second and Third Chain Lakes and above Third Lake. Because the best areas lie six or seven miles from the access, we recommend this trip primarily for paddlers seeking exercise or planning to camp. From the access, we would head north into Second Chain Lake, though if you have time you might want to explore the southern part. A few houses stand near the outlet, but some interesting islands also beg to be explored, and the shallow water will discourage most motorboaters.

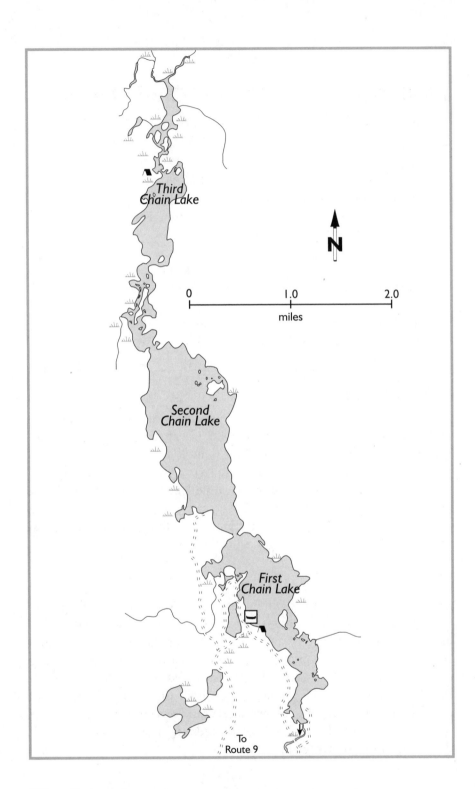

Third
Chain Lake

Second
Chain Lake

First
Chain Lake

0   1.0   2.0
miles

N

To
Route 9

In Second Chain Lake's marshy coves look for great blue heron, wood duck, moose, and beaver. For more of a wilderness feel, paddle through Second Lake into the boggy channel between Second and Third lakes. Though it is only about a mile in length, if you paddle around islands and explore all the inlets and coves, you could easily paddle two or three times that distance. Watch for pitcher plants and the many different heaths that grow here (rhodora, bog laurel, bog rosemary, leatherleaf, highbush blueberry, and lowbush blueberry).

Rhodora, a member of the heath family, puts on a dazzling display of showy purple flowers before leaf emergence in the spring.

The few rustic cabins along the southwest shore of Third Chain Lake do not spoil its beauty. Farther north, some absolutely gorgeous lichen- and moss-covered boulders extend down into the water. A beautiful campsite perches on a large boulder at the lake's north end. You can also paddle the slowly meandering Chain Brook Stream, which you can explore for another mile or so.

A quiet paddle through the marshy connector stream between Second and Third Chain Lakes.

34

Clifford Lake and Silver Pug Lake
T26 ED BPP and T27 ED BPP

MAPS: Maine Atlas, Map 35
   USGS Quadrangle, Clifford Lake

AREA AND MAXIMUM DEPTH: Clifford Lake, 954 acres, 50 feet;
   Silver Pug Lake, 198 acres, 39 feet

HABITAT TYPE: lake with large peninsula, many coves and islands

FISH: smallmouth bass (not many, but trophy size), white perch,
   chain pickerel

CONSERVATION: to help conserve this area, make contributions to
   the Downeast Lakes Forestry Partnership, www.neweng land-
   forestry.org/projects/dlfp.asp, 207-796-2100

EXPECT TO SEE: scenic hillsides, bald eagle, moose possibile

TAKE NOTE: no personal watercraft; fire permits, Maine Forest
   Service, 207-827-1800; some authorized sites do not require
   permits

GETTING THERE

From Calais, go west on Route 9. From the Crawford picnic area on the East Machias River, go 1.1 miles (1.1 miles), and turn right at the Wesley town-line sign. Go 8.2 miles (9.3 miles) to the access on the left (pass the Silver Pug Lake access at 5.0 miles [6.1 miles]).

Coming from the west on Route 9, after the junction with Route 192, go 2.9 miles, turn left, and continue as above.

Clifford Lake is a beautiful spot: remote, undeveloped, and small enough that you don't feel too exposed in an open boat. The west arm of the lake's horseshoe configuration connects by stream to Silver Pug Lake. Many attractive islands and shoreline granite boulders dot Clifford Lake's surface. During our first ten minutes on the east arm, we saw five loons; traveling about, we saw several more. You may see eagles here; they routinely return to the same nest year after year, enlarging it each spring.

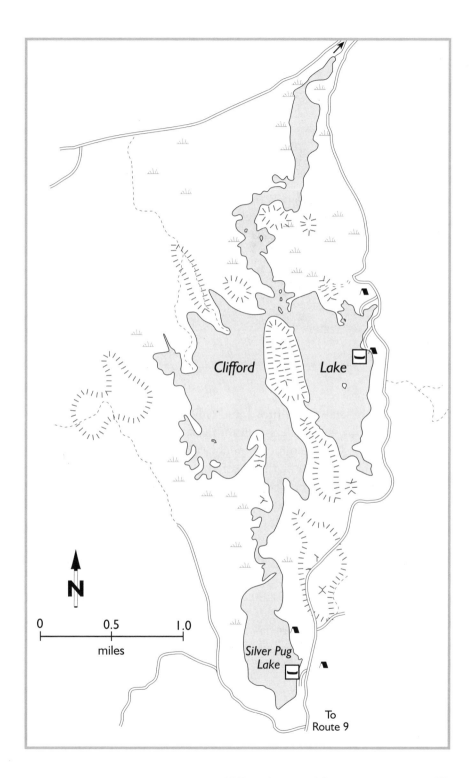

Clifford

Lake

Silver Pug
Lake

N

0   0.5   1.0
miles

To
Route 9

Cormorants

Both fairly shallow, Clifford and Silver Pug lakes harbor warm-water fish species, primarily smallmouth bass that hide out among the numerous rocks. Lacy hemlock branches drape out over the water, and lime-green lichens festoon the dead trees along shore. A variety of conifers, including spruce, red and white pine, and hemlock, cover the surrounding hillsides. Occasional maples and other deciduous trees break the monotony of the thick conifer canopy.

We saw several cormorants; ring-necked, wood, and black ducks; great blue heron; and lots of songbirds. Numerous coves, begging for exploration, line the shore, and you can paddle all the way up to the small dam at the lake's north end. This wild place seems to get few visitors and will provide hours of paddling in solitude. The Downeast Lakes Forestry Partnership has undertaken a campaign to acquire a conservation easement that includes both of these lakes.

35

Bearce Lake
Baring PLT and Meddybemps

MAPS: Maine Atlas, Map 36
   USGS Quadrangle, Meddybemps Lake East
AREA: 275 acres; 17,200 acres in National Wildlife Refuge
HABITAT TYPE: wooded hillsides, some marshland
FISH: chain pickerel
MOOSEHORN NATIONAL WILDLIFE REFUGE: moosehorn.fws.gov,
   207-454-7161
EXPECT TO SEE: bald eagle
TAKE NOTE: no motors, no development

GETTING THERE

From Machias, go north on Route 191 to the junction with Routes 214. Continue on Route 191 for 3.0 miles (3.0 miles), turn right, and go 0.3 mile (3.3 miles) to the access.

From Calais, take Route 1 north (highway actually goes south-west here), and turn left (south) onto Route 191. Go 4.0 miles (4.0 miles), turn left, and go 0.3 mile (4.3 miles) to the access.

Visitor Center: From the access road, go north on Route 191 for 4.0 miles (4.0 miles), and turn right onto Route 1. Go 2.3 miles (6.3 miles), turn right, go 1.8 miles (8.1 miles), and turn right into refuge headquarters. We watched a porcupine wandering about the headquarters grounds.

A porcupine munches balsam fir bark at the Moosehorn National Wildlife Refuge Visitors Center near Bearce Lake.

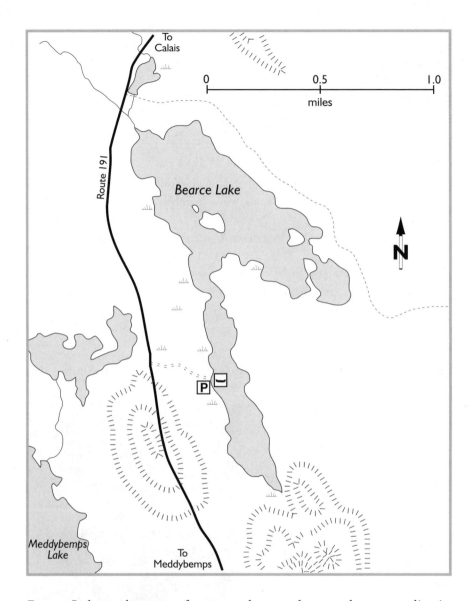

Bearce Lake—a long way from anywhere, unless you happen to live in Calais on the New Brunswick border—provides a great place to paddle. It lies wholly within the 4,680-acre wilderness section of Moosehorn National Wildlife Refuge.

The refuge provides unspoiled habitat for the American woodcock, a strange-looking bird (but perhaps not to other woodcock) with an inordinately long bill that probes the mud of alder swamps and other wetlands for whatever wiggles. Perhaps more interesting to most visitors, however, are the nesting bald eagles. As many as three pairs have nested at a time on the refuge. Since 1991, a pair has nested on a small platform within a couple hundred feet of the main highway, a few miles from Bearce Lake, apparently oblivious to the steady stream of cars.

Many different types of trees border this beautiful lake. We noted white birch, spruce, white pine, northern white cedar, tamarack, hemlock, red maple, and gray birch. A well-developed understory and several marshy areas contribute to the high plant-species diversity. Look here for beaver, moose, wood duck, and black duck. When we visited, a huge flock of bank swallows darted continually over the water, trying its best to reduce the flying-insect population, also huge.

Granite boulders lining the shore and poking up from the water add another dimension to Bearce Lake. Be careful paddling here, because the barely submerged boulders contain jagged, protruding quartz crystals, the kind that produce deep gouges in passing hulls.

The branches of a paper birch drape over the placid waters of Bearce Pond in the Moosehorn National Wildlife Refuge.

36

Pocomoonshine, Mud, and Crawford Lakes

Alexander, Crawford, Princeton, and No 21 Twp

MAPS: Maine Atlas, Map 36
 USGS Quadrangles, Princeton and Crawford Lake

AREA AND MAXIMUM DEPTH: Crawford Lake, 1,677 acres, 27 feet; Pocomoonshine Lake, 2,464 acres, 40 feet

HABITAT TYPE: shallow lakes with many islands; boggy connector streams; 4,200-acre peatlands, among the largest in Maine, and bog ecosystems abound

FISH: smallmouth bass, white and yellow perch, chain pickerel; largemouth bass in the river; eel at the Crawford Lake dam; considered among the best smallmouth bass lakes in Maine

OUTFITTERS: Sunrise County Canoe Expeditions, 207-942-9300, www.sunrise exp.com

EXPECT TO SEE: loon, osprey, bald eagle, otter, moose, typical bog plants

TAKE NOTE: fire permits, Maine Forest Service, 207-827-1800

GETTING THERE

Pocomoonshine Lake has three access points. The East Machias River trip starts at the southeast arm access. If you are not doing the river trip, choose any access. With wind from the south, use the southeast access, circle around to the west, and head down to the Mud lakes and Crawford Lake. With wind from the north, use one of the two northern access points.

Southeast Access: From Calais, go north on Route 1. Turn left onto Route 9, go about 8.0 miles, turn right onto South Princeton Road, and continue straight down hill to the access as South Princeton Road goes right.

Northeast Access: Turn right off Route 9 as above, go 1.1 miles (1.1 miles), and turn right, staying on South Princeton Road. Go 4.0 miles (5.1 miles), and turn left onto Lake Road (Woodland Road goes right). Go 0.4 mile (5.5 miles) to the access. Alternatively, from Woodland, go west on Woodland Road for about 5 miles to the access.

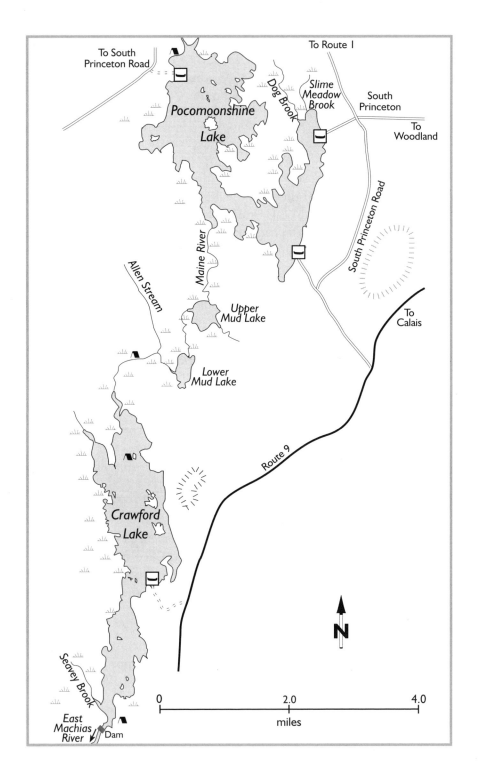

To South
Princeton Road

To Route 1

Dog Brook

Slime
Meadow
Brook

South
Princeton

To
Woodland

Pocomoonshine
Lake

South Princeton Road

Maine River

Allen Stream

To
Calais

Upper
Mud Lake

Lower
Mud Lake

Route 9

Crawford
Lake

N

Seavey Brook

East
Machias
River

Dam

0   2.0   4.0

miles

Pocomoonshine, Mud, and Crawford Lakes   119

Northwest Access: From the junction of South Princeton and Lake roads (near northeast access), go north for 3.2 miles (3.2 miles), and turn left. Go 3.6 miles (6.8 miles), and turn left into the access and campsite. You can reach this access from Route 1, about two miles east of Princeton—see *Maine Atlas.*

East Machias River Trip

We paddled Pocomoonshine twice, in July and August. The southeast access marks the start of the East Machias River trip: down the Maine River, through Upper and Lower Mud lakes, Crawford Lake, and into the East Machias River. You can take out on Crawford or Round lakes; you can continue on Rocky Lake Stream, taking out in Rocky Lake; or you can continue down the East Machias River through Second Lake, taking out at Hadley Lake or in East Machias. During July of a dry year, we opted for a long two-day, middle-distance trip, taking out at Rocky Lake (see page 100).

We would avoid the river trip in late summer or during low water. Below Crawford Lake, we walked our boats for about three miles through boulder-laden riffles, seriously scratching our shins and boats to about the same degree. In the spring during higher water, you supposedly can sail right through this stretch. According to the AMC River Guide, even those with limited whitewater experience can navigate the modest rapids. If you have questions about water conditions, contact Sunrise County Canoe Expeditions, which can also arrange a car-ferrying service.

From the southeast access, paddle across to the far southwestern cove, and head south, staying to the left. The forested shoreline of Pocomoonshine gives way to the slowly meandering Maine River. After traveling a mile or so through typical bog and floating-plant vegetation, the stream widens out, twice in quick succession, into Upper and Lower Mud lakes. Following the channel through these weed-choked waterways presents a challenge. We stayed to the right and battled our way through rushes, sedges, and pickerelweed until we found the west-leading outlets of each lake. In Lower Mud Lake, stay in the more open water until well down the lake; then look for an obvious channel leading off to the right (west). Dabbling ducks love these shallow lakes, and we tried our best not to disturb their foraging.

As you head west out of Lower Mud Lake, after a couple hundred yards Allen Stream enters from the right; you can paddle up this marshy stream quite a distance. Look for a campsite on the left where Allen Stream flows in and another on one of the northernmost islands as you enter Crawford Lake, just off a peninsula jutting out from the left shore. A sloping granite boulder off the southwestern shore provides the best take-out.

Crawford Lake, five miles long and narrow, funnels wind and churns up swells and whitecaps whenever the wind blows north or south. At the lake's southern end, besides finding a campsite, you can double back up the meandering, marshy Seavey Brook; it looks to be a truly wild place, perfect for moose watching.

At the end of Crawford Lake, you have come more than eleven miles, and with any wind, you will not be able to paddle this round trip in just one day. It makes an ideal two-day trip, allowing time for side-channel exploration.

Pocomoonshine Lake

With wind from the north, we would explore the northern arms of Pocomoonshine Lake. From the South Princeton access, Dog Brook presents a beautiful paddle up a meandering, wide, slow-flowing inlet. Conifers dominate the shoreline, set quite far back from the channel.

While designed for ocean paddling, sea kayaks appear more frequently on Maine's lakes and ponds. Kayaks offer speed and ease of paddling for the solo paddler.

White pine, tamarack, spruce, and hemlock grow in profusion. Dwarfed red maples grow out from the shore; grasses and low-growing bog vegetation lead down to the stream channel, covered with yellow pondlily, fragrant waterlily, pickerelweed, and other aquatic vegetation.

After about a mile the channel narrows and gets quite rocky. If you pick your way back through the rocks for another quarter-mile, a series of beaver dams appears. We did not portage above the dams, leaving further exploration for another visit.

If you paddle the northeast arm, check out Slime Meadow Brook. Beaver have opened a narrow channel, allowing you to paddle quite a way back in. Of course, when you try to turn your boat around, that's when you get slimed.

Putting in on the northwest arm, a relatively large open expanse of lake, dotted with a few islands, will face you. The seemingly never-ending series of marshy coves, starting directly across from the access and extending south down the large peninsula separating the northern arms, provide the most interesting areas to explore.

37

Big Lake, Clifford Stream, Little River, and Little Musquash Stream

Grand Lake Stream PLT, ND 21 TWP, and T27 ED BPP

MAPS: Maine Atlas, Maps 35 and 36
　　USGS Quadrangles, Big Lake, Clifford Lake, Monroe Lake, and Princeton

AREA AND MAXIMUM DEPTH: 10,305 acres, 70 feet

HABITAT TYPE: large, shallow lake with many islands and marshy coves; rivers through marshlands

FISH: salmon, smallmouth bass, white perch, chain pickerel

CONSERVATION: to help conserve this area, make contributions to the Downeast Lakes Forestry Partnership, 207-796-2100, www.newenglandforestry.org/projects/dlfp.asp

EXPECT TO SEE: bald eagle, osprey, loon, bobolink, muskrat, moose

TAKE NOTE: under windy conditions, main lake can be very treacherous; fire permits, Maine Forest Service, 207-827-1800

GETTING THERE

From Calais, go north on Route 1 through Princeton. Turn left at the sign for Grand Lake Stream, go 10.2 miles (10.2 miles), turn left onto Water Street, and go 3.0 miles (13.2 miles) to the access.

We include this section not so much for Big Lake but for the several marshy streams that flow into the lake. Big Lake, though huge at over 10,000 acres, seems much smaller because of the large number of islands that populate its waters. We would stick to the lake's west end near the access, which suffers least from winds. When winds blow from the northwest, you should be able to paddle down the west shore and into the feeder streams.

Because marshlands abound around the lake, we would camp on the islands, where you will need a permit to build a fire. It will take a

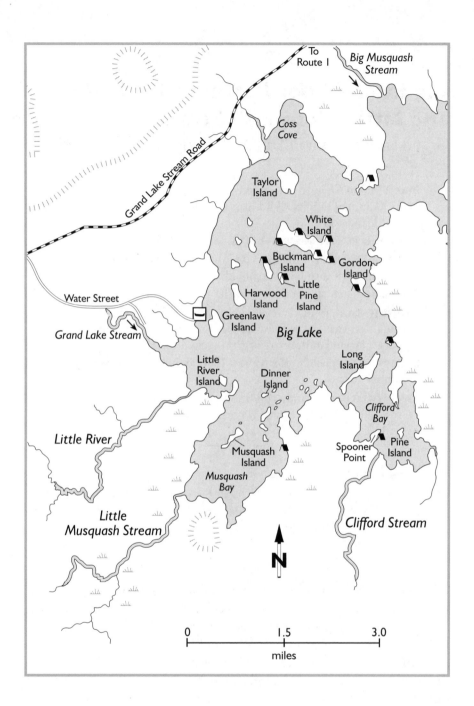

To
Route 1

*Big Musquash
Stream*

Grand Lake Stream Road

Coss
Cove

Taylor
Island

White
Island

Buckman
Island

Gordon
Island

Little
Pine
Island

Harwood
Island

Water Street

Greenlaw
Island

Big Lake

Grand Lake Stream

Little
River
Island

Dinner
Island

Long
Island

*Clifford
Bay*

Little River

Spooner
Point

Pine
Island

Musquash
Island

*Musquash
Bay*

*Little
Musquash Stream*

Clifford Stream

N

0   1.5   3.0

miles

couple of days to explore thoroughly the lake's west end, islands, and inlet streams. The Downeast Lakes Forestry Partnership has undertaken a campaign to acquire a conservation easement that includes all of the streams included here, as well as most of Big Lake's shore.

On the lake you should see osprey, bald eagle, loons, and ducks. Look for muskrats, snapping turtles, bobolinks, red-winged blackbirds, yellowthroats, yellow warblers, and other typical marshland birds along the feeder streams. In addition to the muskrats that you will see swimming, keep a lookout for otters. Paddle here in the spring or later in the season after the ubiquitous blackflies and mosquitoes have abated.

38

Big Musquash Stream
Grand Lake Stream PLT

> **MAPS:** Maine Atlas, Map 35
> USGS Quadrangles, Big Lake and Waite
> **STREAM LENGTH:** 6 miles
> **HABITAT TYPE:** slowly meandering marshy stream, flowing
> through a broad, treeless valley
> **FISH:** smallmouth bass, chain pickerel
> **EXPECT TO SEE:** bobolink, black duck, ring-necked duck, otter,
> moose
> **TAKE NOTE:** paddle here when wind makes lake paddling treacherous

---

GETTING THERE

From Calais, go north on Route 1 through Princeton. Turn left at the sign for Grand Lake Stream, and go 4.1 miles to the access on the right, just before the bridge.

Big Musquash Stream, at least 100 feet across for much of its length, flows several miles through a broad, treeless valley. Pointed firs of the northern boreal forest border the meadow; a few white birch, aspen, and red maple mix in among the conifers. Some shrubby alders border the water in places, along with bog rosemary, leatherleaf, and sweetgale that bloomed when we paddled here.

We spotted a weasel hunting for mice along the shore and found piles of mussel shells left by feeding otters. In addition to the common yellowthroats and yellow warblers that graced the shores, we saw many bobolinks—a ground-nesting oriole and one of the few birds with a light back and a dark belly.

As you paddle back up the valley, you can also paddle into some of the feeder streams for a ways. Though a good place to paddle at any time, paddle here especially when winds keep you off larger lakes. We suspect that the stream sees little traffic, making it a great spot to look for moose in the early morning and in the evening.

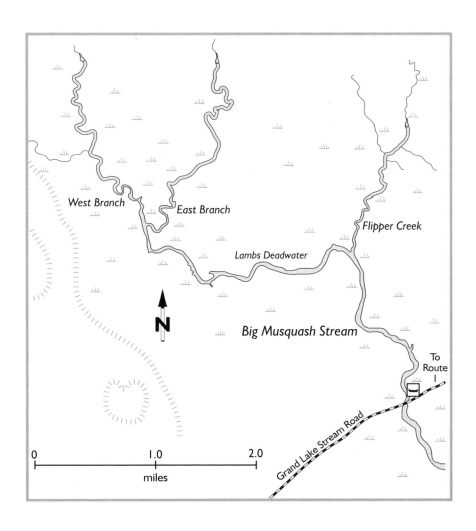

West Branch

East Branch

Flipper Creek

Lambs Deadwater

N

Big Musquash Stream

To
Route
1

Grand Lake Stream Road

| 0 | 1.0 | 2.0 |

miles

Blackflies and Mosquitoes
Scourges of the North

Mosquito

Anyone who has spent any time in Maine's North Woods knows insects all too well. They can detract from outdoor fun throughout the summer and can make most of June virtually off-limits to outdoor recreation in the state's northern reaches. Though it will not take away the itch, understanding these insects may help us accept them as part of the ecosystem we enjoy.

Blackflies. Blackflies belong to the family Simuliidae ("little snub-nosed beings"), and most species of concern to us belong to the genus *Simulium*. Scientists have identified more than 1,500 species of blackflies worldwide, 300 in North America, and about 40 species in Maine. Only 10 to 15 percent of blackfly species suck blood from humans or domestic animals.

In parts of northern North America, blackflies cause considerable livestock losses—mostly from weight loss but they actually can kill cattle. In parts of Alberta, mortality rates from blackflies range from 1 to 4 percent. Blackfly problems in North America, however, pale compared to problems in Africa and Central America, where the aptly named species *Simulium damnosum* has infected an estimated 20 million people with onchocerciasis, or river blindness (a disease caused by roundworms transmitted by the fly).

Blackflies begin their lifecycle in streams and rivers. Adult females deposit eggs in the water, and emerging larvae attach themselves to rocks, plants, and other surfaces in the current. Two tiny, fanlike structures sweep food particles into their mouths. A several-hundred-foot stretch of a narrow stream can support more than a million larvae. In a river, the population can number in the multibillions per mile.

Each larva builds a pupal case in which it metamorphoses into an adult blackfly. When ready to emerge, it splits the pupal case and rides to the water's surface in a bubble of oxygen that had collected in the case.

Adult blackflies have one primary goal: to make more blackflies. The trouble begins when females seek a blood meal to nourish their eggs. Only females bite (actually puncture and suck); pacifist males sip nectar from flowers, and they may be important pollinators of blueberries. Blackflies rely heavily on eyesight to find prey, so they remain active mostly during daylight—and at temperatures above 50°F.

No blackfly species preys exclusively on humans. We are too new on the evolutionary chain to be a specific host to blackflies, which arose during the Jurassic period 180 million years ago. An estimated 30 to 45 blackfly species in North America feed on humans. One species (*Simulium euryadminiculum*) feeds only on loons.

Mosquitoes. The other major Maine Woods insect nemesis is the ubiquitous mosquito. Mosquitoes, members of the Culicidae family, number more than 3,400 species worldwide, with 170 in North America. Three-quarters of the mosquito species in the United States and Canada belong to three genera: *Aedes* (78 species), *Culex* (29 species), and *Anopheles* (16 species).

As with blackflies, mosquito larvae live an aquatic life; unlike blackflies, most mosquitoes adapted to *still* water. In any quiet bog or muskeg, you can find mosquito larvae wriggling about. They eat algae and other organic matter they filter out of the water with brushlike appendages. Both larvae and pupae breathe through air tubes at the water's surface.

Adult mosquitoes have short lifespans. Most females live approximately one month, while males live only one week. The high-pitched buzz comes from beating their wings at about 1,000 beats per second. Females generate a higher-pitched whine that helps males locate mates. Using a hand lens, look for the male's much bushier antennae, used to locate females.

Both males and females feed on plant nectar as their primary energy source, but females of most species also require a blood meal to fuel egg production. As with the blackfly, a mosquito does not really bite. Rather, she stabs through the victim's skin with six sharp *stylets* that form the proboscis center. Saliva flows into the puncture to keep the blood from coagulating. Most people have an allergic reaction to the saliva. Upon repeated exposure to mosquito bites, one gradually builds immunity.

While mostly a nuisance in the Northeast, mosquitoes cause more deaths in the tropics than any other animal. They carry more than 100 different diseases, including malaria, yellow fever, encephalitis, filariasis, dengue, and West Nile virus. The most destructive of these, malaria, kills about one million people a year, mostly children, and as many as 200 million people worldwide carry the disease.

Southern latitudes have far greater mosquito-species diversity, but the numbers of individuals generally increase farther north. In the Arctic, with fewer than a dozen species, adults can be so thick they literally blacken the skies. In one experiment, several rugged Canadian researchers bared their torsos, arms, and legs to Arctic mosquitoes and reported as many as 9,000 bites per minute! At this rate, an unprotected person could lose half of his or her blood in two hours.

Blackfly and Mosquito Control. For mosquito control, we drained thousands of square miles of salt marsh during the 1930s and 1940s with long, straight drainage ditches—many still visible. (As much as half of the wetland area in the United States has been lost during the last 200 years—partly for mosquito control and partly for development and agriculture.) Along with eliminating habitat, we used thousands of tons of pesticides in the battle against mosquitoes. DDT remained the chemical of choice for decades because of its supposed safety to the environment—a claim that proved tragically untrue. Since the banning of DDT and other deadly chlorinated-hydrocarbon pesticides in 1973, osprey, bald eagle, and peregrine falcon populations have made a comeback.

Today, most attention focuses on biological control of these insects, relying on natural enemies of the pest: viruses, protozoa, bacteria, fungi, and parasites. A bacterium, *Bacillus thuringiensis* variety *israelensis,* generally known as Bti, discovered in 1977 from samples of sand collected in the Negev Desert, has exhibited the most successful control. Bti bacteria produce protein crystals that react with other chemicals in the insects' stomachs, producing a poison that kills the larvae.

While Bti currently enjoys high success rates, hidden problems could arise, just as with DDT, especially as bioengineers incorporate the Bti gene into plants. This widespread and indiscriminate spreading of the Bti protein could easily lead to pest resistance. Entomologists and conservation biologists also worry that monarch butterflies, on their 1,000-mile-plus migrations to their Mexico wintering grounds, will suffer huge mortality from Bti-engineered corn.

Protecting Yourself from Biting Insects. Largely because of biting insects, May and autumn remain our favorite times for paddling in the north country. During all but the height of the blackfly season in June, however, these insects should not spoil your trip. Out on the water where breezes often blow, paddlers can usually escape insects.

Proper clothing forms the most important line of defense. During blackfly season, wear long-sleeved, tight-knit shirts and pants with elastic cuffs, or tuck your pant legs into your socks. Blackflies land on your clothing and search for openings, such as wrists, ankles, and necks. A mosquito-cloth head-net works well, but with a collared shirt, blackflies will usually find a route in. Cotton gloves can help, too.

Mosquitoes can penetrate soft clothing better than blackflies, so more rugged materials work well for shirts and pants. Wearing two light shirts also works. Tight cuffs are not as important because mosquitoes usually fly directly to their dining table. With mosquito-cloth head-nets, try to keep the mosquito cloth away from your skin.

Insect repellents generally repel mosquitoes better than blackflies. DEET (N,N-diethylmetatoluamide) remains popular in the north country. Fortunately, one of our coauthors is a chemist and able to pronounce this name. Unfortunately, he also knows enough about its chemical structure to be concerned about potential long-term toxicity to humans. Because DEET works by evaporating into the nearby air to clog insects' odor receptors, you have to keep slathering it on. While we admit to keeping some concentrated DEET around when the bugs get really bad, we recommend clothing as the primary defensive strategy.

Some new, more natural repellents, such as Bite Blocker, Buggspray Vanilla, and Avon Skin-So-Soft Bug Guard Plus, may work for you. Eventually, natural-products chemists will find very effective, totally nontoxic alternatives to DEET.

Is There Anything Good about Blackflies and Mosquitoes?
One wonders what might possibly be good about the little beasts. The answer lies in the role they play in aquatic ecosystems, where they provide a vital food source. Many game fish rely on blackfly and mosquito larvae for at least part of their diets. One study found that blackfly larvae comprise up to 25 percent of the brook trout diet. Even if blackfly and mosquito larvae do not provide a *direct* food source for our favorite game fish and waterfowl, chances are pretty good that they form a vital part of the food chain upon which these animals rely. If we appreciate angling for brook trout, listening to the call of the loon, or watching the stately great blue heron, we should recognize that these species might not be here without blackflies and mosquitoes. Yes, even blackflies and mosquitoes have an important place in the aquatic ecosystem.

39

Third Machias Lake
T5 ND BPP, T42 MD BPP, and T43 MD BPP

MAPS: Maine Atlas, Map 35
USGS Quadrangles, Dark Cove Mountain, Fletcher Peak, and Monroe Lake
AREA AND MAXIMUM DEPTH: 2,612 acres, 31 feet
HABITAT TYPE: long, shallow lake with marshy inlet stream
FISH: smallmouth bass, white perch, chain pickerel, eel in fall at outlet
EXPECT TO SEE: loon, bald eagle, red-breasted merganser, ring-necked duck, moose, beaver in stream
TAKE NOTE: no personal watercraft; only one cabin; The Nature Conservancy undertook a project in 2004 to purchase the surrounding land; fire permits, Maine Forest Service, 207-827-1800

GETTING THERE

From Machias, go north on Route 192 to Route 9. Go west (left) on Route 9 for 10.9 miles (10.9 miles), and turn right. Go 3.7 miles (14.6 miles), and bear right at the fork; go 5.0 miles (19.6 miles), and bear right. Go 0.1 mile (19.7 miles), jog right, go across the Machias River bridge, and take an immediate left. Go 4.3 miles (24.0 miles), turn left, and go steeply downhill. Continue straight as roads enter from the right for 0.9 mile (24.9 miles) to the access on the right, just before the bridge.

Paddling out from the access and indeed throughout most of the southwest arm, notice the beautiful, enormous granite boulders deposited at random by retreating glaciers. Many of them protrude well out into the lake, making this a very picturesque spot. Conifers cover most of the shoreline and retreat up the hillsides into the distance. A well-developed understory right at the water's edge consists of small birches, red maples, and a variety of shrubs.

Staying to the right as you leave the small arm at the access, note the extensive sand beach around to the left. Paddling out among the boulders

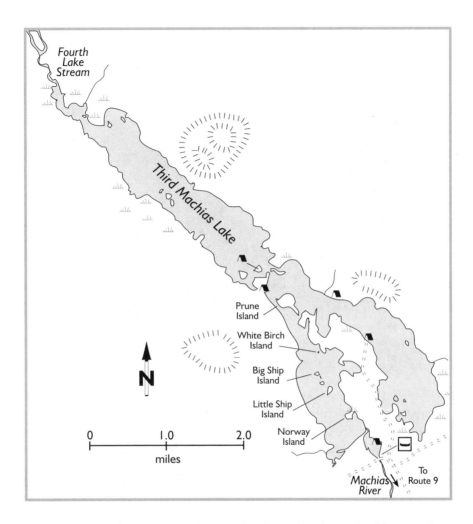

Fourth
Lake
Stream

Third Machias Lake

Prune
Island

White Birch
Island

N

Big Ship
Island

Little Ship
Island

Norway
Island

0   1.0   2.0

miles

To
Route 9

Machias
River

and islands, you may notice that Little Ship Island is indeed bigger than Big Ship Island and that red pines cover White Birch Island. Tons of large granite boulders guard the large cove off to the right just after Norway Island. A small amount of marshland gives way to scrub vegetation on the shore, followed by a uniform stand of pines on higher ground.

After threading our way through the islands at the top of the southwest arm, we turned right (south) into the east arm and paddled down to campsite 6 on the west shore. A road leads to this spot, but we liked the other campsites better, particularly those on the island and peninsula that separate the lake's north and south ends.

If you have time, check out the inlet, Fourth Lake Stream, in the far northwest that drains Fourth Machias Lake. You can paddle back

Because they live in low-nutrient soils, pitcher plants trap insects for food. Insects fall into the leaf "pitchers," where rainwater mixes with digestive enzymes. Downward-pointing hairs keep them from climbing out.

almost a mile before boulders and riffles block your way. Beaver lodges and recent cuttings fill this peaceful, marshy area. Although we did not see any moose here in midafternoon, this would be a good place to look for them. Indeed, we did watch a cow moose feeding in a similar marshy area on Fourth Machias Lake. In the spring one can paddle down from Fourth Machias Lake, through Third Machias Lake, all the way to the town of Machias.

While paddling here, we saw few other people and lots of red-breasted mergansers, ring-necked ducks, loons, and other birds. In the early morning and evening you should have no trouble finding beaver willing to slap their tails on the water as they dive out of sight. One could easily spend several days exploring this beautiful, wild place.

40

Nicatous Lake
T40MD, T41MD, and T3ND

> **MAPS:** Maine Atlas, Map 34
>   USGS Quadrangles, Gassabias Lake, Spring Lake, and West Lake
>
> **AREA AND MAXIMUM DEPTH:** 5,165 acres, 56 feet
>
> **HABITAT TYPE:** huge lake with many islands
>
> **FISH:** smallmouth bass, white perch, chain pickerel
>
> **EXPECT TO SEE:** loon, osprey, bald eagle, moose possible
>
> **TAKE NOTE:** under windy conditions, Nicatous Lake can be treacherous; do not take novice paddlers here; no personal watercraft; some development; much of the shoreline preserved; fire permits, Maine Forest Service, 207-827-1800; several authorized sites do not require permits

---

GETTING THERE

From I-95, Exit 54, go east on Routes 155 and 188. Turn right on Route 188 when Route 155 goes left; follow signs to Nicatous Lodge. Go 5.6 miles from the end of the pavement to the access (at 4.6 miles, go right, following access signs).

Nicatous Lake, much more accessible than many other large lakes in eastern Maine, suffers from the same drawback: Because glaciers crept down out of the north in this region, most large lakes point north-south, meaning that wind blowing strongly from the north or south causes treacherous waves. Under these conditions, retreat to the nearby smaller bodies of water, such as Great Pond; Bearce Lake; Folsom, Crooked, and Upper ponds; or Bog Brook Flowage.

The northern and middle sections of Nicatous Lake, the most interesting to paddle, contain many islands, several campsites, and little development away from the access. In contrast, the southern end below the Narrows widens out and consequently has more open water—and more development. It would take a few days to explore the entire

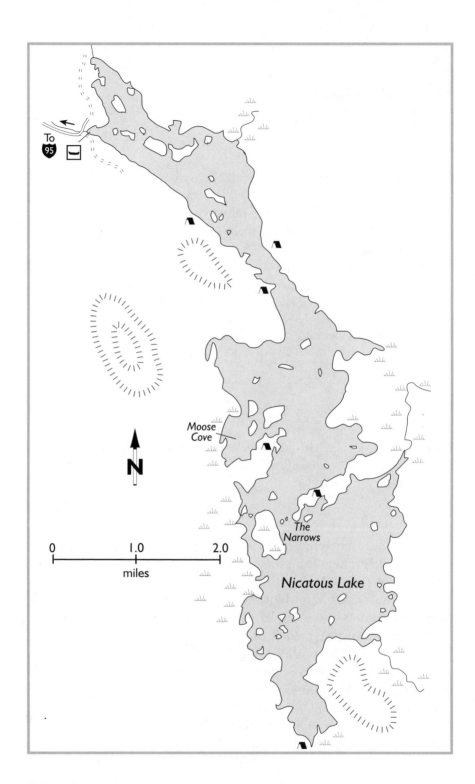

To
95

Moose
Cove

The
Narrows

Nicatous Lake

N

0   1.0   2.0
miles

shoreline and all of the islands of this 9-mile-long lake. One gets the feeling, in this beautiful setting with forested hillsides all around, that the lake does not see much motorboat traffic, especially on the north end.

Paddling out from the access, we were struck by the granite boulders and white cedars that dominate the shoreline. Lots of sugar maples occur here, as well as birch, hemlock, spruce, and white and red pine. Tall, mature trees populate the heavily forested islands, most dominated by conifers, some with dense stands of red pine, with a few birch and red maple thrown in.

In addition to exploring the islands, paddle quietly down into Moose Cove—with the most extensive marshy area—to look for wildlife. One of the nicest campsites on the lake occurs on a little peninsula on the west shore, just above the Nicatous Club. Sparse vegetation should allow the breeze in to keep the bugs down.

In 2000, The Trust for Public Land, Forest Society of Maine, and Maine Coast Heritage Trust obtained a 20,767-acre conservation easement—at the time the largest in Maine—working with the owner, Robbins Lumber, that includes large parts of Nicatous Lake. In addition, the state bought 76 of the lake's islands.

A moose surprises us as we drift around a point and into a cove. Note the line of flies on its nose.

41

Fourth Machias Lake
T5 ND BPP and T42 MD BPP

MAPS: Maine Atlas, Map 35
USGS Quadrangles, Dark Cove Mountain, Duck Lake,
Fletcher Peak, and Gassabias Lake

AREA AND MAXIMUM DEPTH: 1,539 acres, 26 feet

HABITAT TYPE: shallow, marshy lake

FISH: white perch, yellow perch, chain pickerel

THE PINES: www.thepineslodge.com, 207-557-7463; lodge with
guest rooms plus cabins

EXPECT TO SEE: loon, moose, scenic hillsides

TAKE NOTE: only one cabin; Downeast Lakes Land Trust is purchasing 27,000 acres surrounding the lake's northern half; fire
permits, Maine Forest Service, 207-827-1800

GETTING THERE

From Calais, go north on Route 1 through Princeton. Turn left at the sign for
Grand Lake Stream, and go 10.3 miles (10.3 miles), passing through Grand
Lake Stream, to pavement's end. Go 0.3 mile (10.6 miles), and take the right
fork, following the sign for Elsemore Landing (on Pocumcus Lake). Go 11.2
miles (21.8 miles), and stay left (right goes to The Pines on Sysladobsis Lake).
Go 0.9 mile (22.7 miles), turn left, and go 0.2 mile (22.9 miles) to the access.

Fourth Machias Lake represents the essence of eastern Maine's wild
lake country. Remote, marshy, nestled beneath gentle mountains, and
filled with wildlife, it receives few visitors. One could explore the whole
lake and its tributaries in one long day, but a leisurely two-day exploration would allow more time to absorb the beauty of this setting and
to enjoy its abundant wildlife.

In the evening and early morning, explore for moose in the extensive marshes surrounding the five inlet streams. The largest expanse of
marsh surrounds Dead Stream, which flows northwest into the lake's
upper arm. Occasional tamaracks dot this broad valley's otherwise flat

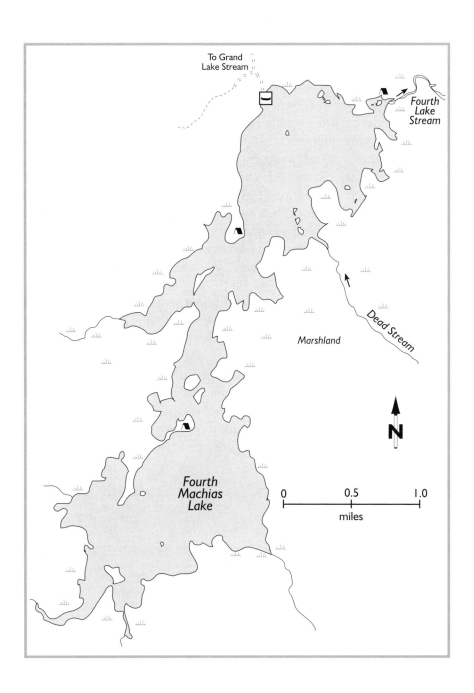

To Grand
Lake Stream

Fourth
Lake
Stream

Dead Stream

Marshland

N

Fourth
Machias
Lake

0   0.5   1.0
miles

terrain. When we paddled here in mid-June, we went back in about a mile, past Canada geese with their fluffy yellow goslings, to find a cow moose wallowing in the water, buried up to her nose. We watched her long ears bat away hordes of blackflies. We even forgot for a moment the accumulating bites on the backs of our necks as we glided silently past the cavorting moose.

On higher ground, away from the huge expanses of marshland, you will find large stands of white and red pine, with a few spruce thrown in. Birch and red maple grow along the shore, along with scattered hemlocks. Tamarack, black spruce, northern white cedar, and red maple grow on the swamp's higher hummocks.

Extensive marshes surround Fourth Machias Lake, affording little high ground to support campsites. We found suitable campsites on peninsulas on the right-hand side at the beginning and end of the connector between the lake's upper and lower arms and at the mouth of Fourth Lake Stream. Of course, if you want to enjoy a respite from the bugs, you can stay at The Pines, a lodge a short way back down the road on Sysladobsis Lake.

In the spring, you can paddle Fourth Lake Stream down into Third Machias Lake. From there you can continue on the Machias River trip, eventually taking out at Machias. In the middle of June in a high-water year, the water did not quite cover the rocks. In a low-water year in September, the stream was down to a trickle.

42

Pocumcus, Junior, and Sysladobsis Lakes

Lakeville, T5 ND BPP, and T5 R1 NBPP

MAPS: Maine Atlas, Map 35
   USGS Quadrangles, Dark Cove Mountain, Scraggly Lake, Bottle Lake, and Duck Lake

AREA AND MAXIMUM DEPTH: Pocumcus Lake, 2,201 acres, 44 feet; Junior Lake, 3,866 acres, 70 feet; Bottle Lake, 281 acres, 42 feet; Sysladobsis Lake, 5,376 acres, 66 feet

HABITAT TYPE: large lakes with many marshy coves

FISH: lake trout, brook trout, salmon, smallmouth bass, white perch, chain pickerel

EXPECT TO SEE: bald eagle, loon, otter, moose

OUTFITTERS: Sunrise County Canoe Expeditions, www.sunrise-exp.com, 207-942-9300; Maine Wilderness Camps, www.mainerec.com/mwcamps.shtml, 207-738-5052

THE PINES: www.thepineslodge.com, 207-557-7463; lodge with guest rooms plus cabins

CONSERVATION: to help conserve this area, make contributions to the Downeast Lakes Forestry Partnership, 207-796-2100, www.newenglandforestry.org/projects/dlfp.asp

TAKE NOTE: under windy conditions, these lakes can be very treacherous; do not take novice paddlers here; fire permits, Maine Forest Service, 207-827-1800; required for nearly all campsites except Elsemore Landing

---

GETTING THERE

From Calais, go north on Route 1 through Princeton. Turn left at the sign for Grand Lake Stream, and go 10.3 miles (10.3 miles), passing through Grand Lake Stream, to the pavement end. Go 0.3 mile (10.6 miles), and take the right fork, following signs for Elsemore Landing. Go 6.1 miles (16.7 miles), and turn right at the Elsemore Landing sign. Go 0.8 mile (17.5 miles), and bear right toward the water at the state campground.

Pocumcus, Junior, and Sysladobsis lakes in the heart of eastern Maine's lake country offer one of the best extended quietwater loop trips in the state, especially when one detours for a few days into Scraggly Lake. These lakes flow into the St. Croix River, which forms the southeastern border between Maine and New Brunswick. Because you can end up where you started, the trip requires just one car.

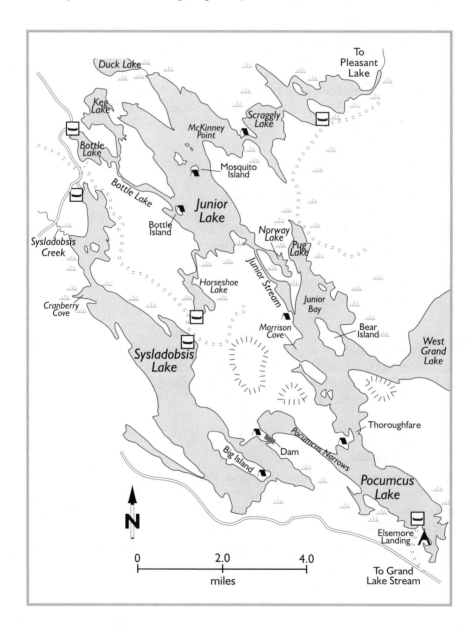

The ease of this trip depends on water levels. With relatively high water levels (usually until midsummer), you can paddle from Junior Lake into Sysladobsis Lake via Bottle Lake Stream, Bottle Lake, and a half-mile carry into Sysladobsis. With lower water levels, the Bottle Lake take-out may be inaccessible. In that case, the carry would require either disembarking on someone's yard (heavy development on Bottle Lake) or making a much longer carry from the state access at the north end. So from midsummer through fall, you might want to plan an up-and-back trip, rather than making a loop trip. The loop trip described here takes anywhere from three to five days or longer.

Elsemore Landing on Pocumcus Lake to Junior Lake

Elsemore Landing, near the south end of Pocumcus Lake (pronounced po-COM-ses, locally known as Compass Lake) has a state-run campground with boat access. The campground can be rowdy on popular summer weekends.

Pocumcus Lake, a mile across at its widest point, stretches for about five miles in length. Make sure you explore the boggy islands of Deer Brook Cove, about two miles up on the left. We watched a cow moose browsing on underwater vegetation near the cove's north end, observed lots of beaver activity, and paddled by a week-old loon chick riding on its parent's back. On the sphagnum islands and floating logs, look for the small, reddish leaves of sundews. On a windy day, this cove provides a nice respite from the main lake.

To reach Junior Lake, paddle north through the Thoroughfare, and after clearing it you can explore several interesting islands and a deep cove along the west shore. To the east you will see the quarter-mile-wide outlet into West Grand Lake, too big to paddle enjoyably, except in very calm conditions. Head north between Morrison Cove and Bear Island into Junior Bay.

Near Bear Island's north end on the western shore, Junior Stream drains Junior Lake. You'll find a great campsite here (no fire permit required), with picnic tables, outhouses, and plenty of tent locations. If you camp here, spend a few hours around daybreak looking for the moose that frequent the marshy coves of Junior Bay, Pug Lake, Junior Stream, and Norway Lake. Also watch for otter, deer, loon, and bald eagle.

With favorable weather, you can make the Junior Stream campsite a lunch stop and continue on to Junior Lake, where you will find some island campsites. We chose to continue on—and regretted it. Most of the morning we had paddled with a light tail wind, but by early afternoon, when we got out onto Junior Lake, the wind had picked up. Our two laden canoes (with precious cargo of four- and seven-year-old daughters) bobbed in the increasingly rough water as we made our way for an island campsite near the lake's center. We got there all right, but just in time, as the wind-driven waves rose to two feet.

We camped on the aptly named Mosquito Island; two stagnant lagoons, one at each end, bred a healthy crop of mosquitoes that became all too apparent when the wind died down. Bottle Island, where we also camped, farther to the south and a bit west, has far fewer mosquitoes. McKinney Point hosts another campsite. On one of the islands just north of McKinney Point, a bald-eagle nest perches in a tall white pine; be careful not to get too close.

The McKinney Point island area has a very wild and remote feel to it. Huge granite boulders dot the undeveloped shoreline. Watch out for boulders lurking just beneath the water's surface. From the eastern arm of Junior Lake, you can make a wonderful trip into Scraggly Lake to the east (see page 147). The deep coves extending to the north and Duck Lake to the northwest offer hours—and miles—of exploration.

You can take another interesting side trip from Junior Lake's southwest shore into Horseshoe Lake. The channel narrows to just a few yards across in places, and a few spots swarmed with mosquitoes, but we loved this little out-of-the-way alcove. On the west shore, just before the channel widens into the lake, look for a floating bog. The thick sphagnum mat floats and harbors pitcher plant, sundew, bog laurel, leatherleaf, and two species of orchid: rose pogonia and calopogon, both in full bloom at the beginning of July. We watched a deer drink, and it looked like a great area for moose.

Junior Lake to Sysladobsis Lake

From Bottle Island, paddle northwest up Bottle Lake Stream into Bottle Lake, where you can portage into Sysladobsis. The two-mile marshy stream abounds with cattail, pickerelweed, yellow pondlily, and many tree stumps, along with some development. As part of a 1979 land settlement, the government returned extensive tracts to the Passamoquoddy and Penobscot tribes. Facing financial difficulty, the tribes sold large tracts to developers, who in turn subdivided into 40-acre lots. Cottages appeared on Bottle Lake Stream and parts of Junior Lake in an area heretofore undeveloped. Fortunately, Maine's strong regula-

Paddling across Junior Lake

tions controlling development next to water require significant set-backs and stringent septic design. Conservation organizations are hard at work preserving several hundred thousand acres of land in this area.

Just before you paddle into Bottle Lake proper, a channel to the right leads into Keg Lake, which we didn't explore. Bottle Lake's heavy development represents the kind of place we prefer to paddle through as quickly as possible.

You can use the north-end access, but to get to Sysladobsis, a small cove extending to the south provides much closer access. As mentioned above, low water levels may make access difficult. To find the portage, paddle around a small peninsula (almost an island) and behind a boat-house (gray when we visited). Though not marked or maintained, we are told this is an acceptable access for the half-mile carry to or from Sysladobsis. From the boathouse, walk south on the dirt road a few hundred feet, then bear right. In a few hundred yards, cross a larger gravel road and continue south for another few hundred yards until you see an access stream on the left. You can launch into this access stream or carry down the road next to the main lake.

Sysladobsis, or Dobsis (pronounced DOB-see), stretches for about 9 miles northwest to southeast and extends about a mile and a half across at its widest. You will become well aware of its size with even a modest breeze from the north or south.

Some development occurs along the shores, but nothing like on Bottle Lake. Some summer residents pump their drinking water right out of the clear lake, and anglers catch good-size salmon regularly. You can explore the few coves and inlets along the lake if weather conditions permit leisurely paddling. We paddled a few hundred yards up Sysladobsis Creek, but rapids eventually blocked our way.

Few campsites exist along the lake; we failed to find the one near Cranberry Cove. Away from established campsites, finding a place to set up a tent among the rocks and hillocks is difficult.

Sysladobsis to Pocumcus Lake and Elsemore Landing

Near the south end of Dobsis, Big Island stretches almost two miles in length on a northwest-southeast axis. As you paddle southeast, keep to the left of the island (unless you have time to explore around it). Stick to the shoreline, and you will reach the lake outlet at Dobsis Dam and Dennison Portage about three-quarters of a mile from the second point. A road-accessible campsite that gets heavy use exists here (fire permit required).

From the campsite, carry around the dam to Pocumcus. Launch into the stream on the dam's left (west) side for the five-mile paddle back to Elsemore Landing. We loved paddling the marshy section through Pocumcus Narrows, with its cattails and stumps of long-dead trees.

～ 43 ～

Scraggly Lake (Southern) and Pleasant Lake
Kossuth Twp, T5 R1 NBPP, and T6 R1 NBPP

MAPS: Maine Atlas, Maps 35 and 45
  USGS Quadrangle, Scraggly Lake

AREA AND MAXIMUM DEPTH: Scraggly Lake, 2,758 acres, 42 feet;
  Pleasant Lake, 1,574 acres, 92 feet

HABITAT TYPE: shallow lake with marshy coves and long shoreline

FISH: Scraggly Lake: smallmouth bass, white and yellow perch,
  chain pickerel, also some salmon and lake trout; Pleasant
  Lake: salmon, lake trout, brook trout

EXPECT TO SEE: bald eagle, osprey, loon, common tern, otter,
  moose

CAMPING: Maine Wilderness Camps, 207-738-5052

TAKE NOTE: no development except a campground on Pleasant
  Lake; fire permits, Maine Forest Service, 207-827-1800, or
  Maine Wilderness Camps

GETTING THERE

There are several options for getting to Scraggly Lake.

Scraggly Lake Access: From I-95, Exit 55, go east on Route 6 for about 38 miles, and turn right onto Amazon Road (3.8 miles after Maine Wilderness Camps entrance). Go south on Amazon Road for 9.0 miles (9.0 miles), turn right into the Hasty Cove access, and go 0.3 mile (9.3 miles) to the water. Roads may be impassable in spring; the last 0.3 mile usually requires a high-clearance vehicle.

From Pleasant Lake: As above, but turn into Maine Wilderness Camps, and go 3.5 miles to the campground. Portage from Pleasant Lake's south end into Scraggly.

From Pocumcus Lake: Launch at Elsemore Landing on Pocumcus Lake (see previous section), and paddle north through Junior Lake into Scraggly. Plan at least a day to get to Scraggly Lake; in windy conditions it may take longer and could be treacherous.

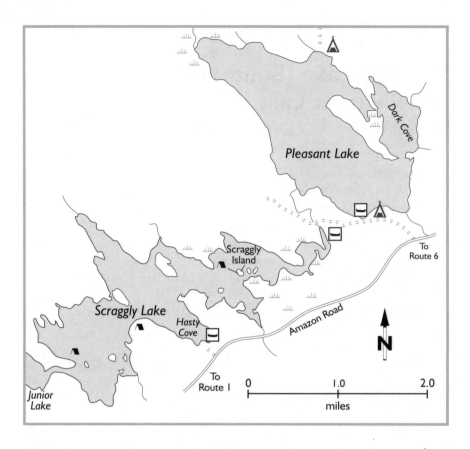

We call this Scraggly Lake "southern" to distinguish it from another Scraggly Lake farther north (see Trip 79). Though only 3.5 miles long, the lake's highly varied shoreline extends nearly 20 miles along marshy coves and undeveloped islands. Wild and remote, this is the paddler's ideal lake: too shallow for most motorboaters, and with difficult access so that you have to do some work to get there.

We paddled into Scraggly as part of a loop trip starting at Elsemore Landing on Pocumcus Lake, extending through Junior and Sysladobsis lakes. Scraggly makes a wonderful two- or three-day detour. A more common one-way trip starts at Maine Wilderness Camps on Pleasant Lake's northern shore, with a portage to the northeastern tip of Scraggly, then on through to Junior Lake and either Pocumcus or West Grand Lake. Maine Wilderness Camps can shuttle you to a starting or ending point.

While paddling along Scraggly's northern shore in the first light of morning, we surprised a magnificent bald eagle feeding at the water's edge. We saw a number of eagles here, along with wood duck, loon, ring-necked duck, deer, and a huge snapping turtle. During a morning paddle from Scraggly up into Pleasant Lake, we watched a playful family of otters in the glass-smooth water. We did not happen to see any moose, even though Scraggly sports superb moose habitat. You may also see common terns; we suspect they nest on large boulders visible from the Scraggly Island campsite.

A number of designated campsites dot Scraggly Island, the nicest a permitted site (no fire permit required); the other two require permits. The island's camping areas include fire rings, picnic tables, outhouses, and lots of space for tents. During a visit at the end of June we found surprisingly few mosquitoes on Scraggly Island, though some surrounding marshy areas had many bugs. We enjoyed exploring the marshy area east and south of the island. At high water, you can find a passage around the large marsh.

A Side Trip to Pleasant Lake

To go from Scraggly Lake into Pleasant Lake, paddle to the eastern tip and take your boat out at a steep ramp (too steep for trailers). Carry up to the road (about 50 feet), then to the right (east). You can carry all the way to the campground and launch onto Pleasant Lake (about a half-mile), or you can cut over to Pleasant Lake on a portage trail. When we paddled here, the trail seemed poorly marked and hard to follow due to recent logging activity.

We particularly enjoyed exploring Dark Cove. Hundreds of boulders sticking out of the water and hiding just beneath the surface near the mouth help to keep down motorboat traffic. In the very clear water, you will see thousands of freshwater mussels poking out of the sand. White cedar, the dominant tree here, grows alongside balsam fir, spruce, and white pine. Alder, bog laurel, sweetgale, and other northern species grow in profusion along the shore. We found a very pleasant campsite near the north end, nestled beneath a grove of red pines.

Cold Stream
Passadumkeag

> **MAPS:** Maine Atlas, Map 33
> USGS Quadrangle, Passadumkeag
> **STREAM LENGTH:** 5 miles
> **HABITAT TYPE:** meandering stream though large marsh
> **FISH:** smallmouth bass
> **EXPECT TO SEE:** osprey, northern harrier, beaver, moose, typical bog vegetation
> **TAKE NOTE:** no development; paddle here when wind makes lakes unsafe to paddle

GETTING THERE

From I-95, Exit 54, go east on Routes 6 and 155. After crossing the Penobscot River, turn right (south) onto Route 2 east. Go 4.4 miles (4.4 miles), and turn left onto Pleasant Street. Go 2.0 miles (6.4 miles), turn right onto Goulds Ridge Road, and immediately pass over the Passadumkeag River bridge. Access is on the left, just over the bridge.

Cold Stream drains a huge bog in the towns of Passadumkeag and Lowell, about 20 miles north of Old Town. The stream itself, with all of its meanderings, only stretches for about five miles. Together with its Little Cold Stream tributary, Cold Stream flows into the Passadumkeag River, which immediately empties into the Penobscot River.

From the access on the Passadumkeag, paddle right, upstream, for a very short way, then take a left into the mouth of Cold Stream. At the confluence of the two rivers, you will find dwarf willow and alder. These give way to typical low-growing bog vegetation along the border of the 40-foot-wide channel. Sweetgale and several members of the heath family grow right to the water's edge. At one point the channel wanders nearer high ground, where you will find a thick grove of silver maples.

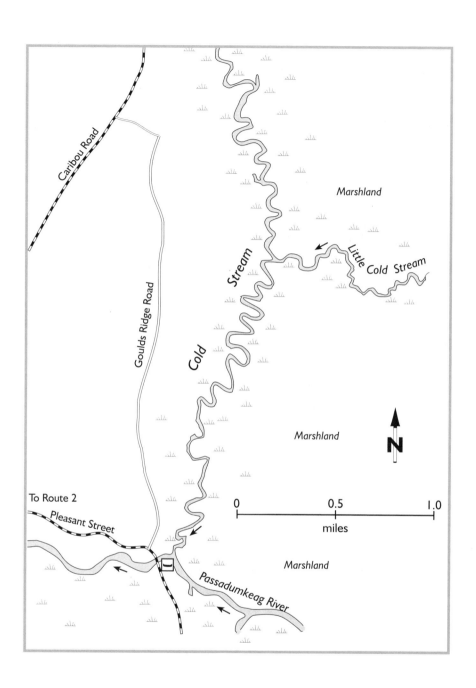

Wild country that sees few visitors, except for an occasional fisherman, it is a great place to look for moose. Although we did not see any, we saw much evidence of their presence. We watched an osprey hover overhead, seemingly oblivious to us, waiting to dive on an unsuspecting fish. We also watched a northern harrier glide over the marsh, skimming the tops of the vegetation, waiting to pounce on any rodents foolhardy enough to be out in the middle of the morning. Formerly called marsh hawk, the harrier's distinguishing characteristics include a white rump patch and its habit of buoyantly gliding over fields and marshes, tipping its upraised wings from side to side.

As we rounded one of the never-ending bends in the channel, we surprised a beaver. In typical fashion, it dove, resurfaced, and slapped its tail on the water, splashing us as it dove again. Wherever you see patches of alder, look for beaver and beaver activity. We saw numerous cuttings, lodges, side channels dug out to provide access to lusher vegetation, and mud banks where they had collected mud to plaster on their lodges and dams. If you paddle here in the evening, you should see several of these industrious little engineers.

You can also paddle quite a way up Little Cold Stream, at least during high water. We would paddle these two streams when wind turns nearby lakes and the Penobscot River to froth.

Beaver

～45～

Folsom, Crooked, and Upper Ponds
Lincoln

MAPS: Maine Atlas, Maps 34 and 44
USGS Quadrangle, Lincoln East

AREA AND MAXIMUM DEPTH: Folsom Pond, 282 acres, 19 feet;
Crooked Pond, 220 acres, 30 feet; Upper Pond, 506 acres,
31 feet

HABITAT TYPE: shallow ponds

FISH: smallmouth bass, white perch, chain pickerel

EXPECT TO SEE: loon, bald eagle, ducks

TAKE NOTE: limited development; fire permits, Maine Forest
Service, 207-827-1800

GETTING THERE

Folsom and Crooked Ponds: From Lincoln, at the junction of Routes 2, 6, and 155, go south on Route 155 for 1.1 miles (1.1 miles), and turn left onto Transalpine Road at the Penobscot Valley Hospital. Go 2.4 miles (3.5 miles), and turn left onto Folsom Pond Road. Staying on the main road, go 1.6 miles (5.1 miles), and take the right fork downhill. Go 0.6 mile (5.7 miles), and go right again. Go 0.6 mile (6.3 miles), turn left onto a rutty dirt road, and go 0.4 mile (6.7 miles) to the access on the right.

Upper Pond: From Folsom Pond access, go back 0.4 mile (0.4 mile), turn left, and go 0.9 mile (1.3 miles) to the access.

Folsom and Crooked Ponds

These ponds harbor very little development and lie in a gorgeous setting, with rolling hills in the background. Their three shallow sections, separated by narrow channels, grow thick with waterlilies and pickerelweed. A few small islands poke up here and there, and lush vegetation grows down to the water's edge. High tree-species diversity characterizes this area, with white cedar, white pine, lots of hemlocks, white birch, and red maple in evidence.

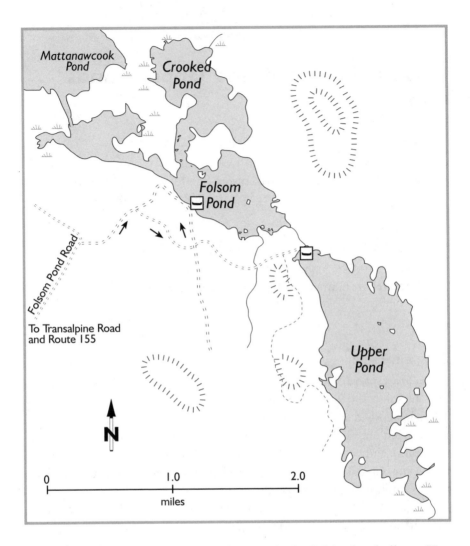

We saw at least ten loons, and many ducks fed in the shallows. You may also see the resident bald eagles here. Explore the extensive marshy areas in the farther reaches of the undeveloped arms for wildlife, especially in early morning or in the evening.

Speaking of wildlife, they say that after about 500 mosquito bites in a season, you become immune, no longer swelling at the site of each attack. Anyone who paddles a lot in the spring in Maine should come to Folsom Pond in June. Spend about ten minutes out there, and you will not have to worry about mosquitoes for the rest of the season. Driving to the access, we had to go slowly because of hundreds of patrolling

Four loons cavort on Folsom Pond in the calm waters of early morning.

dragonflies. Clearly, however, they were not doing their job of controlling the mosquito population.

Upper Pond

A small stream separates Upper Pond from Folsom and Crooked ponds, and you have to drive to the Upper Pond access. Though much larger than the other two, it has only one marshy area, on the south shore, but aquatic vegetation appears regularly along the shoreline. The tree-species assembly resembles that of Folsom and Crooked ponds, and we saw just as many loons here—at least ten.

Western Lakes
& Mountains

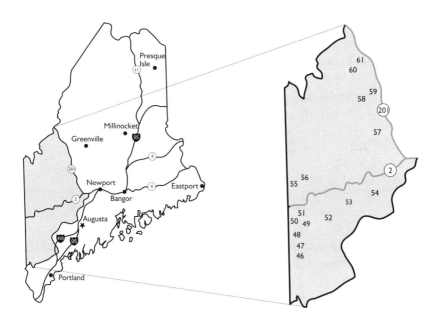

Rugged mountains and abundant lakes populate this region. Flagstaff is the state's fourth largest lake, and the Rangeley Lakes—a system of 112 interconnected streams, lakes, and ponds—dominate the landscape and provide a paddler's paradise. The Western Lakes and Mountains Region borders New Hampshire, and encompasses the eastern portion of the White Mountain National Forest. Featured trips include Lake Umbagog (Trip 55), with its abundant moose, loons, osprey, and occasional bald eagle; huge Flagstaff Lake (Trip 57), where you may spot otters and rafts of migrating waterfowl; and Attean and Holeb Ponds and the Moose River Bow Loop (Trip 61), which provides a several-day trip on the Rangeley Lakes system with beautiful mountains as a backdrop.

Brownfield Bog
Brownfield

MAPS: Maine Atlas, Map 4
    USGS Quadrangle, Brownfield
AREA: 5,700 acres in the Wildlife Management Area
HABITAT TYPE: shallow marsh with limited open water
EXPECT TO SEE: ducks, geese, turtles, muskrat, deer, beaver, moose, and osprey possibly
TAKE NOTE: extremely slow paddling because of boggy islands, shallow water

GETTING THERE

From Fryeburg, go southeast on Routes 5 and 113 to East Brownfield, and turn left onto Route 160. Go 1.5 miles (1.5 miles), and turn left onto Lord Hill Road. Go 0.1 mile (1.6 miles), and turn left onto the access road. Go 0.8 mile (2.4 miles) to a small shed with a list of rules. Park here and put your boat in about 50 feet down the road. Go 1.5 miles (3.9 miles) to a more interesting place to paddle (stay left at the fork 0.3 mile [2.7 miles] from the shed).

During the summer, when canoers overrun the nearby Saco River, you can paddle undisturbed on Brownfield Bog. The Brownfield Bog Wildlife Management Area, maintained by the state, contains hundreds of acres of marsh to explore. When we paddled here on a warm, sunny October day, bigtooth aspen leaves reflected golden light onto the water as we enjoyed a beautiful view of snow-dusted White Mountains off in the distance. An extensive grassy area at road's end would make a scenic spot for a picnic.

Brownfield Bog, very wild but relatively accessible, teems with wildlife. In addition to nesting waterfowl, you should see deer, beaver, muskrat, turtles, and—if you paddle here early in the morning or at dusk—an occasional moose. Just about every type of bog vegetation abounds, from pitcher plants and sundews to waterlilies, sweetgale, and rhodora. Because of the huge amount of beaver activity and extensive

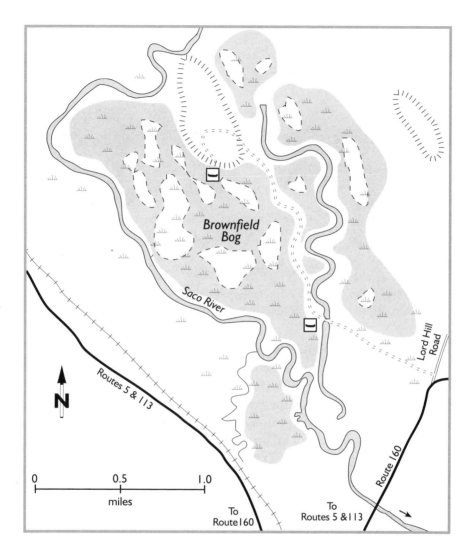

bog vegetation, we progressed slowly through the hidden pathways. If you need more space, just push aside the small floating islands dotting the marsh. Because of the large landmass within the marsh, you can paddle here unaffected by wind.

This area and south of here provides an ideal spot to look for oaks. White and red oaks cover the higher ground within and on the hillsides surrounding the marsh. Thought to have originated in Mexico and then radiated out to other areas, oaks comprise a genus with more than 500 species found throughout the warmer parts of the north temperate region. Native oaks species number 58 in the United Statess, but as you

Oak-covered hillsides form a backdrop for Brownfield Bog. Marshy islands keep these waters calm when wind-driven waves make more open ponds unsafe.

would expect, the number of species present in a given area dwindles the farther you get from Mexico. For example, Texas has 29 species of oak, Illinois 20, Pennsylvania 18, New York 12, and Vermont 7. Maine has 8 species, with most of the rarer ones concentrated along the lower New Hampshire border and along the coast.

With some searching at Brownfield Bog and along the southern New Hampshire border, expect to find swamp white oak, chestnut oak, bear oak, black oak, and scarlet oak, along with white oak and the ubiquitous northern red oak. Only bur oak, found in the Machias region, is absent from this area. We found a thick stand of bear oak along the shore of Black Pond in Porter, the next town south of Brownfield.

Brownfield Bog typifies the kind of wilderness experience that becomes increasingly difficult to find in Maine these days. It seems that even the most remote ponds and lakes sprout cabins and camps overnight, and unfortunately more and more people adopt the sedentary TV-generation lifestyle by forsaking the traditional hand-powered Maine canoe for motorboats. Because the state owns the bog, it will not sprout cabins; and because of its shallow and weedy character, those addicted to throbbing horsepower will have to get their thrills elsewhere. Gazing off through fall-colored, yellow-leaved birches and aspen at the layered hillsides and mountains, we are thankful that Brownfield Bog remains wild and protected in such a heavily vacationed area.

～47～

Pleasant Pond
Brownfield, Denmark, and Fryeburg

MAPS: Maine Atlas, Map 4
   USGS Quadrangles, Brownfield and Fryeburg
AREA AND MAXIMUM DEPTH: 604 acres, 15 feet; river length,
   1.5 miles
HABITAT TYPE: shallow, marshy pond
FISH: smallmouth bass, white perch, chain pickerel
CANOE RENTAL AND CAMPGROUNDS: Saco River bridge, Route
   160; Camp N Canoe, 207-935-2529, www.woodlandacres.com
   River Run Canoe Rental, www.riverruncanoe.com,
   207-452-2500
EXPECT TO SEE: views of White Mountains, muskrat, deer
TAKE NOTE: do not attempt to paddle here unless you can easily
   paddle upstream; novice paddlers should avoid this area during high water; wear PFD; fire permits, Maine Forest Service,
   207-624-3700

GETTING THERE

From Fryeburg, go east on Route 302, cross the Saco River bridge, and park
in the designated area on the right. The lot fills on summer weekends, with
cars spilling out onto the adjacent road shoulders.

The Saco River, born among the highest peaks of the White Mountains in New Hampshire, gathers feeder streams and momentum as it
roars down the steep valleys. By the time it reaches Fryeburg, though,
it morphs into a tame, meandering, marshy meadow stream, popular
with weekend canoeists. Thousands of people paddle this water on
summer weekends. Very few of them, however, take the time to paddle
out onto Pleasant Pond, accessible only from the Saco River. With layered hills and lofty peaks of the White Mountains as a backdrop, sitting
out in the middle of the pond, gazing off at the multihued pastel layers
retreating into the distance, we found it difficult to leave even as the

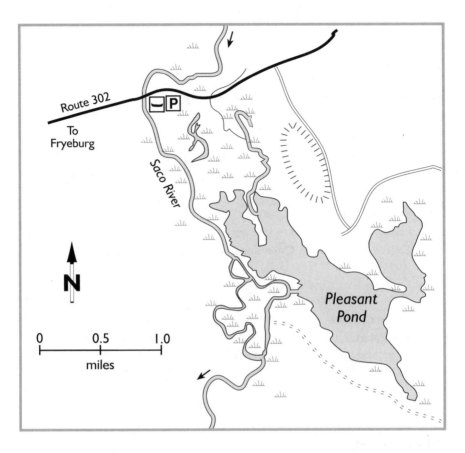

sun set over the mountains, though our delay would mean paddling back in the semidark. A magical place, indeed.

The Saco's banks make it difficult to see out into the surrounding marsh. Though the current flows at a modest pace in the summer and fall, leave sufficient time to paddle back (at least 50 percent more time than it takes to paddle down to Pleasant Pond). Watch closely for the access stream off to the left on a sharp, sweeping curve to the right. A black and orange No Trespassing sign appears in front of you; high in a tree, a broken paddle says Pleasant on it.

Oaks line the Saco's banks, along with occasional groves of hemlock and scattered white pine. In addition, silver maple shows up in large numbers in some places. You can distinguish silver maple from the other swamp dweller—the red maple—by the deeply cleft, five-lobed leaves with silvery undersides. Red maples have shallow-cleft, three-lobed leaves. Silver maples have the largest-winged seeds of all native maples, reaching three inches in length and providing important food for squirrels, foxes, and mice, plus pine and evening grosbeaks. We spied a fat gray squirrel clambering among the silver maples, searching for seeds.

Pleasant Pond—shallow and marshy, especially along the north end where the access stream enters—would take a few hours to explore fully. Look for beaver, muskrat, red-winged blackbird, turtles, and deer lurking in the marshy inlets and coves. At quieter times, especially on the pond's north end, one might be lucky enough to see a moose browsing on the abundant vegetation.

Because of the extensive marshes, we found few areas where one could pitch a tent. It would be far easier to camp out under the oaks on unposted land along the Saco River. Please treat this private property with respect.

During spring high water, you will not be able to paddle the 1.5 miles back to the Route 302 bridge. You could take out at the Route 160 bridge, five or so miles downstream from Pleasant Pond. Given the summer crowds, we prefer to paddle here in the fall, when the hillsides have turned to golds, reds, and browns. We paddled here in October and saw not another soul; when we visited in June and August, cars jammed the parking areas, and canoes dotted the river.

48

Kezar Pond

Fryeburg

> **MAPS:** Maine Atlas, Maps 4 and 10
>   USGS Quadrangles, Fryeburg and Pleasant Mountain
> **AREA AND MAXIMUM DEPTH:** 1,851 acres, 12 feet
> **HABITAT TYPE:** lake with extensive marshes along the perimeter
> **FISH:** smallmouth bass, largemouth bass, white perch, yellow
>   perch, chain pickerel
> **EXPECT TO SEE:** views of White Mountains, loon, bald eagle,
>   osprey, great blue heron, marshland species
> **TAKE NOTE:** wind can make paddling here dangerous; novice
>   paddlers should avoid this area during windy conditions; wear
>   PFD; under windy conditions, stay on the old course of the
>   Saco River

GETTING THERE

From the junction of Routes 5 and 302 in Fryeburg, go east on Route 302 for 5.5 miles (5.5 miles), and turn left onto Hemlock Bridge Road. Go 3.0 miles (8.5 miles) to the Hemlock Covered Bridge. Park on right before the bridge or on left across the bridge. If you launch before the bridge, paddle to the right—not under the bridge. If you launch after the bridge, paddle under the bridge, and take the right channel to Kezar Pond.

You can also explore the old channel of the Saco River either up to North Fryeburg or down to its junction with the Saco River and Pleasant Pond (see page 161).

Kezar Pond, given its relatively round shape, might not seem like a great paddling spot, but we had a great time here, despite a stiff southern breeze that made paddling difficult. From the beautiful covered bridge on the Saco River's old course, paddle north into the Kezar Pond outlet stream, which meanders gently along on a barely perceptible current for about a mile, the sides lined with silver maple, gray birch, white pine, red maple, viburnum, and a few red oak. The creek

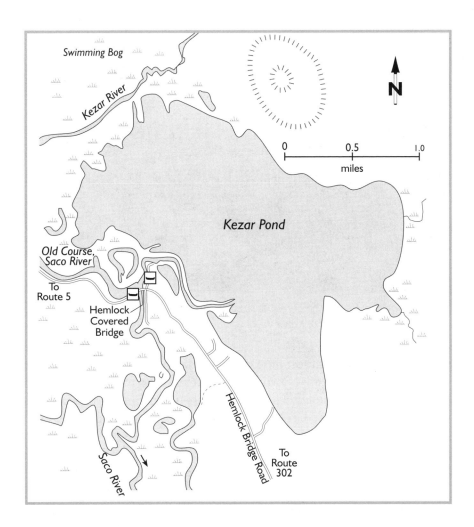

traverses the 400-acre Kezar Pond Fen that contains Long's bulrush *(Scirpus longii)*, a globally rare and federally threatened species.

The main pond affords an impressive and extensive view of the White Mountains to the west and of Smarts Hill, extending up from the pond's northeast side. From the outlet stream, to the right lie a few marshy coves full of pickerelweed, bulrush, and waterlily, with great blue herons fishing the shallows. A few cottages on the southern lobe comprise the bulk of the pond's modest development. After exploring the south end, we paddled across to avoid the developed areas, then around the pond counterclockwise.

Two inlet streams on the east side provide great little side explorations. The more southerly one—somewhat difficult to find—heads

Hemlock Bridge, a historic wooden-truss structure built in 1857, spans the Old Course of the Saco River just south of Kezar Pond.

off near the northernmost house along the pond's east side. Silver maple, royal and sensitive fern, and sweetgale line the deep, narrow, winding, sandy-bottomed channel. Near the creek outlet you will also find cranberries, whose large red berries in the fall dwarf the tiny oval leaves of this heath (related to blueberry and laurel).

In the pond's northeast lobe, you can explore some hidden coves and an inlet creek, also very easy to miss. We paddled a couple hundred yards up this creek—our pace quickened by the mosquitoes in this wind-shielded area—until a beaver dam blocked our progress. Without the mosquitoes, we might have portaged over the dam and explored upstream, but we retreated back to the main pond and its protective wind. (One learns to love and hate the wind!)

We favor the north end, extending around to the western tip. This section adjoins an area known as Swimming Bog, a Maine priority wetland conservation area. Hillocks of grasses and pickerelweed dot the shallow shoreline here. When whitecaps fill the pond itself, the matrix of tiny islands damp the waves, keeping it fairly calm. We explored lazily through these hillocks and the acres of pondlilies. As we snaked our way west, we watched a bald eagle we had first spotted from the pond's east end (nearly two miles away) that had perched atop an old silver maple (see page 65 for more on bald eagles).

49

Five Kezar Ponds

Lovell, Stoneham, and Waterford

MAPS: Maine Atlas, Map 10
USGS Quadrangle, North Waterford

AREA AND MAXIMUM DEPTH: Middle Pond, 72 acres, 51 feet;
Back Pond, 62 acres, 33 feet; Mud and Unnamed Pond, 45
acres, 35 feet

HABITAT TYPE: Mud Pond—minerotrophic fen; wooded ponds

FISH: brook trout, smallmouth bass, chain pickerel

EXPECT TO SEE: loon, pitcher plant, sundew, tamarack, black
spruce, beaver in evening

TAKE NOTE: 10-HP limit

GETTING THERE

From the junction of Routes 35 and 118 in North Waterford, go south on
Route 35 for 0.2 mile (0.2 mile), and turn right onto Lovell Road/Five Kezars
Road (the right fork). Go 3.0 miles (3.2 miles) to a small turnout on the left
(do not take any right turns, no matter how enticingly named). Carry down
over the bank to the pond.

Of the Five Kezar Ponds, we cover Mud, Middle, Back, and one
unnamed pond here. Jewett Pond, not connected to the other four, has
no public access. Although the ponds have pockets of development, we
include this series of small, forested ponds because unusual natural features abound. With relatively little boat traffic, especially in the spring
and fall, one can find hours of quiet paddling.

After paddling up the unnamed pond, before passing under the
bridge on the left into Middle Pond, keep going northwest, curving
around to the right into Mud Pond, a splendid example of a peatland
minerotrophic fen. Scientists only recently started to distinguish
between raised peatlands with no streams flowing through, calling them
bogs, and peatlands on slopes with water flowing through, calling them
fens. *Minerotrophic* means "mineral nourished" from the flow-through

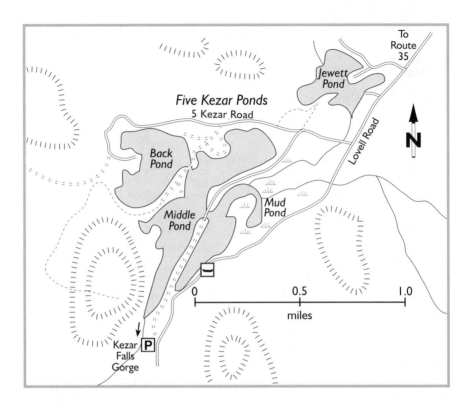

of water. In contrast, in the classic domed bog with no flow-through—the huge 4,300-acre Great Heath, twenty miles due west of Machias—almost all nutrients come from rainfall and the air. In contrast to the dwarfed shrubs and trees of nutrient-poor bogs, the relatively large tamarack, red maple, and black spruce of the Mud Pond fen benefit from water flow-through that brings necessary minerals and carries away acids produced by sphagnum and plant degradation.

Beaver thrive in the shrubby environment of Mud Pond, opening watery paths to higher ground to drag succulent branches of alder, birch, and red maple back to their submerged winter food caches. Look for them by paddling quietly here in the evening. Pitcher plants and sundews, as well as many species of marshland shrubs, abound on the raised sphagnum clumps. It is so rare that one can paddle back into such a beautiful, unspoiled peatland that this alone makes a trip to Five Kezar Ponds worthwhile.

But one more unusual natural feature draws us here: Kezar Falls Gorge. Paddle back out of Mud Pond, and turn right under the bridge to Middle Pond. Turn left, and paddle southwest to the five ponds'

The Mud Pond fen

outlet. Where the pond narrows, pull your boat up on shore, and hike the short distance to Kezar Falls Gorge. A surprising amount of water tumbles down through a steep-walled, beautifully sculpted canyon. To get a better view, climb up above on the left. You can also reach the gorge by continuing down the access road.

50

Horseshoe Pond
Lovell and Stoneham

MAPS: Maine Atlas, Map 10
   USGS Quadrangle, Center Lovell
AREA AND MAXIMUM DEPTH: 132 acres, 40 feet
HABITAT TYPE: narrow lake in wooded valley
FISH: brown and brook trout, smallmouth bass
EXPECT TO SEE: mountain views, merganser, great blue heron,
   osprey and moose a possibility
TAKE NOTE: 6-HP limit

GETTING THERE

From Fryeburg, go north on Route 5. When Routes 5 and 5A split, go left on Route 5 for 0.8 mile (0.8 mile), and turn left onto West Lovell Road at the sign for Kezar Lake and The Narrows. Go 1.0 mile (1.8 miles) to The Narrows bridge, continue for 1.7 miles (3.5 miles), and turn left onto Foxboro Road (West Lovell Road goes right). Go 1.6 miles (5.1 miles), and turn right (New Road goes left). Go 0.7 mile (5.8 miles), turn right onto Horseshoe Pond Road, and go downhill 1.0 mile (6.8 miles) to the access.

Horseshoe Pond's magnificent setting, with steep hills hovering on all sides and two very different nearby hiking trails, prompted us to include it. Small and out of the way, Horseshoe Pond provides paddling solitude, especially when wind whips up whitecaps on Kezar Pond. A few small cabins stand on the pond's southern end, but the White Mountain National Forest protects the north end. The tree-covered hillsides give way to dense shrubbery along the shore. Rhodora, a type of rhododendron that boasts clusters of beautiful rose-purple flowers in late May, dominates the shoreline. Nearby Moose Pond more than makes up for the lack of marshy areas.

The presence along the shoreline of mostly shallow-rooted trees such as spruce, red and white pine, hemlock, and white birch indicates

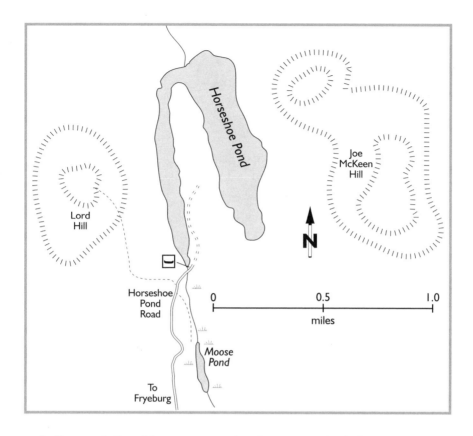

a shallow soil. In addition to stands of pines on the hillsides, you will find lots of oak and sugar maple. An osprey, great blue heron, and flock of common mergansers—a colorful, fish-eating, diving duck with a narrow, serrated bill—greeted us as we paddled the narrow western arm.

While you are here, hike the short trail into Moose Pond. The Nature Conservancy maintains the Sucker Brook Nature Trail, which begins along the road on the left, just uphill from the access. When we hiked here in October, a moose had made fresh tracks on the road. After a short hike into Moose Pond, we found denuded red maple and alder trunks where a moose had recently browsed.

A trail found immediately across the road leads up to Lord Hill, which towers 720 feet over Horseshoe Pond's west edge. Look for an abandoned mica mine at the top, and enjoy the beautiful view of the pond and the Sucker Brook valley.

～51～

Virginia Lake
Stoneham

> **MAPS:** Maine Atlas, Map 10
>   USGS Quadrangle, East Stoneham
> **AREA AND MAXIMUM DEPTH:** 128 acres, 28 feet
> **HABITAT TYPE:** small wooded lake
> **FISH:** brook trout, largemouth bass, black crappie, white perch,
>   chain pickerel
> **EXPECT TO SEE:** mountain views, alder flycatcher
> **TAKE NOTE:** no personal watercraft; deposits of at least 67 miner-
>   als found in Stoneham: www.mindat.org

GETTING THERE

From Fryeburg, go north on Route 5, and turn left onto Birch Road just as you get to Keewaydin Lake. Go 0.4 mile (0.4 mile), and turn left onto Virginia Lake Road (Birch Avenue goes right). Go 0.6 mile (1.0 mile), and take the left fork (right fork goes to Virginia Lake Farm) 0.3 mile (1.3 miles) to the access.

Since 1987 a part of the White Mountain National Forest, Virginia Lake sits just south of a string of peaks that stretches to 2,000 feet in elevation, 1,200 feet above the lake. Virginia Lake, a real gem, sees little boat traffic, aside from a few fishermen. You can explore this scenic lake fully in a few hours.

The forested shores on the west, south, and east, primarily oak, give way to marshy inlets on the north that drain the surrounding peaks. During spring high water, you should be able to paddle back into the swamp a little way. Besides the typical marsh vegetation, look for an alder swamp, the summer home of an uncommon and very drab warbler-sized bird, called, appropriately enough, the alder flycatcher. An inconspicuous little bird with an olive-brown back and pale-yellow belly, with two white wing bars and a small white eye ring, this flycatcher—and the eight other similarly drab species found throughout the United States and Canada—sits upright on exposed branches,

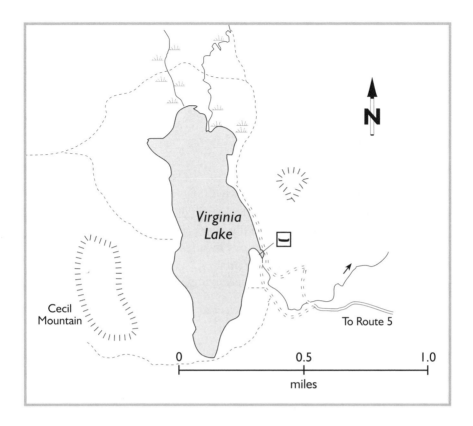

Virginia Lake

Cecil Mountain

To Route 5

| 0 | | 0.5 | | 1.0 |

miles

waiting to pounce on juicy insects that fly by. Listen for its song, a distinctive, falling, buzzy *fee-bee-o* anytime you are near alder stands in the spring and early summer.

When we paddled here in October, the alder flycatchers had long ago departed for warmer climes, those still abuzz with insects. The birches and maples along the northern shoreline had turned bright yellow and red, and the hillside oaks, with their burnished reds, stood in contrast to the dark green of scattered conifer groves. Huge clumps of multicolored leaves clogged the surface of the lake's south end, driven there by breezes from the north, the same ones that carry ducks and geese southward. The reflection of the brightly colored hillsides shimmered on the lake's rippled surface. Though the paddling season would end, sadly, with leaf fall, we were reminded that one can paddle in complete solitude almost anywhere in Maine anytime after Labor Day, enjoying the gloriously colored fall foliage and the cool air, free of biting insects.

North Pond
Norway

> **MAPS:** Maine Atlas, Maps 10 and 11
>   USGS Quadrangle, West Paris
> **AREA AND MAXIMUM DEPTH:** 147 acres, 10 feet
> **HABITAT TYPE:** shallow marsh slowly filling in
> **FISH:** largemouth bass, white perch, chain pickerel
> **EXPECT TO SEE:** loon, heath family members in profusion, bog
>   orchids, loon, turtles, waterfowl in fall, osprey, moose possible
> **TAKE NOTE:** Perham's gems and minerals, West Paris:
>   homepage.mac.com/rasprague/PegShop/perham.html

GETTING THERE

From the junction of Routes 26 and 117 in Norway, go west on Route 117 for about 1.5 miles, and turn right onto Crockett Ridge Road and the causeway over Pennesseewassee Lake. Go 2.5 miles (2.5 miles), and turn left onto Round the Pond Road. Go 2.2 miles (4.7 miles), and turn right into the access on North Pond Dam Road.

Wild and beautiful, particularly on the north and west ends, North Pond should be a sure bet for moose. The heavily forested hillsides of hemlock, birch, aspen, white pine, oak, maple, and many other tree species should provide refuge during the day, while acres and acres of marsh vegetation should provide food by night. Although we paddled here quietly at sunset, however, we did not see any moose.

We did not spend much time paddling the southeast arm because of the several houses there that stand in stark contrast to the pond's pristine northern and western reaches. The north end's twisting channels meander their way in and out among islands and floating chunks of marsh vegetation. One could spend several hours paddling north along the east side then down the west side, exploring each of the extensive channels reaching back up into the surrounding hills.

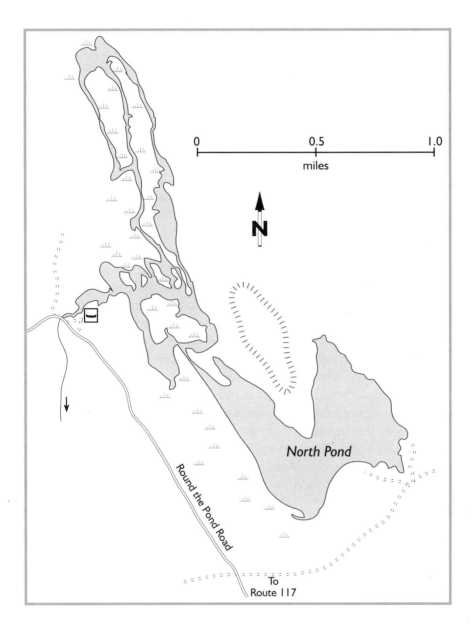

A fire tower rises on a hill in the north, and you can see a few farms off in the distance. From the access, paddle by an island covered with big white pines, almost to the eastern shore, and turn north, heading for the fire tower. You can paddle up this channel all the way back to the farms on those hills, exploring the many side channels along the way.

While tamarack, black spruce, and white pine populate several low-lying islands, shrub vegetation predominates. Waterlilies float in shallow channels lined with cattails, and members of the heath family, many of them with evergreen leaves, dominate the swamps of North Pond. Some sport showy flowers, such as rhodora, with its beautiful rose-purple flowers that emerge before the leaves in May; the summer-blooming swamp azalea, with its long, showy white flowers (near the northern limit of its range here); and the similar sheep laurel and bog laurel, with clusters of bright pink flowers. You can distinguish the latter two easily by the location of their flower whorls: Bog laurel's flowers occur at the ends of stems, whereas with sheep laurel, a cluster of new leaves grows above the flowers.

Other members of the swamp-loving heath family include Labrador tea, with its woolly brown leaf undersides; bog rosemary, with its two-inch-long, quarter-inch-wide leaves with white undersides, and its small, pink, urn-shaped flowers; and leatherleaf, with its aptly named leaves and long lines of upside-down, white, bell-shaped flowers. Perhaps the best-known members of the heath family include highbush and lowbush blueberries, huckleberries, and cranberries.

You can find some of these heaths in great numbers in and around North Pond. Although we loved exploring the channels and identifying the plants, we really wanted to see moose.

People also travel here for the geology. Common minerals include pegmatite—a very large-crystal granite—and gem-quality crystals of quartz, amethyst, and tourmaline. For directions to area mines—or to see what others have found—visit Perham's in West Paris.

～53～

Bunganock Pond and Brook
Hartford

MAPS: Maine Atlas, Map 11
   USGS Quadrangle, Canton
AREA AND MAXIMUM DEPTH: 51 acres, 12 feet; stream length, 1.3 miles
HABITAT TYPE: shallow, weedy pond and stream
FISH: largemouth bass, yellow perch, chain pickerel
EXPECT TO SEE: great blue heron, marsh birds, painted turtle,
   marsh vegetation
TAKE NOTE: no motors

GETTING THERE

From Auburn, go north on Route 4, and turn left onto Route 219 in North Turner. Turn right onto Route 140, go 0.5 mile (0.5 mile), and turn right. Go 0.8 mile (1.3 miles) through a sand pit on a very straight dirt road to the access. It is difficult to turn around on this narrow road; have someone guide you as you make a multipoint turn.

The outlet stream, far more interesting to the quietwater paddler than Bunganock Pond itself, sees hardly any visitors. The undeveloped pond has only one visible cabin, but its small, relatively round nature does not offer a lot of interesting features. We paddled the complete shoreline in less than an hour and then spent our remaining time paddling down and back on meandering Bunganock Stream.

Bunganock Pond
Many large white pines hug Bunganock Pond's shoreline, along with maple, birch, and other deciduous trees. Explore the marshy coves, and enjoy the view of forested hills to the west. An abundance of vegetation, especially waterlilies, populates the pond's waters. Most floating-leaved pond vegetation, such as fragrant waterlily, yellow pondlily, watershield, and bladderwort, cannot grow in more than about four feet of water, though some less common aquatic plants tolerate deeper water.

Bunganock Brook

Although we paddled here in July, we found relatively high water levels. We suspect that in late summer or during dry years, the outlet stream may be somewhat less navigable. Indeed, we had difficulty even getting into the pond's outlet stream, sliding the boat down the overgrown bank next to the bridge, then following its path. We found the first hundred feet of the stream the most difficult, and we had to get out of the boat three times, portaging over beaver dams and through shallows before the channel widened out to an easily paddleable thirty feet. If

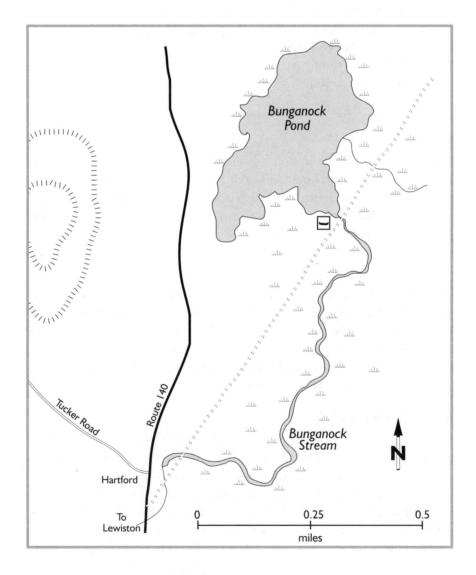

Fragrant waterlilies and pickerelweed abound in the shallow, marshy areas of Bunganock Pond.

your boat floats in this widened channel, you probably will find enough water to paddle to the end.

Wildlife, marsh vegetation, and solitude fill this place. We saw Eastern kingbird, great blue heron, song sparrow, and painted turtles that poked their heads up through floating vegetation and dived down through tea-colored water as we approached. Abundant fragrant waterlilies and yellow pondlilies, along with pickerelweed and grasses, line the channel. Sweetgale and other shrubs crowd the shore in places, and water-tolerant trees such as tamarack and red maple encroach on the banks wherever the ground rises slightly above the marsh.

At bends in the stream, occasional large granite boulders stand like sentinels guarding the passageway. In those areas, beware of submerged boulders. We had little trouble if we stayed in the middle of the channel when near visible boulders.

The stream snakes around the large pine island in the middle of the marsh, and it looks like it disappears at a dwarf-tamarack and red-maple forest. Instead, the stream abruptly turns right, continuing on for another few hundred yards before taking a sharp left turn down a narrow rocky channel. At this point you have reached the road at Hartford Center; barely submerged rocks fill the narrow channel.

~ 54 ~

Parker Pond
Mount Vernon and Vienna

> **MAPS:** Maine Atlas, Maps 12 and 20
>   USGS Quadrangles, Fayette and Farmington Falls
> **AREA AND MAXIMUM DEPTH:** 1,610 acres, 76 feet
> **HABITAT TYPE:** large, clear lake
> **FISH:** salmon, smallmouth bass
> **EXPECT TO SEE:** loon, osprey, kingfisher, granite boulders, pine-covered islands
> **TAKE NOTE:** modest development; motors limited by rocks; winds from the north or south can make paddling here treacherous; novice paddlers should avoid this area during windy conditions; wear PFD

GETTING THERE

From Augusta, go west on Route 17 to Readfield where it joins Route 41. When Routes 17 and 41 split, turn right (north) onto Route 41. From the public access sign on Echo Lake in West Mount Vernon, go 3.7 miles (3.7 miles), and turn sharply left onto Seaveys Corner Road. Go 1.5 miles (5.2 miles) to the access on the left.

We include this large, scenic pond because there is so much to explore and because numerous islands that dot the western shore screen much of the development. Even if you paddle past these islands, trees hide most of the houses. With all the coves, bays, inlets, peninsulas, and islands, it would take all day to explore Parker Pond.

After leaving the access, head right. What appears to be a peninsula is really a series of islands. On the far side of these islands, a huge flat rock provides a great spot for swimming and picnicking. After exploring these islands, head for the northwest cove around to the right. A series of beautiful pine-covered islands, many suitable for picnicking and swimming, extend down the whole western side of the pond, standing sentinel over the many coves.

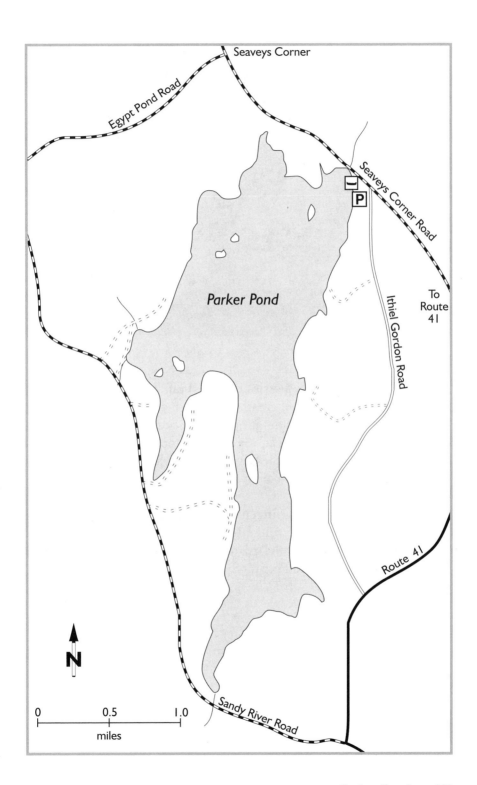

Seaveys Corner

Egypt Pond Road

Seaveys Corner Road

P

To
Route
41

Ithiel Gordon Road

Parker Pond

Route 41

N

Sandy River Road

0   0.5   1.0
miles

A common loon (Gavia immer) *plies the clear water of Parker Pond.*

Well out from shore, a series of large boulder formations extends up from the water's surface, creating more great places for swimming or picnicking, especially when biting insects seem to patrol every patch of vegetation. The quite clear water gives good views of the pond's rocky floor. We suspect that the large boulders gleaming up at us everywhere except in the pond's center help to keep the motorboat traffic down.

We saw osprey, loons, fifteen ring-billed gulls resting on a bare rock formation, kingfishers, and dozens of swallows. Besides the beautiful white pines covering the islands, balsam fir, hemlock, red and sugar maples, red oak, and gray birch line the western shore.

Umbagog Lake
Magalloway PLT and Cambridge and Errol, New Hampshire

> **MAPS:** Maine Atlas, Maps 17 and 18; New Hampshire Atlas, Map 51
>   USGS Quadrangles, Umbagog Lake South and Umbagog Lake North
>
> **AREA AND MAXIMUM DEPTH:** 7,850 acres, 48 feet
>
> **HABITAT TYPE:** large, shallow, marshy lake with numerous coves and rivers
>
> **FISH:** brook trout, smallmouth bass, pickerel, northern pike, yellow perch
>
> **LAKE UMBAGOG NATIONAL WILDLIFE REFUGE:** lakeumbagog.fws.gov, 603-482-3415
>
> **CAMPING:** Umbagog Lake Campground, www.nhstateparks.org, 603-482-7795; backcountry sites require reservations; towing to remote sites available for a fee
>
> **EXPECT TO SEE:** moose, loons, bald eagle, osprey, wood duck, merganser
>
> **TAKE NOTE:** wind can make paddling treacherous; motorboat and personal watercraft traffic heavy on popular summer weekends

---

GETTING THERE

Southern End: From Bethel, go north on Route 26 to the New Hampshire border. Access is on the right, about a mile after entering New Hampshire. Backcountry campsite users can put in at the Umbagog Lake Campground, 0.7 miles east of the public access.

Androscoggin River: From Errol, New Hampshire, go south on Route 26 for about 100 yards after crossing the Androscoggin River bridge, and turn left onto North Mountain Pond Road at the sign Access to Public Water. The lake is about 3 miles up the river.

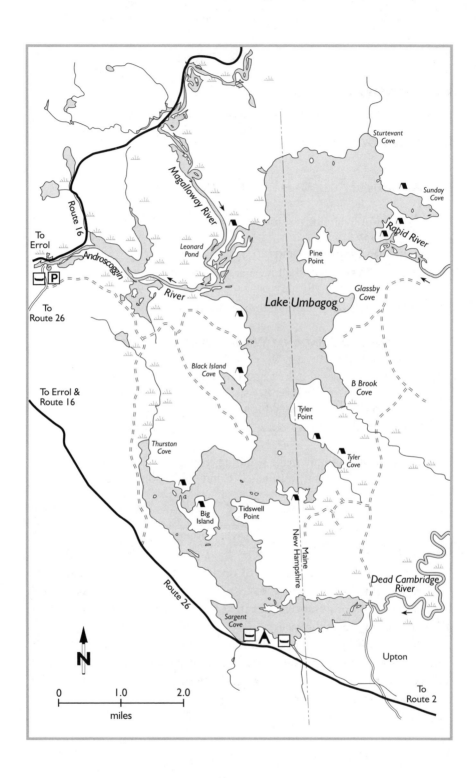

Sturtevant Cove

Sunday Cove

Rapid River

Magalloway River

To Errol

Route 16

Leonard Pond

Pine Point

Glassby Cove

Androscoggin

River

Lake Umbagog

To Route 26

Black Island Cove

B Brook Cove

Tyler Point

To Errol & Route 16

Thurston Cove

Tyler Cove

Big Island

Tidswell Point

Sargent Cove

Maine
New Hampshire

Dead Cambridge River

Upton

Route 26

N

0   1.0   2.0

miles

To Route 2

With the tremendous variety of wildlife and the number of ducks nesting here, it should not surprise us that Umbagog Lake has become one of the newest national wildlife refuges. Established in November 1992, the Lake Umbagog National Wildlife Refuge encompasses about 16,300 acres with another 2,600 acres protected by the states of Maine and New Hampshire.

Umbagog, pronounced *um-BAY-gog*, straddles the Maine–New Hampshire border, covering more than 12 square miles. Oriented generally north-south, with a highly varied shoreline that extends for more than 50 miles, plus dozens of islands, this magnificent lake exudes wildness. Readily accessible to the backcountry paddler, Umbagog Lake Campground manages 30 wilderness sites around the lake. A few private cottages and camps dot parts of the lake, and unfortunately, motorboat traffic has increased in recent years. We should all encourage New Hampshire and Maine to restrict motorboat and personal watercraft use for the protection of moose and nesting ducks, loons, and bald eagles—and for the solitude that belongs in this beautiful spot.

A very shallow lake—*Umbagog* means "shallow water"—with average depths of only about 15 feet, the many marshy areas provide ideal nesting habitat for such species as ring-necked, black, mallard, and wood ducks, and hooded and common mergansers. Wood ducks and hooded mergansers (our two common cavity nesters) use the approximately 100 nesting boxes around the lake.

Leonard Pond, the largest marshy area, in the lake's northwest corner, sports an extensive, thick, grassy marsh that from 1989 to 2001 supported nesting bald eagles. In 1989, the first chick died, but biologists added a chick from a captive pair; the eagles adopted and raised the foster chick. In the spring of 1994 during nesting, the male died from lead sinker ingestion. (On January 1, 2000, New Hampshire banned the use of lead sinkers weighing one ounce or less, to protect loons and other waterfowl; Maine followed suit two years later.) The female abandoned the lone egg but found a new mate. In the summer of 1997, nesting failed, but in 1998 they raised two young. In 1999, they raised another pair, but in 2000, the hatchlings died. However, in 2000, a second eagle pair began nesting on Umbagog's southern end and has successfully raised young. Unfortunately, the northern nest disappeared in fall 2001 after 13 years and raising 16 fledglings. For more about eagles, see page 65.

Moose teethmarks on a red maple.

Osprey, meanwhile, have had an even better time of it. Approximately 25 pairs nest in the vicinity of Umbagog in a typical year and rear about 35 chicks. Loons have had mixed success. Many loons summer on the lake —of 22 territorial pairs, 13 pairs actually nested, fledging a total of 11 chicks in 1994. However, in late July of 1997, when we paddled here, biologists told us that few chicks survived the late, cold spring. More recently, the number of nesting pairs dropped by half; as of 2004, biologists had not yet figured out why. During May, June, and July, be particularly careful about nesting loons. Even a quiet paddler inadvertently getting too close to a nest can result in abandonment, and loons always nest very close to water.

Our favorite places on Umbagog include Leonard Pond, the coves along the inlet of the Rapid River on the northeast, and the small coves and islands east of Tidswell Point. Big Island, purchased by the Society for Protection of New Hampshire Forests in the 1980s, is also wonderful and includes six campsites. For camping with kids, sites on the north shore of Tyler Cove stand out because of the protected sandy swimming beach.

We also enjoy paddling the slow-flowing, meandering Androscoggin and Magalloway Rivers. Paddling toward Umbagog on either river, a number of marshy ponds both to the right and left await your exploration. Keep an eye out for moose, otter, and mink.

Moose abound. Look for them standing belly deep in the Magalloway River, in ponds off to the left of the Androscoggin, or in any of the numerous coves on the lake. In the early morning light, in a cove just east of Tidswell Point, we watched three moose browsing by the water's edge. At the far southeastern end—the most developed part of the lake—we got our closest look at a moose not 200 yards from a cottage near the mouth of the Dead Cambridge River. We have also watched them swim across open water in the early morning, moving along at a brisk pace.

The varied vegetation around Umbagog includes conifers that predominate in most areas: balsam fir, spruce, northern white cedar, hemlock, and white pine; in other areas, deciduous trees, including yellow and paper birches, red maple, and an occasional red oak, predominate. We also saw a few relatively rare jack pines.

Potentially dangerous winds and waves crop up very quickly on this large lake, making open-boat paddling hazardous at times. Paddling around the lake during a two-day period in August, we got into heavy winds both afternoons, even though the water was as smooth as glass on each of those mornings. Wind blowing from the north or northwest across several miles of water can build up sizable waves.

Lots of fish inhabit the lake—as evidenced by the large osprey population. In mid-August, we caught yellow perch, smallmouth bass, and lots of lake chub (a whitefish with large scales and a deeply forked tail) up to a few pounds. With the right bait, lures, or flies, one should not have too much trouble pulling a few tasty meals out of the lake.

～ 56 ～

Upper and Lower Richardson Lake
Magalloway PLT, Richardsontown Twp, and Twp C

MAPS: Maine Atlas, Map 18
> USGS Quadrangles, Richardson Pond, Middle Dam, Metal-lak Mountain, Andover, and Oquossoc

AREA: Upper Richardson 4,200 acres; Lower Richardson, 2,900 acres

HABITAT TYPE: deep, clear lakes; scenic hillsides

FISH: salmon, lake trout, brook trout

WILDERNESS CAMPSITES: South Arm Campground, www.southarm.com, 207-364-5155

PINEGREE FOREST PARTNERSHIP:
> www.newenglandforestry.org/projects/Pingree.asp; Pingree family and New England Forestry Foundation developed 762,000 conservation easement, including west shore of Upper Richardson (the state owns the east shore) and north shore of Lower Richardson

EXPECT TO SEE: loon, bald eagle, osprey, moose, otter

TAKE NOTE: treacherous paddling under windy conditions; inexperienced paddlers should avoid this lake; no personal watercraft; fire permits, Maine Forest Service, 207-827-1800

GETTING THERE

South End: From Rumford, go west on Route 2 for several miles, and turn right (north) onto Route 5. At Andover, turn right onto Route 120, go 0.4 mile, cross the Ellis River bridge, and turn left onto South Arm Road at a sign for the South Arm Campground. Go 9.1 miles to the access on the left, 0.4 mile past the campground entrance (9.9 miles from Andover).

North End: From Rangeley, go west on Routes 4 and 16. When they split, go west on Route 16 for 14.4 miles (14.4 miles), turn left onto Mill Brook Road, and go 1.0 mile (15.4 miles) to the access.

Upper and Lower Richardson, once distinct lakes, merged at The Narrows with construction of 22-foot Middle Dam on Lower Richardson

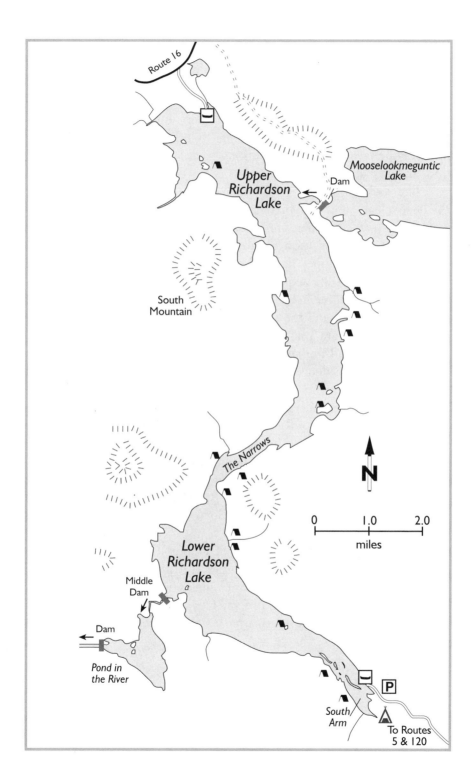

Route 16

Upper
Richardson
Lake

Dam

Mooselookmeguntic
Lake

South
Mountain

The Narrows

N

0   1.0   2.0
miles

Lower
Richardson
Lake

Middle
Dam

Dam

Pond in
the River

P

South
Arm

To Routes
5 & 120

in the early 1900s. The combined lake covers more than 11 square miles and extends roughly 15 miles in an S-curving, north-south direction. The lake ranges in width from a few hundred yards at The Narrows to about 1.5 miles at the widest section of Lower Richardson.

Their size and orientation make them quite dangerous in bad weather, where wind-driven waves can build up over more than five miles of open water. In bad conditions, wear life vests, use extreme caution, and stay close to shore.

The rocky shoreline gives way to a generally sandy bottom, and the deep, clear water supports an excellent coldwater trout and salmon fishery. Spruce, fir, cedar, and white pine predominate in this young forest, extensively cut prior to state acquisition.

Nearly all of Upper Richardson's eastern shore consists of public reserve land. The state acquired 80 percent of this 22,800-acre tract in 1984 from the Pingree heirs (Seven Islands Land Company) and James River Corporation, and the other 20 percent in 1978 from the Brown Company. The state manages the Richardson Unit for recreation, wildlife habitat, and timber. Within sight of the lake, the first two uses generally take precedence over the last. The Appalachian Trail passes a few miles east.

Thirty-eight primitive campsites, managed by South Arm Campground, dot the shores of Richardson Lake and its islands. Some of the nicer campsites you will pass paddling north from the campground include Spirit Island, Sand Banks (which has a great sandy beach area), Portland Point at The Narrows with a protected sandy cove, Pine Island, and Metallak Island in Upper Richardson (Pine Island used to have a bald eagle nest), Half Moon Cove on the west shore with two campsites, and Big Beaver Island.

If you paddle in the north end of Upper Richardson, also check out Cranberry Cove, the most remote and protected part of either lake. At low-water levels, you have to pick your way carefully among the rocks. The shoreline of Cranberry Cove harbors a typical northern fen ecosystem, with tamarack, leatherleaf, bog rosemary, pitcher plant, and sphagnum.

～ 57 ～

Flagstaff Lake

Bigelow Twp, Carrying Place Town Twp, Dead River Twp, Eustis, Flagstaff Twp, and T3 R4 BKP WKR

> **MAPS:** Maine Atlas, Maps 29 and 30
> USGS Quadrangles, Little Bigelow Mountain, Stratton, and The Horns
> **AREA AND MAXIMUM DEPTH:** 20,300 acres, 50 feet
> **HABITAT TYPE:** large, shallow lake with numerous coves and islands
> **FISH:** brook trout, salmon, chain pickerel
> **NORTHERN FOREST ALLIANCE:**
> www.northernforestalliance.org/explore.htm
> **EXPECT TO SEE:** loon, ducks, osprey, raven, moose, otter
> **TAKE NOTE:** no personal watercraft; wind can make paddling hazardous; fire permits, Maine Forest Service, 207-827-1800

GETTING THERE

From the south, take either Route 16 or Route 27 north to Stratton. In Stratton, where Routes 16 and 27 divide, go north on Route 27 for 4.3 miles (4.3 miles), and turn right onto the access road. Go 2.3 miles (6.6 miles) to the access, staying straight and on the main road.

The beautiful Bigelow Mountains just to the south carry the Appalachian Trail to 4,000 feet, or 3,000 feet above the lake's surface. To the north, Flagstaff Mountain stretches to 2,500 feet while layered hillsides recede into the distance at other compass points. The beautiful setting amid the northern boreal forest, with its pointed spires of fir, spruce, and tamarack, provides reason enough to travel to this remote area in the Rangeley Lakes Region.

You could spend a week exploring the islands, coves, and shoreline of huge Flagstaff Lake—Maine's fourth largest—as it courses west to east for more than 18 miles through the dammed-up Dead River valley. Though wind could present hazardous conditions, you should be able

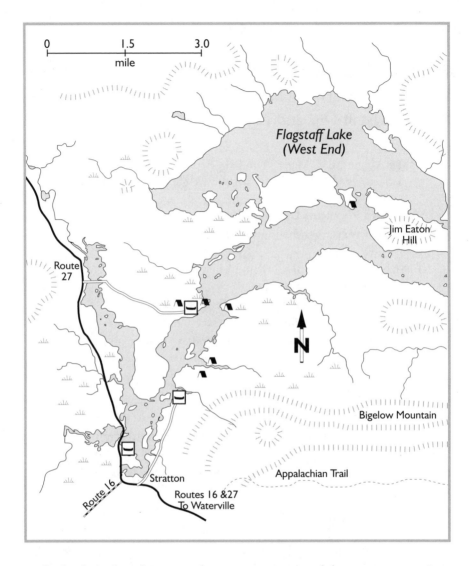

Flagstaff Lake
(West End)

Jim Eaton Hill

Route 27

N

Bigelow Mountain

Appalachian Trail

Stratton

Route 16

Routes 16 &27
To Waterville

0   1.5   3.0
mile

to find relatively calm water from one or more of the ten access points (see the *Maine Atlas*). When we paddled here on a day with south winds, we snuck behind islands and into protected coves. In one of those coves, we watched an otter fish the waters as a pair of ravens called overhead. In other coves, we found fish carcasses on rocks, leftovers from otter feasts. With west winds, we would explore the North Branch of the Dead River, which you can paddle up for several miles.

Much of the land surrounding Flagstaff Lake, particularly the southern shore, lies within Maine Public Reserve Lands, which pro-

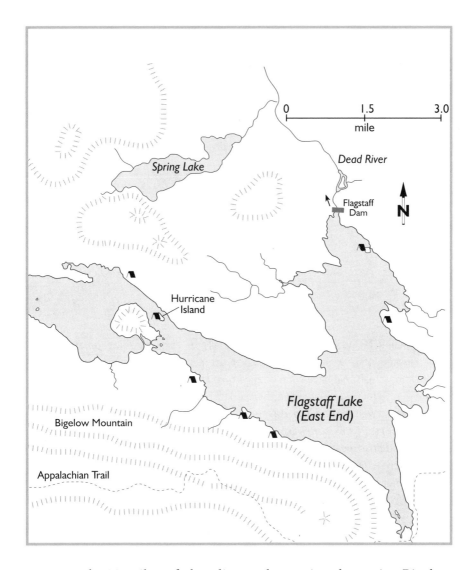

Spring Lake

Dead River

0   1.5   3.0
mile

Flagstaff
Dam

N

Hurricane
Island

Flagstaff Lake
(East End)

Bigelow Mountain

Appalachian Trail

tects nearly 20 miles of shoreline and contains the entire Bigelow Range within its 35,000 acres. The Western Mountains Project of the Northern Forest Alliance is working to protect the remaining sections. In this wild country, expect to see moose, otter, beaver, bear, mink, loon, osprey, and lots of other wildlife.

The Playful River Otter

Paddling Maine's remote lakes, especially in early morning or at dusk, sooner or later you will see a river otter—or perhaps a family of these sleek mammals. We have seen dozens throughout Maine. Their playful antics and masterful swimming make them one of our favorite species to observe.

The river otter, *Lutra canadensis,* once inhabited virtually every U.S. watercourse, from sun-warmed southwestern rivers to icy far-northern lakes and streams. Today, because of 200 years of trapping, water pollution, and encroaching development, the otter has retreated to the far corners of its former range. Because they eat at the top of the food chain, otters also suffer from pollution and toxic chemicals in the environment, such as heavy metals, DDT derivatives, dioxin, and PCBs.

The river otter, with its long, thin body and relatively thick, sharply tapered tail, can reach four feet in length and weigh up to 25 pounds. Long prized by trappers, its dense dark-brown fur above gives way to lighter colors on the belly and throat.

Otters have adapted well to the aquatic environment. Their noses and ears close when underwater, and their webbed toes aid in swimming. Though otters swim fast enough to catch trout in open water, they usually opt for slower-moving suckers, minnows, crayfish, tadpoles, and salamanders. When hunting, otters usually come up for air every 30 seconds or so, though they can remain underwater for up to two minutes. When they surface, their heads generally pop way up in the air with a loud exhale as they look around—quite different from beavers and muskrats, which barely rise above the water's surface.

Though adapted for water, otters do pretty well on land as well, their undulating gate typical of weasel family members. Clocked at up to 18 miles per hour on land, they can travel as many as 100 miles overland in search of new territory. Otters generally place their dens—natural cavities under tree roots or abandoned beaver lodges—at the water's edge, with an underwater entrance.

Otters consume smaller fish and crayfish in the water, while they take larger prey to shore or to a protruding rock. In shallow water, look for an otter's tail sticking out of the water as it roots around in the mud for food. Ingenious hunters, otters sometimes herd fish into shallows, making prey capture easy. They may even puncture a beaver dam, then wade in and feast on fish flopping in the receding water. Because otters hunt so successfully, they have plenty of time to play—a famous otter trait.

The young of many mammal species play. Animal behaviorists believe such play provides practice for future hunting, territorial interactions, and courtship. But otters do not stop playing when they reach adulthood. They roll in the water, chasing one another, or climb repeatedly up on a snow- or mud bank and slide down into the water. Animal behaviorists have not yet found reasons for otters' play, other than simply to have fun.

Otters mate in the late winter or early spring, but birth does not follow until almost a year later. As with many members of the weasel family, embryo implantation is delayed, and development stops until the following fall or winter, followed by birth to two to four cubs in a well-protected den anytime between November and April (usually February to April). The cubs emerge fully furred, but with eyes closed and no teeth. They will not venture outside the den for about three months, remaining completely dependent on their mother for at least six months. Though the mother provides all care for the young cubs, the father may rejoin the family and help with care and teaching after they reach about six months. Otters become sexually mature after two years.

Though otters are curious animals and relatively bold, keep your distance when observing them. Interference from humans may cause them to move away and search for more remote streams or ponds.

Gilman Pond
Lexington Twp and New Portland

MAPS: Maine Atlas, Map 30
   USGS Quadrangle, New Portland
AREA AND MAXIMUM DEPTH: 242 acres, 10 feet; stream length,
   2.5 miles
HABITAT TYPE: shallow pond with inlet and outlet streams
FISH: brown trout, chain pickerel
EXPECT TO SEE: loon, osprey, kingfisher
TAKE NOTE: private access; small fee charged

GETTING THERE

Access is at the Gilman Pond Campground, which is no longer in operation. The pleasant fellow who ran the adjacent farm and the campground still allows launching for a small fee. It is unknown how much longer this will continue.

From Waterville, go north on Route 139 to Norridgewock, then go northwest on Routes 8 and 201A to North Anson. Turn left (west) onto Route 16, and follow to North New Portland. After taking a sharp left in the village, go 1.1 miles (1.1 miles), and turn right onto Gilman Pond Road. Go 1.9 miles (3.0 miles), and look for several white trailers on the right.

Gilman Pond, a delightful little out-of-the way pond in the Rangeley Lakes region, nestles into a valley surrounded by forested hills. This picturesque pond offers the opportunity for several hours of quiet paddling, especially if you paddle down to Route 16, a round-trip distance of about five miles. Paddle here when the wind blows on nearby Richardson and Flagstaff lakes.

Although we found the outlet stream the most interesting, we also enjoyed paddling the pond's north end, choked with sedges, equisetum, buttonbush, and other aquatic vegetation. Note Sandy Stream flowing down through scattered silver maples along the northern

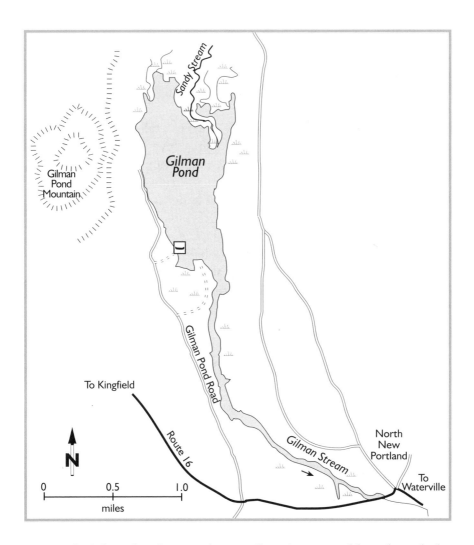

peninsula. Though it has good water flow, impenetrable sedges choke the waterway, indicating that boats do not ply these waters in great numbers. The cove on the peninsula's northeast side is quieter and marshier than the one on the other side. The shoreline sports a wide variety of tree species, including cedar, birch, spruce, hemlock, and balsam fir on the north end.

As you travel down the eastern shore (a small amount of development clusters along the western shore) to the outlet, note the large number of tall red oaks. White and yellow birch, aspen, and maple show up in good numbers as well. When we paddled here, loons called from the pond, kingfishers darted down the shore in front of us, and an osprey fished near the outlet. The presence of these three fish-eating birds together indicates a healthy fish population. Local fishermen told us fishing is pretty good for chain pickerel and an occasional lunker brown trout.

Paddling down the outlet, note the very tall tamaracks on the right-hand shore. An extensive marshy area covers the left-hand side. After passing it, you can turn left and paddle into it. In mid-July when we visited, the still-high water covered the roots of many shoreline trees, especially red maples. Their leaves had started to wilt, obviously not because of lack of water. Instead, standing water impeded gas exchange between the air and their roots.

Many beautiful wild swamp roses bloomed up and down the outlet, and extensive dogwood and viburnum blooms abounded. Islands of buttonbush, with its terminal Osage orange–like green balls that later turn into large, round, puffy white flowers, occurred in large clumps out in the water. Rushes filled the side channels. Sweetgale, with aromatic leaves that give off a wonderful scent when crushed, dot the shoreline in marshy areas. With the diversity of plants and the opportunity to see many flowers in bloom, this is a great spot for plant lovers.

～ 59 ～

Pierce Pond and Upper Pierce Pond
Pierce Pond Twp

MAPS: Maine Atlas, Map 30
  USGS Quadrangles, East Carry Pond and Pierce Pond

AREA AND MAXIMUM DEPTH: 1,650 acres; Pierce Pond, 185 feet;
  Upper Pierce Pond, 66 feet

HABITAT TYPE: deep, clear ponds

FISH: salmon, brook trout

CAMPS: Harrison's Pierce Pond Camps, 207-672-3625; Cobb's
  Pierce Pond Camps, 207-628-2819

EXPECT TO SEE: loon

TAKE NOTE: conservation easements protect the shoreline from
  further development; no personal watercraft; camping at
  established sites only; no fires

GETTING THERE

Otter Pond Cove: Requires high-clearance vehicle. If you get stuck, there is a caretaker at Otter Pond Cove. From Bingham, go south on Route 16. After crossing the Kennebec River, turn immediately right onto Ridge Road. Go 4.2 miles (4.2 miles), and turn right onto progressively deteriorating Carry Pond Road, following signs to Harrison's Pierce Pond Camps. Go 11.3 miles (15.5 miles), and turn right up the hill; watch out for rocks. Go 3.9 miles (19.4 miles) to Harrison's Pierce Pond Sporting Camps (on left); just after the bridge, the Appalachian Trail crosses the road. Go up the hill for 1.2 miles (20.6 miles), turn left onto the access road, fork left after 1.3 miles (21.9 miles), and go 0.4 mile (22.3 miles) to the access.

Harrison's Access: If you are staying at the camp, you can launch your boat there.

Lindsay Cove: Fee to launch here. Follow the directions as above, but instead of turning right after 15.5 miles, turn left. Go 6.3 miles (21.8 miles) on the main road, and turn right. Go 0.3 mile (22.1 miles), and stay left, following signs for Cobbs. Go 0.7 mile (22.8 miles), and turn right. Go 0.4 mile (23.2 miles), and turn right off the main road; the gate is open from 6:30 A.M. to 9:30 P.M.

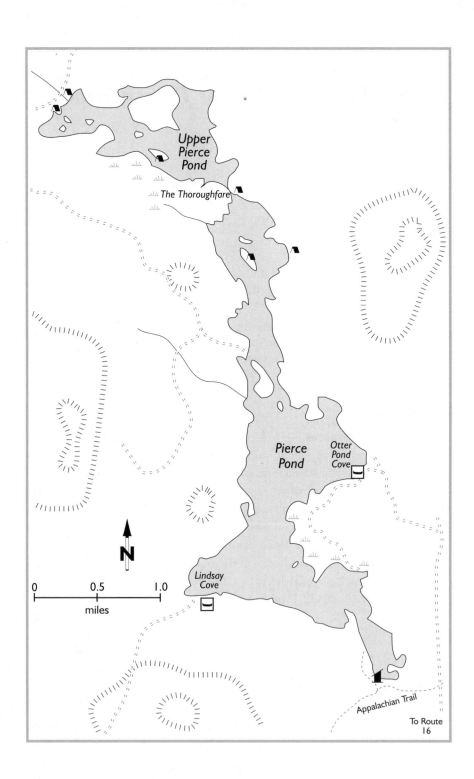

Upper
Pierce
Pond

The Thoroughfare

Pierce
Pond

Otter
Pond
Cove

N

Lindsay
Cove

0   0.5   1.0

miles

Appalachian Trail

To Route
16

Pierce Pond's deep, cold, well-oxygenated substratum makes this an excellent coldwater fishery and brings a fair number of fishermen to its shores. Because of the difficult access and more than 2.5 square miles of surface area, you can paddle in relative solitude here.

Beautiful forested hillsides surround both ponds, with conifers dominating the eastern shore and mixed conifers and deciduous trees sharing the western shore. Heavily forested islands lend a scenic quality, especially to the northern section. The islands break up the view of open water, making the ponds seem deceptively small. Lots of beautiful boulders poke up everywhere, especially guarding channels going up the right side of the middle and northern sections of Pierce Pond and in Upper Pierce Pond. The huge number of these rocks, some barely submerged, belie the depths under open water.

There seems to be a camping spot on the Thoroughfare that connects the two ponds, as well as sites in the upper bay of Pierce Pond, one on the eastern shore and one on the western side of the two islands out in the middle. If you camp here, you will have to share the shore with a monster beaver lodge and its inhabitants. Upper Pierce Pond has a couple of camping spots, one on the south end of an island to the left. When we paddled here, passing between the ponds required a portage over some slippery boards, dodging the beaver cuttings. The depth here is deceptive because of the very clear water.

Lots of loons plied the clear waters of the ponds as we paddled this wild place nearly alone on a beautiful late-July weekend. Purple damselflies, with their backswept wings, landed on our paddles and arms. Northern white cedar, white birch, white pine, and red pine covered the islands and hillsides. One could easily spend several days exploring this wonderful spot.

Spencer Lake and Fish Pond
Hobbstown Twp and T3 R5 BKP WKR

> **MAPS:** Maine Atlas, Map 39
> USGS Quadrangles, King and Bartlett Lake and Spencer Lake
> **AREA AND MAXIMUM DEPTH:** 1,819 acres, 135 feet
> **HABITAT TYPE:** deep, clear lake
> **FISH:** lake trout, brook trout, salmon, yellow perch
> **EXPECT TO SEE:** loon, osprey, raven, Canada goose, spectacular views
> **TAKE NOTE:** no personal watercraft; fire permits, Maine Forest Service, 207-827-1800

GETTING THERE

From Bingham, go north on Route 201. After passing The Forks, continue for 13.9 miles (13.9 miles), and turn left onto Hardscrabble Road, just after the Parlin Pond access. Go 4.6 miles (18.5 miles), and take the left fork. Go 0.7 mile (19.2 miles), and take the right fork. Go 8.1 miles (27.3 miles), turn left, and go through a gate onto the access road. Go slowly down a potholed road lined with balsam fir and red and striped maples, arriving at the Fish Pond access.

Breathtaking views of surrounding mountains—Number 5, Three Slide, Hardwood, and Hardscrabble—await you as you drive to these bodies of water. At the Fish Pond access, several families of Canada geese grazing on flat grasslands across the pond greeted us. As we watched the low afternoon sun turn the billowing clouds hovering over Spencer Mountain to shades of gold and red, we knew we had come to a wild place. Other than the few people who come to fish for trout and salmon, you should paddle here pretty much alone.

Nestled between two parallel ridges and ringed with peaks rising 1,300 feet above the water level, Spencer Lake fills a deep gorge, giving

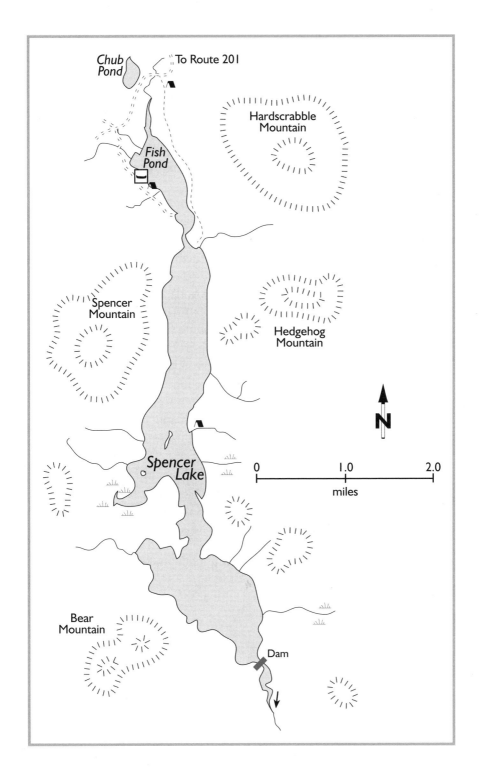

it depth not found in other lakes in this area. Depth keeps the lower layers—down to 135 feet—quite cold, much to the liking of the lake trout, brook trout, and salmon populations.

When we paddled here, ravens croaked out their hoarse cries, and loons filled the air with haunting songs, adding to the already incredible feeling of wilderness. Ospreys, great blue herons, and kingfishers fished the surface waters. Spotted sandpipers bobbed their tails along the shore, and warblers hunted for insects in the trees hanging out over the water.

As we paddled through the access stream between Fish Pond and Spencer Lake, we encountered submerged stumps, a sand beach, and shallow water, which could be a problem at low water levels. The expected conifers—white and red pine, spruce, balsam fir, and northern white cedar—dominate the shoreline, intermingling with white birch, red maple, and alder. Conifers and hardwoods share the western hillsides about equally, but deciduous trees dominate the eastern hillsides. Past logging practices may have altered the species composition here in this area of the northern spruce, pine, and fir forest.

As you paddle south into Spencer Lake, a lodge with several cabins appears on the left, and farther down the lake, after passing a series of islands and a large peninsula on the right, another cluster of cabins appears on the left. A fair amount of marshland surrounds the large peninsula, while a rocky shoreline contains the rest of the lake. Several campsites occur on Fish Pond and Spencer Lake. Continued access and shoreline use lie in the hands of cable-TV billionaire John Malone, who purchased the remaining shoreline of Spencer Lake in July 2000 from Plum Creek for $1,330 per acre. Earlier he had purchased a 7,400-acre parcel surrounding the lake from International Paper for $470 per acre. The good news is that he is a national director of The Nature Conservancy and has expressed strong interest in land conservation.

~61~

Attean Pond, Holeb Pond, and Moose River Bow Trip
Attean Twp, Bradstreet Twp, Holeb Twp, and T5 R7 BKP WKR

MAPS: Maine Atlas, Map 39
  USGS Quadrangles, Attean Pond, Catheart Mountain, and Holeb

AREA AND MAXIMUM DEPTH: Attean Pond, 2,745 acres, 55 feet; Holeb Pond, 1,055 acres, 52 feet

LENGTH: 34-mile loop trip

HABITAT TYPE: large shallow lakes; Attean Pond dotted with islands; marshy stream

FISH: salmon, brook trout

EXPECT TO SEE: loon, bald eagle, osprey, moose, beaver

TAKE NOTE: wind from the west can make paddling these large ponds treacherous; no personal watercraft on Attean Pond; all sites require fire permits, Maine Forest Service, 207-827-1800

GETTING THERE

From Jackman at the railroad crossing on Route 201, go south 0.6 mile, turn right onto Attean Road (signpost; Routes 6 and 15 go left here), and follow to the end at the Attean Pond access.

We cover Attean and Holeb ponds together because they form part of the popular Moose River Bow trip. We paddled this scenic 34-mile loop in August over a three-day weekend. To maximize wildlife viewing and allow thorough exploration of the two ponds and some side channels on the river, four days would be better. To avoid crowded campsites on the river, try to start your trip on a Thursday or earlier in the week.

The Maine Public Land Reserve system protects Attean and Holeb ponds and the neighboring part of the Moose River. Bogs, fens, and marshes cover the landscape, supporting a large moose population.

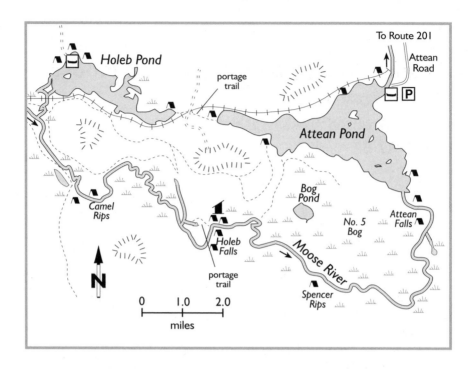

We saw two moose on our trip, and friends who made the same trip a year earlier saw five. In the evening, beaver swam before us, eventually slapping the water with their tails before diving out of sight as we ventured too near.

The Moose River Bow loop totally encloses Number 5 Bog, a National Natural Landmark. Inaccessible except by foot down an old logging road taking off north from Spencer Rips, this unique, pristine fen of more than 1,500 acres may be the most remote of the Northeast's large peatlands. Formed 10,000 years ago as glaciers retreated and now protected from logging and other development, Number 5 Bog sports large stands of jack pine, tamarack, and white cedar. Its sphagnum-covered open areas provide habitat for many plant species, including several rare orchids. The area, wetter than most other peatlands in Maine, such as the Great Heath just northeast of Cherryfield, even boasts a substantial 90-acre pond, Bog Pond.

Other natural wonders abound in this area, starting with Attean Pond. Extraordinarily scenic, the pond's nearly 60 islands scatter over four square miles, with forested mountains all around. As you approach Jackman on Route 201, stop at the turnout overlooking the pond for a bird's-eye view of this often-photographed wonder.

A mature bald eagle surveys its domain from a large white pine on the shores of Holeb Pond. Nearly driven to extinction by pesticides, this majestic raptor now inhabits many lakes in Maine.

The loop trip starts at the Attean Pond access. After paddling to the right (west) for 4.0 miles across Attean Pond, portage for 1.2 miles into Holeb Pond on a well-marked trail with boardwalks across swampy areas. When you get to the wide logging road after 1.0 mile, turn right, cross the railroad track, watch for a small sign, and take an immediate left for the last little segment down to Holeb Pond. Paddle across Holeb Pond to its outlet, Holeb Stream, which joins the Moose River, which, in turn, flows back into Attean Pond.

Holeb Pond, smaller than Attean and with many fewer islands, also sits among beautiful surroundings, with mountains off in the distance. Large granite boulders at the put-in enhance the scenic quality. Holeb Pond generally sees less traffic because of more difficult access, much to the liking of the mature bald eagle we watched as it perched in a large white pine. If you have time, explore the coves and islands on the right, midway down the pond.

Note the tall steeplelike spires of the many large balsam firs along the Moose River. Some very large tamaracks mix in among the firs, while alders cover the shoreline for miles and miles. Occasional marshy openings intrude on the alders, and these locations, along with entering streams and side channels, provide moose viewing opportunities.

In most places, the Moose River moves along slowly, but because the water drops 73 feet between Holeb and Attean ponds, you must portage around a few falls; some you can run during high water. By August in most years, you must portage Camel Rips and Spencer Rips, along with Holeb Falls and Attean Falls. Mercifully, these relatively short portages—some just a few feet—do not compare with the long portage into Holeb Pond. Campsites occur adjacent to these portages.

Finding the portage at Holeb Falls can present quite a challenge. As shown on the map, paddle to the left into the side channel and then take an immediate right (look for moose to the left). Go over two short drops on this, the Moose River's left channel. Then, after about a half-mile, take a sharp left down an easy-to-miss, very narrow side channel, and go about 150 feet to the take-out.

Holeb Falls, just past the trip's midpoint, is back out on the main river. To see it, after the portage, cross the river to the campsite at the base of the riffle. From there a trail takes you up to the falls.

Between Holeb and Attean falls, the river can seem a little monotonous. Eventually, you will hope never to see alders again, and you will

Calm water at dawn reflects surrounding hills from the boat access at the end of the portage into Holeb Pond.

A great horned owl perches on a broken-off yellow birch that hangs out over the Moose River.

wholeheartedly root for the beaver in its attempt to gorge on alder bark. To break the monotony, take the time to explore the streams, side channels, and marshy areas along the banks. The marshiest area on the loop—and the best area to look for moose— lies between the falls. Just as the river turns north toward Attean Pond, Catheart and other tall mountains appear off to the east and should help take your mind off the endless alders.

Two short, marked portages confront you at Attean Falls, the first on the left, the second on the right. You paddle a few hundred feet between them.

Upon returning to Attean Pond, it will look as though the pond has shrunk. Most of the islands cluster between the Moose River inlet and the take-out point, blocking the rest of the lake from view. These islands effectively damp wind-driven swells that might be a problem on more open water. Navigating through them can be somewhat of a challenge, especially if you don't use your compass. A hint: three narrow valleys, with no hills, lead down to the water. You have just left one, the Moose River. The one to the left leads to Holeb Pond. Head for the one to the right to get to the access by paddling north-northwest for about two miles and then northeast.

Greater Moosehead Lake & 100-Mile Wilderness

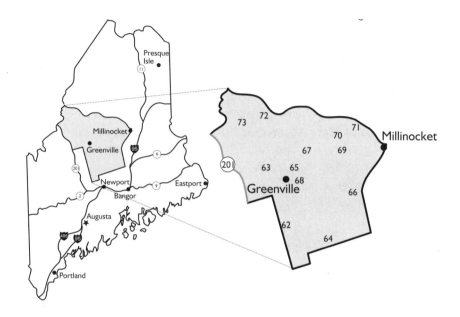

The region spans hundreds of miles of forests, lakes, rivers, and mountains in central and northwestern Maine. Moosehead Lake, at 117 square miles, is the largest lake contained within a single state east of the Mississippi. Just to the east lies the 100-Mile Wilderness, running from Monson to Baxter State Park and Mount Katahdin. Within this region, the AMC's Katahdin Iron Works property contains Long Pond (Trip 68), with its spectacular views of surrounding mountains, as well as many other ponds, some of which boast increasingly rare populations of native brook trout. In 2004, the AMC began to operate the Little Lyford Pond Camps, a traditional Maine sporting camp dating back to 1874, which serves as an excellent base to explore the area. For more information, see "The Maine Woods," on page 246. Other featured trips include Bald Mountain Pond (Trip 62), nestled along the Appalachian Trail, where you should see moose; Debsconeag Lakes (Trip 70), protected in a 41,000 acre wilderness, where you paddle with Mount Katahdin as a backdrop; and spectacular Lobster Lake (Trip 72), with its unique geology and stands of old growth red pine.

～62～

Bald Mountain Pond
Bald Mountain Twp

MAPS: Maine Atlas, Map 31
   USGS Quadrangle, Bald Mountain Pond
AREA AND MAXIMUM DEPTH: 1,152 acres, 62 feet
HABITAT TYPE: deep, clear pond; forested hillsides
FISH: brook and blueback trout
FRIENDS OF BALD MOUNTAIN POND: pond preservation effort,
   www.mainetoys.com/Links/BMP_home/BMP_home.html
EXPECT TO SEE: loon, moose
TAKE NOTE: no personal watercraft; fire permits, Maine Forest
   Service, 207-827-1800

GETTING THERE

From Bingham, at the junction of Routes 16 and 201, go east on Route 16 for 5.4 miles (5.4 miles), and turn left onto Townline Road. Go 2.8 miles (8.2 miles), and turn right onto Deadwater Road. Go 0.1 mile (8.3 miles), and take the left fork. Go 2.1 miles (10.4 miles), and take the right fork. Go 1.9 miles (12.3 miles), and turn diagonally right onto Bald Mountain Pond Road. Go 5.7 miles (18.0 miles), circling around Austin Pond, and take the right fork. Go 2.1 miles (20.1 miles) straight to the access.

The Appalachian Trail skirts Bald Mountain Pond's northern shore, part of the Maine Public Reserve Land system. A wild place in a beautiful setting, aptly named Bald Mountain dominates the western skyline. Unfortunately, the Plum Creek timber company owns most of the surrounding land and has built several new roads and clear-cut some of the area. The Friends of Bald Mountain Pond has mounted a preservation effort. The pond also draws large crowds on summer weekends—although fewer people camp here than at nearby Austin Pond. A visit here would be more satisfying during the week or after Labor Day.

   When we paddled out on the last Sunday in July at 6:30 A.M., the resident loons and we made the only ripples on the placid surface for

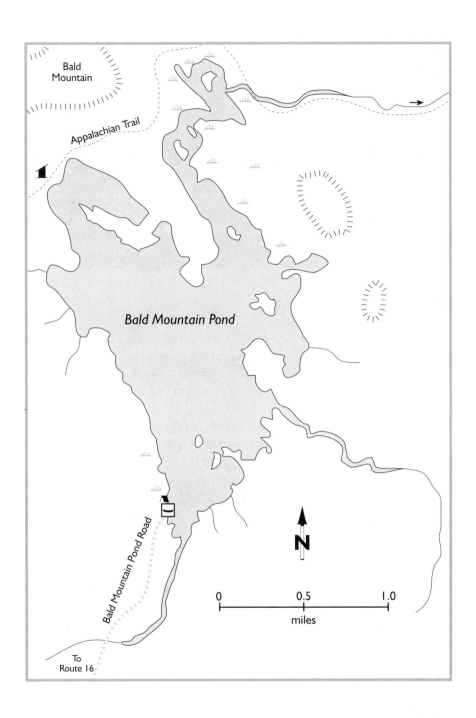

Bald
Mountain

Appalachian Trail

1

Bald Mountain Pond

Bald Mountain Pond Road

To
Route 16

N

0   0.5   1.0
miles

A cow moose seeks relief from a buzzing horde of biting flies at the north end of Bald Mountain Pond.

the first hour and a half after sunrise, while the weekend partiers slept in. The only noise, other than an occasional loon call, came from the large population of white-throated sparrows, with their "Old Sam Peabody, Peabody, Peabody" call. We saw lots of wildlife, including a cow moose in the northeast cove, submerged to her nostrils, trying to escape a huge cloud of biting flies. Several of these tenacious flies broke off from the pack and annoyed us for about a half hour after our encounter with the moose.

Heavily forested islands enhance the picturesque nature of Bald Mountain Pond. Hundreds of granite boulders dimple the surface in places; unfortunately for boat hulls, many of these rocks hide out barely submerged. Go cautiously when paddling near shore and when exploring the many inlets. The boulder-strewn northern inlet comprises one of the most scenic areas, making paddling up there well worthwhile.

White and red pine, cedar, balsam fir, and spruce grow right down to the water, and a fair number of yellow birch, maples, and white birch appear in and among the conifers. Fragrant waterlilies abound in the coves and shallower parts. Bird species include ring-billed gull, red-breasted merganser, loon, black duck, belted kingfisher, and double-crested cormorant.

Because of the many coves and inlets dotting the shoreline, it takes several hours to explore fully this wonderful place. Paddle out early to maximize wildlife viewing, and come during the week to avoid the weekend camping parties.

63

Indian Pond

Big Moose Twp, Indian Stream Twp, and Sapling Twp

MAPS: Maine Atlas, Map 40
  USGS Quadrangles, Indian Pond North and Indian Pond South

AREA AND MAXIMUM DEPTH: 3,746 acres, 118 feet

HABITAT TYPE: large, deep pond

FISH: lake trout, brook trout, salmon, smallmouth bass

INDIAN POND CAMPGROUND: 800-371-7774

EXPECT TO SEE: loon, bald eagle, osprey, moose, beaver

TAKE NOTE: wind from the south can cause treacherous conditions; fire permits, Maine Forest Service, 207-827-1800

GETTING THERE

There are three access points. The easiest, by far, is the southern access.

Southern Access: From Bingham, go north on Route 201, and turn right onto Lake Moxie Road at The Forks. Go 5.3 miles (5.3 miles), and turn left onto Indian Pond Road. Go 7.9 miles (13.2 miles) to Indian Pond Campground and the access.

Northeast Access: The access road had a ditch across it when we visited; with road repairs, this would be a relatively easy access. Check the *Maine Atlas* for directions.

West Outlet: High clearance vehicle necessary. From Rockwood, go south on Route 6. Just after leaving town and 0.2 mile before the bridge over West Outlet, turn right onto Milligan Farm Road. Go 4.8 miles (4.8 miles), turn left, and go 2.8 miles (7.6 miles) to the access.

Indian Pond, large and very scenic, truly is the country of the pointed firs. Little development intrudes on the shoreline, and the few boats plying the water have 35 miles of shoreline and nearly six square miles of surface to share. This wildlife paradise sports healthy populations of deer, moose, bear, coyote, fox, beaver, osprey, eagle, loon, and fish. One must be wary of winds, but it still represents a great opportunity for a two-to-four-day family trip.

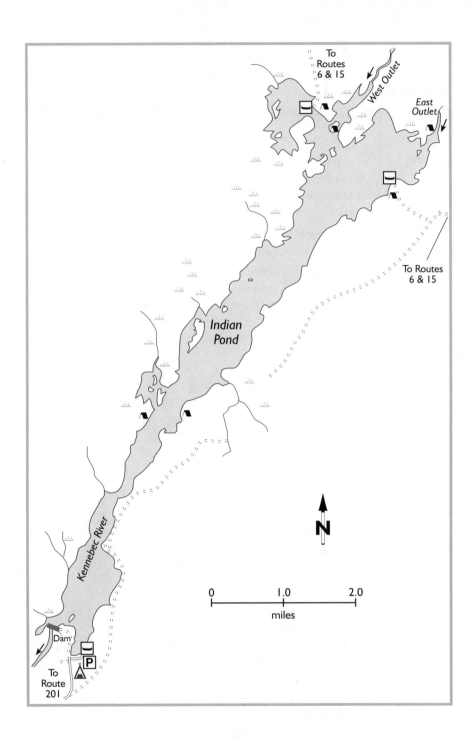

In preparation for your trip here, you can camp overnight at the Indian Pond Campground (reservations advised). A tremendous amount of congestion occurs on the roads and at the pond's southern end, most of it from rafters and kayakers testing their ability to float after getting dumped on the Class IV and V rapids of the Kennebec River Gorge below Indian Pond. When we paddled here, as we gazed out from the access over the picturesque southern end of Indian Pond, we could see only one other boat.

Make sure that you paddle the more scenic north end. It sees far fewer people and motorboats. Most of the marshy areas and islands occur from the midpoint up to the north end, the heart of moose country; we saw five moose along the road while driving from Greenville to Rockwood late one evening. The shallow, marshy northern end provides the best chance for seeing moose. Be sure to explore the two large, marshy coves about halfway up the left side. Both contain plenty of moose habitat.

White and red pines, balsam fir, tamarack, cedar, and spruce blanket the shores and islands on the lake's north end. Occasional red maple and white birch occur here and there, and a well-developed understory lines the shore. Lots of drowned stumps populate the northwest arm, a legacy of the fifty-year-old Harris Dam at the south end.

We saw many species of birds here in addition to osprey and loon, including song sparrow, spotted sandpiper, hermit thrush, ring-billed gull, and cedar waxwing.

A telephoto lens gives a close-up view of the northern diver, the common loon.

64

Branns Mill Pond
Dover-Foxcroft

MAPS: Maine Atlas, Map 32
   USGS Quadrangle, Garland
AREA AND MAXIMUM DEPTH: 271 acres, 15 feet
HABITAT TYPE: shallow, marshy pond and stream
FISH: brook trout, smallmouth and largemouth bass, white perch,
   chain pickerel
EXPECT TO SEE: loon, high aquatic plant diversity
TAKE NOTE: some development

GETTING THERE

From I-95, Exit 39, go north on Routes 7 and 11. Continue north on Route 7 when Route 11 splits off. From Dexter where Route 23 splits off, go north 7.0 miles (7.0 miles) on Route 7, and turn right (east) onto Merrills Mills Road. Go 1.4 miles (8.4 miles), turn right onto Notch Road, and go 0.8 mile (9.2 miles) to the access on the left.

From Bangor, go north on Route 15 to Dover-Foxcroft, then turn left (south) onto Route 7. Go 5.6 miles, turn left onto Merrills Mills Road, and continue as above.

Branns Mill Pond, a real gem, brims with wildlife and provides a wonderful place to explore, especially in the early morning or late afternoon. On a windy day when other lakes in the area bristle with whitecaps, this pond remains much quieter and more suitable for paddling.

From the access, paddle southeast through the pond's narrow section into the inlet brook. This lazy channel winds for about a mile through biologically rich and highly diverse marsh habitat. Floating aquatic plants, especially yellow pondlily, crowd the channel by early summer. In places, dense stands of cattail occur, but elsewhere, sedges, rushes, alder, sphagnum, and heaths dominate the marsh. Part of the creek lies within the Penobscot-Piscataquis Wildlife Management Area.

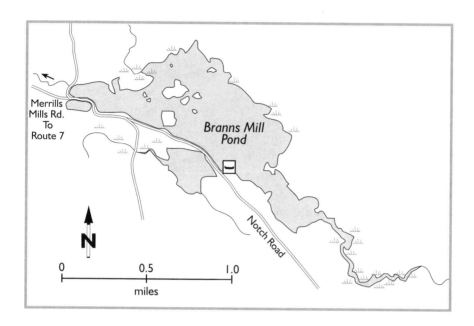

As we paddled quietly along here, we suddenly heard a distinct munching sound. Muskrat? Beaver? Then, 15 feet away the bushes rustled, and out swam an otter. From the sound, one can only conclude they enjoy eating as much as they seem to enjoy everything else. As dusk approached, we also saw a muskrat swimming along the creek and several beaver that loudly announced our passage with slapping tails.

As you paddle up the creek, the channel narrows gradually and the current picks up. After poling over the remains of an old beaver dam, the sound of running water meant we neared the end of our upstream explorations. At the end of the channel we came to a large stone wall and the ruins of a structure—probably Branns Mill, but we have not been able to learn anything of the history.

Notice that trees growing on the banks get progressively shorter closer to the stream, evidence of a narrowing channel. Aquatic plants and sphagnum gradually expand out over the water's surface. Then shrubs such as leatherleaf and alder take hold. As a root mat builds up, tamarack and cedar become established. You can see this succession clearly as you look from the water's edge to the forest on higher ground.

An interesting geology underlies this area. Unlike the granite covering most of central and northern Maine, sedimentary rock lies here. In places, the layered rock tilted up before the stream channel eroded it, so you'll pass jagged rocks extending out of the water like tombstones. Use caution paddling here; unlike rounded granite boulders, this jagged shale could puncture your boat.

While we would choose the inlet channel first for exploration, we enjoyed the rest of the pond, as well. The narrow section between the access and the inlet creek, as well as the far western tip by the dam, suffer from development, but most of the pond remains fairly natural. Marshy areas, rich with wildlife, extend along the northern shore. We saw at least one loon pair and suspect they nest on one of the many islands, relatively

Tamarack

safe from predators. Open areas on a few of these islands would make nice picnic spots, but we do not suggest overnight camping.

65

Prong Pond
Beaver Cove and Greenville

> **MAPS:** Maine Atlas, Map 41
>   USGS Quadrangle, Lily Bay
> **AREA AND MAXIMUM DEPTH:** 427 acres, 27 feet
> **HABITAT TYPE:** shallow pond with many marshy areas
> **FISH:** brook trout, smallmouth bass, white perch, yellow perch
> **CAMPING:** Lily Bay State Park, www.state.me.us/doc/parks/
>   reservations or 207-695-2700; reservations strongly
>   recommended
> **EXPECT TO SEE:** loon, bog vegetation
> **TAKE NOTE:** fire permits, Maine Forest Service, 207-827-1800

GETTING THERE

From Greenville, where Routes 6 and 15 turn left, go north on Main Street/Lily Bay Road for 6.8 miles (6.8 miles), following signs for Lily Bay State Park, and turn right onto Prong Pond Road. Almost immediately, turn right again, and go 0.2 mile to the access (7.0 miles).

To reach Lily Bay State Park, turn right on Lily Bay Road after leaving Prong Pond, and go 1.7 miles north to the state park entrance.

Prong Pond, a little-noticed pond on the southeast side of giant Moosehead Lake, can provide a pleasant day of paddling, especially when wind has whipped Moosehead and other large lakes in the region to a froth. Though it looks small, the pond offers 9 miles of perimeter to explore, extending in several long, narrow arms, or prongs. Cedar, white pine, spruce, paper birch, and hemlock line the pond's rocky shoreline. Along some sections, stately red pine groves rise from the shore; a nice campsite lies under some of these pines on a point of land along the pond's eastern shore.

Narrow arms extending east and west provide a great opportunity to observe northern bog flora, including pitcher plants—with their nodding flowers extending above the grasses—sedges, sweetgale,

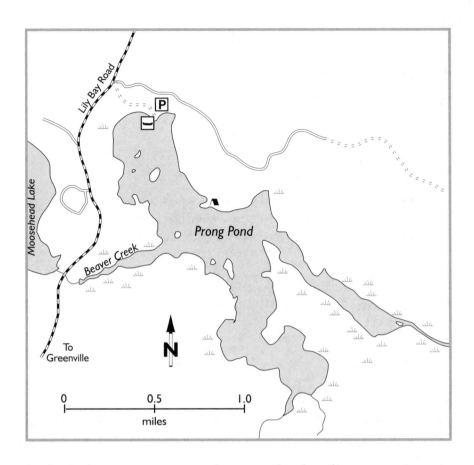

leatherleaf, swamp rose, cranberry, and other low vegetation. At ground level, amid the sphagnum, look for the diminutive red leaves of sundew. Both pitcher plants and sundews obtain some of their nourishment from insects (see page 88).

Though by no means as common as pitcher plants and sundews, keep an eye out for two of Maine's most beautiful orchids: rose pogonia and calopogon, or grass pink. We saw several good-size patches of rose pogonia (*Pogonia ophioglossoides*), which has one or two flowers on the stem and a small lanceolate leaf. We saw only two calopogon orchids (*Calopogon pulchellus*), which has three or more flowers and long, grasslike leaves. We watched a fascinating and beautiful crab spider on the calopogon flower, waiting for an insect to come along. The spider, all white except for a pink band on either side of its globelike body and well camouflaged against the flower backdrop, sat motionless with four long legs outstretched and fangs no doubt ready to impart a fatal dose

Watch out for rocks in Beaver Creek at the western tip of Prong Pond.

of venom to a visiting pollinator. This spider has the ability to adapt its coloration to that of different plants.

The long, shallow east arm has an extremely mucky bottom. Even if your paddle does not sink into the muck, agitation will stir up the sediment and release bubbles of swamp gas (mostly methane). In some places the water seemed to boil behind us as we paddled along. At the prong's far eastern tip, you will reach a beaver dam and lodge.

The boglike arm extending to the west (Beaver Creek) has the same plants as the east arm. We noticed more tamarack, the larger ones farther back from the water marking the encroachment of land into the quiet stream. The many dead trees along here—sun-whitened snags and stumps—provide nesting habitat for tree swallows. We watched a sharp-shinned hawk dart between these snags as it tried to elude some blackbirds.

Along with the possibility of camping on the pond, Lily Bay State Park also offers camping a few miles away. Located on one of the prettiest areas of mammoth Moosehead Lake, dozens of islands protect the bay from wind.

~ 66 ~

Seboeis Lake
Lakeview PLT and T4 R9 NWP

> **MAPS:** Maine Atlas, Map 43
>   USGS Quadrangles, Endless Lake, Ragged Mountain, and
>   Seboeis Lake
> **AREA AND MAXIMUM DEPTH:** 4,201 acres, 69 feet
> **HABITAT TYPE:** large, deep lake
> **FISH:** salmon, brook trout (streams only), smallmouth bass, white
>   perch, chain pickerel
> **EXPECT TO SEE:** loon, bald eagle, osprey, common tern, moose,
>   views of Mt. Katahdin
> **TAKE NOTE:** winds from the north or south can make paddling
>   here treacherous; novice paddlers should avoid this area dur-
>   ing windy conditions; wear PFD; no fire permits needed for
>   designated sites; other sites, no fires allowed

GETTING THERE

From Millinocket, go south on Route 11 for about 13 miles. Watch for a triangular road sign indicating a left turn, and a green sign saying West Seboeis. Turn left, and go 1.1 miles (1.1 miles) to a junction. Go straight for 1.8 miles (2.9 miles) to the northern access.

Go left at the junction to the outlet stream bridge. Cross the bridge, and turn right. Put in here, but do not block access to the cottage or dam.

We paddled Seboeis Lake in July and August, entering from the northern access and from the east arm. The state manages most of the lake as part of public reserve lands.

Seboeis Lake sees relatively heavy traffic from fishermen in small boats. At times, upwards of a dozen boat trailers park at the northern access. Fortunately, this large lake provides plenty of room on its 6.5-square-mile surface. One August morning, we paddled alone until the first boat appeared at 8:30 A.M.

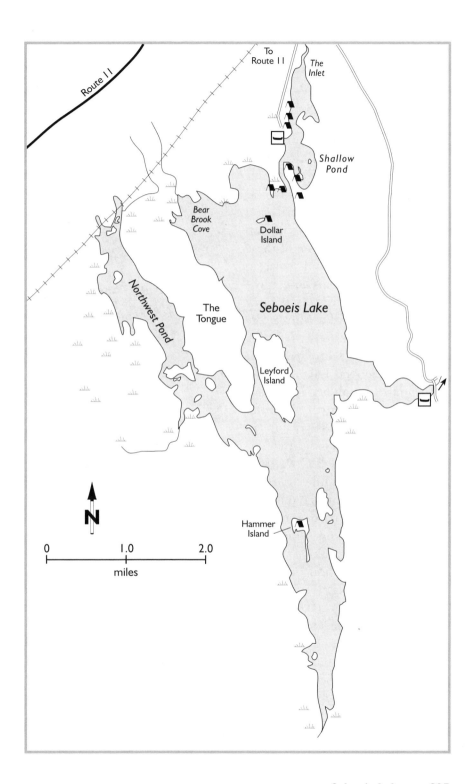

Route 11

To
Route 11

*The
Inlet*

*Shallow
Pond*

*Bear
Brook
Cove*

Dollar
Island

Northwest Pond

The
Tongue

Seboeis Lake

Leyford
Island

N

0   1.0   2.0
miles

Hammer
Island

Several campsites exist, including a few right at the access. Several more appear on the two peninsulas that separate The Inlet from the main lake, three on the left going down the channel and two more on the spit jutting out from the end of the right peninsula. Look for one on Dollar Island and one on the north end of Hammer Island. By evening on a July weekend, each one of these campsites will probably have an occupant. On our trips here, however, we saw at least one open campsite at the access. Sites at the access do not require fire permits.

We use the word *spectacular* to describe Seboeis Lake. You can see Mount Katahdin in Baxter State Park to the north. Beautiful tree-covered islands occur in many places, including the en-

Tall pines line the shores of the large islands in lower Seboeis Lake. The thin soil of these rocky islands supports few large deciduous trees.

trance to Bear Brook Cove, Northwest Pond, down in the southern arm, and up in The Inlet. Large boulders line much of the shore, and if you paddle back into the outlet on the eastern shore halfway down the lake, you will see an extraordinary number of boulders both sticking up out of the water and submerged. A number of fairly large northern white cedars appear along the shore in this cove, along with cattails and other marsh vegetation.

We enjoyed exploring Shallow Pond and The Inlet, particularly the marshy islands of Shallow Pond. Be wary of barely submerged stumps when you paddle in this area. Going down the channel that separates The Inlet from the main lake, you will see large white and red pines lining the eastern shore. Indeed, pines and other conifers dominate the shoreline most everywhere.

Leyford Island, at 237 acres the largest island in the Bureau of Public Lands' eastern holdings, is a special-protection resource, with only camping and hiking allowed. Moose and deer frequent the marshy coves, particularly those along the northwest shore and in Northwest Pond.

One can expect to see bald eagle, osprey, belted kingfisher, dozens of loons, and a colony of common terns, all using different methods to catch fish in these fertile waters. Fishermen come here to angle for landlocked salmon, brook trout, bass, perch, and pickerel.

Morning mists shroud the shore of Seboeis Lake. In late summer the lake's warm surface waters evaporate in the early morning chill, then recondense into a thick fog. As the rising sun burns off the fog, majestic Mount Katahdin appears to the north.

Moose
The Northwoods Giant

Coming across a huge bull moose as you round the bend of a marshy stream is truly awesome—and the high point of many trips into the northwoods. The moose, *Alces alces,* is the world's largest member of the deer family. [Bull moose can stand seven feet tall at the shoulders and range in weight from 900 to 1,400 pounds,] with cow moose typically three-quarters as large. Among North American land mammals, only bison and Alaskan brown bear (a grizzly bear subspecies) commonly exceed the moose in weight; none approaches it in height.

Well adapted to the marsh environment, its long legs allow it to reach tree branches and wade into bogs and snow. During the summer, one can often see moose in ponds and streams, foraging on aquatic plants. Moose sometimes stand neck-deep in water to escape hordes of biting flies, and we have even seen moose totally submerged. By late August or early September, moose generally move into deep woods, where you are less likely to see them. They range over a small territory, usually a few square miles.

Adult moose vary in color from dark brown to almost black, while calves run much lighter in color. Thick, dense fur—sometimes six inches long around the neck and shoulders—helps protect them from biting flies. Moose have a keen sense of hearing and smell, but poor vision. When frightened, they can run at speeds up to 35 miles per hour for short distances. Their incredibly long legs help them run through bogs and muskegs. They swim slowly, but have been known to go as far as twelve miles.

Moose derive most nourishment by browsing on trees and aquatic vegetation but also graze on grasses, mosses, lichens, and low herbaceous plants. Because of their long legs and short necks, they often need to spread their front legs or drop to their knees to feed. They rear up on their hind legs to feed on tree branches and sometimes "ride down" saplings by straddling them to bring upper branches into reach.

The rutting season extends from September through October but may range into November and even early December. After an eight-month gestation period, cows bear one or two calves in May or June. Younger cows generally produce just one offspring. As one might expect, a correlation exists between the incidence of twins and the availability of forage.

We see most moose during the early morning and evening hours, though one can see them at any time. Moose often allow you to approach quite closely, but always use caution when doing so, as cows with calves can be quite aggressive, and bull moose become unpredictable during the rut.

The moose population fluctuated considerably during the last two centuries in the Northeast. During colonial days, they provided an important food source for early settlers. Because they were so easily killed, populations plummeted, and by 1904 only a few northern counties harbored any moose. In 1930, one estimate put Maine's moose population at about 2,000. The state prohibited moose hunting in 1935, and the population gradually recovered. In recent decades, with widespread clear-cutting resulting in the proliferation of low-growing browse, moose populations rebounded dramatically. The Maine moose population today numbers about 30,000, but that may be on the way down as clear-cutting becomes less widespread.

A limited annual moose-hunting season was instituted in 1980, with 700 permits issued. The number of permits issued annually has increased to about 3,000, with hunting now allowed near the coast in an effort to reduce the 600 collisions with cars each year.

Brainworm infestations, fatal to moose, keep populations from building in southern areas because of the presence of large numbers of deer. Though unaffected by these parasites, deer carry them and deposit them in their feces, which passes to land snails. If moose browse on plants hosting snails—a likely occurrence at lower elevations in more southern areas—they contract the disease and die.

We never tire of that awe-inspiring, exhilarating feeling we get paddling into a marshy cove and coming suddenly upon an enormous bull moose or cow with calf. We have seen many dozens of these majestic mammals, and we hope you see as many on your travels.

67

Third and Fourth Roach Ponds
Shawtown Twp

MAPS: Maine Atlas, Map 42
USGS Quadrangles, Wadleigh Mountain and Farrar Mountain
AREA AND MAXIMUM DEPTH: Third Roach Pond, 570 acres,
26 feet; Fourth Roach Pond, 266 acres, 38 feet
HABITAT TYPE: small, shallow ponds
FISH: brook trout
LODGING: Medawisla Sporting Camp, 207-695-2690
EXPECT TO SEE: loon, bald eagle, osprey, moose, otter
TAKE NOTE: no personal watercraft; campsites require a fire
permit, Maine Forest Service, 207-827-1800

GETTING THERE

From Greenville, go north about 18 miles on Main Street/Lily Bay Road to Kokadjo. After crossing the bridge in Kokadjo, go 1.9 miles (1.9 miles), and turn right. Stay on the main road, and only take forks where indicated. Go 4.8 miles (6.7 miles), and take the right fork. Go 3.8 miles (10.5 miles), and go right. Go 2.2 miles (12.7 miles), and go left. Go 5.3 miles (15.8 miles), and go right. Go 0.5 mile (16.3 miles), and turn left at the T. Go 0.9 mile (17.2 miles), and turn left into the access (second of two roads in quick succession). The access road is rough. Carry your gear the 200 yards down to the pond.

The abundant wildlife that awaits you makes the difficulty of getting into Third and Fourth Roach ponds well worth the effort. If you camp at the southeast end of Third Roach, you will likely have the whole place to yourself—along with the moose, deer, otter, eagle, and other wildlife that abounds.

During two days on these ponds in late July, we saw four moose, including a very large bull; a deer with two fawns; two otters; loons, including one pair with two chicks; a large family of common mergansers; and an eagle. In the amount and variety of wildlife we have seen, these ponds rank near the top.

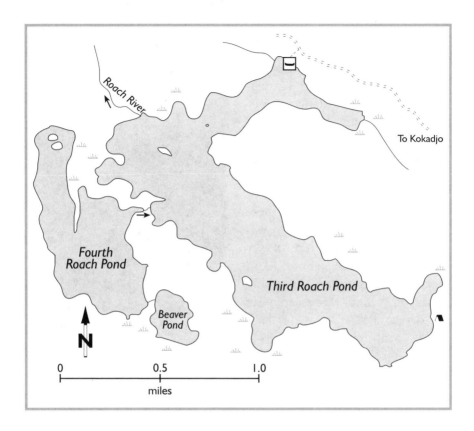

A typical northern Maine woodland of spruce, balsam fir, white pine, cedar, and paper birch extends away from the rocky shoreline. On the long point of land extending south into Fourth Roach Pond, however, you will see a very different red pine forest. You can get out and walk, picnic, or camp under a red pine canopy very easily, unlike most other forest types in this area.

A few marshy areas occur at the ends of the various fingers. At the northeast end of Third Roach, the water becomes very shallow, with yellow pondlilies and other floating vegetation, while grasses and sedges grow along the perimeter. Right at the tip, we watched a bull moose neck-deep in the ooze, grazing on this vegetation while protecting itself from biting flies. It is remarkable how moose can extract themselves after wallowing in the underlying muck.

Third and Fourth Roach ponds connect via a small, rocky stream. In spring, you can probably paddle between these ponds, but by mid-summer you need to wade through the couple hundred feet of this stream, pulling your boat.

From these ponds, you get a clear view of the extensive clear-cutting that has taken place on the surrounding hills. With binoculars we could see evidence of erosion on newer cuts. The so-called beauty strip around the Roach Ponds—that ribbon of uncut woods left along the perimeter of most ponds—seemed almost paper thin. Looking into these woods as we paddled along, it was disconcerting to see bits of sky between the tree trunks. And driving along the paper-company roads to get here, we passed miles of barren, almost desolate, land where sapling hardwoods—mostly birch—had been killed with herbicides to make room for more valuable conifers.

A bull moose makes for the treeline at the northeastern cove on Third Roach Pond.

The wonderful campsite at Third Roach Pond's southeast end backs up against a hill rising 700 feet from the pond and offers a protected sandy beach for a relaxing swim after a day of exploration.

Second Roach Pond, also nice, has difficult public access. For those interested in more refined accommodations, guests staying at Medawisla (Native American name for *loon*) can easily put in on Second Roach Pond. Unlike most sporting camps, Medawisla emphasizes wildlife observation rather than hunting, and its location includes superb moose habitat. The movie *On Golden Pond* used loon recordings made here.

68

Long Pond

Bowdoin College Grant East and West, Elliotsville Twp, and T7 R9 NWP

> **MAPS:** Maine Atlas, Maps 41 and 42
>   USGS Quadrangle, Barren Mountain West
>
> **AREA AND MAXIMUM DEPTH:** 643 acres, 64 feet
>
> **HABITAT TYPE:** narrow pond elongated on an east-west axis
>
> **FISH:** brook trout, lake trout, landlocked salmon
>
> **LODGING:** AMC's Moose Point Cabin (on Long Pond) and Little Lyford Pond Camps (nearby), www.outdoors.org/lodging, 603-466-2727
>
> **EXPECT TO SEE:** loon, white-tailed deer, moose, otter, beaver, forested White Cap, Chairback, Barren, and Baker mountain peaks
>
> **TAKE NOTE:** fire permits, Maine Forest Service, 207-827-1800; camping and entrance fees required (North Maine Woods, www.northmainewoods.org); high-clearance vehicle required; recommend 4WD

GETTING THERE

From Greenville, where Routes 6 and 15 turn left, go north on Main Street/Lily Bay Road for 100 yards, and turn right onto Pleasant Street/East Road. Go straight for 12.4 miles (12.4 miles) to the Hedgehog Checkpoint (pay fees). Continue for 1.8 miles (14.2 miles), and turn right onto Greenville–KI Road. Go 1.1 miles (15.3 miles), and turn right onto Long Pond Road (look for Long Pond Campsite sign on left). Go 2.2 miles (17.5 miles) to the bridge over Trout Brook, and then go another 100 yards, turn left, and go 0.2 mile (17.7 miles) to the campsite. At time of publication, access was being moved but will remain public.

Long Pond, which lies within a 37,000-acre parcel now owned and managed by the Appalachian Mountain Club, provides a wonderful place to paddle, especially when winds from the north or south turn the region's larger lakes into a foaming froth. The lake's east-west axis, islands, and narrow width provide not only wind protection but also a lengthy shoreline to explore. For a map of the greater area, see page 247.

Deciduous trees have repopulated logged areas on the hillsides. Look for large stands of conifers on steeper slopes and on the spectacular distant mountains that you can see from many vantage points around the pond. Portage around the right side of an old dam at the outlet to explore a small flowage of about 75 acres. Look here for deer and moose that often frequent this area. You may also see beaver and otter. Besides the area at the outlet, two more small marshy areas occur on the pond's east side.

The several camps along the shore—including rustic log cabins that date to the 1800s—do not mar the wild feel of Long Pond. The pond is also known for its great spring fishing.

The AMC's Moose Point Cabin, on the southern shore of Long Pond, is a remote, primitive camp just 9 miles away from Little Lyford Pond Camps. For information and reservations, see www.outdoors.org/lodging or call 603-466-2727. (Photo by Gerry Whiting)

Not far from Long Pond, Gulf Hagas is another spectacular water feature in the lush 100-Mile Wilderness. (Photo by Sarah Jane Shangraw)

While in this area, you may wish to visit The Hermitage and Gulf Hagas, both accessible from the Appalachian Trail where it crosses the Greenville–KI Road, about a half mile east of the turnoff onto Long Pond Road. The Hermitage, a National Natural Landmark, consists of a 35-acre stand of Old Growth Pine on a bluff overlooking the Pleasant River West Branch (about a half mile from the road). Gulf Hagas, the "Grand Canyon of Maine," a four-mile chasm with five major and many smaller waterfalls and also a National Natural Landmark, lies along Gulf Hagas Rim Trail. This strenuous loop hike that takes off from the Appalachian Trail about 1.5 miles from the road requires fording the Pleasant River West Branch, which may be decidedly un-Pleasant at times of high water. It will be worth the effort to view the falls and the sheer slate walls rising to 400 feet above the streambed. Viewing the fall foliage in the gorge would make the trip even more spectacular, though watch your footing on the rim trail, particularly when covered by wet leaves or at any time when wet.

For more information about the mountains and hiking opportunities in this area, see *Maine Mountain Guide, Ninth Edition*, from AMC Books (2005).

Little Lyford Pond 1 with Baker Mountain rising in the background. (Photo by Sarah Jane Shangraw)

While in the area, consider a stay at the AMC's Little Lyford Pond Camps, an historic Maine sporting camp offering individual cabins, a bunkhouse, and family-style meals in a central lodge. The camp lies near the two Little Lyford Ponds, and offers additional paddling, fly-fishing, and wildlife-watching opportunities.

69

Jo-Mary Lakes (Middle, Lower, and Turkey Tail)

T4 Indian Purchase, TA R10 WELS, T1 R9 WELS, and T1 R10 WELS

> **MAPS:** Maine Atlas, Map 42
>   USGS Quadrangles, Ragged Mountain, Pemadumcook Lake, and Nahmakanta Stream
> **AREA AND MAXIMUM DEPTH:** Middle Jo-Mary and Turkey Tail, 1,152 acres, 18 feet; Lower Jo-Mary, 1,912 acres, 64 feet
> **HABITAT TYPE:** shallow marshy lakes and streams
> **FISH:** salmon, lake trout (Lower Jo-Mary only), brook trout, white perch, yellow perch, chain pickerel
> **EXPECT TO SEE:** loon, bald eagle, osprey, moose, views of Mt. Katahdin
> **TAKE NOTE:** no personal watercraft on Lower Jo-Mary; fire permits, Maine Forest Service, 207-827-1800

GETTING THERE

From Millinocket, go west on Routes 11 and 157 to the T where Route 157 ends, go left on Route 11 for 7.5 miles (7.5 miles), and turn right onto Turkey Tail Road/Fire Road 3 at South Twin Lake's southern tip. Go 4.2 miles (11.7 miles), and take the right fork. Go 0.4 mile (12.1 miles), and join a larger logging road. Go 0.7 mile (12.8 miles), and go left onto Fire Road 3. Go 0.5 mile (13.3 miles), and stay straight (right fork). Go 1.1 miles (14.4 miles) to road's end at Jo-Mary Stream and Turkey Tail access on the right.

We treasure this rarely explored string of connected lakes—Turkey Tail, Middle Jo-Mary, and Lower Jo-Mary. A few summer homes intrude on Turkey Tail and the south end of Middle Jo-Mary, but you quickly leave those behind as you paddle north toward Lower Jo-Mary.

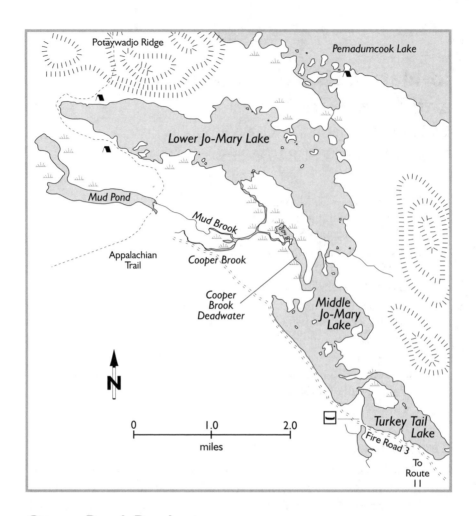

Cooper Brook Deadwater

These lakes include about 25 miles of highly varied shoreline, but we find the winding channel of Cooper Brook between Middle and Lower Jo-Mary lakes the most interesting. This slow-moving creek and the marshy Cooper Brook Deadwater it becomes provide superb, marshy wildlife habitat. We saw two moose here, lots of beaver activity, ring-necked duck, wood duck, great blue heron, American bittern, and songbirds galore.

If you paddle from Middle Jo-Mary to Lower Jo-Mary via this creek, you actually travel upstream initially, then downstream, though on hardly perceptible current. Cooper Brook and Mud Brook enter from the west, and the current divides, with half flowing north into

Lower Jo-Mary and half south into Middle Jo-Mary. By midsummer in a dry year, you might not be able to paddle through easily. We paddled here in mid-May (before blackflies and mosquitoes) with plenty of water.

From the Cooper Brook Deadwater, you might have difficulty finding the brook, especially later in summer with taller vegetation restricting your view. You simply have to explore the area, winding among the grassy islands and floating peat mats that form the shoreline. Once you find it, you should have no trouble following the channel, generally lined with low alder and various heaths (blueberry, leatherleaf, bog rosemary, and sheep laurel). About a half mile from the Deadwater, you will reach a fork in the creek—actually a brook comes in from the left and divides. To get to Lower Jo-Mary, bear to the right (northeast). If you have some time, first explore to the left; from the USGS map it looks as if you could paddle a mile or so upstream on both Cooper Brook and Mud Brook.

As you continue downstream toward Lower Jo-Mary, you pass a rocky area that could be a problem at low water levels. You may have to cross beaver dams, as well. As you paddle out onto Lower Jo-Mary, take a careful look at the several tall white pines so you can find the creek access if you return by the same route.

Lower Jo-Mary Lake

Rounded granite boulders extend above—and lurk just below—the water surface along the rocky south shore. In a cove hidden by an island about a half mile west of Cooper Brook, we watched a moose browse on low cedar branches. We saw a number of loon pairs and watched two bald eagles soaring. Northern white cedar dominates the south shoreline. Thick, generally impenetrable shrubs line the banks.

Traversing the south shore, you get great views of Mount Katahdin across the lake. About a mile from the lake's western tip, the Maine Appalachian Trail Club maintains a wonderful campsite, nestled beneath a stand of tall red pine.

Lower Jo-Mary's north shore—especially the west half with its sandy banks—differs from the south shore. With full southern exposure, the drier woods support more deciduous trees, such as maple, beech, ash, and oak, along with paper birch and aspen. Once the lake widens out farther east, though, and you leave the steep Potaywadjo Ridge, the shoreline returns to the wet, swampy, cedar-dominated vegetation you will see on the south shore and around most of this region's other lakes.

We had hoped to find a portage path into Pemadumcook Lake from the northeastern tip of Lower Jo-Mary, but we could not find one. However, new logging roads could provide a portage path. Also, skilled paddlers could negotiate the fifty yards of whitewater under and below the bridge at the outlet; in mid-May we found this water fairly rough. Returning upstream, though, would be a real chore through almost impenetrable woods, as the connecting stream would be too deep and too fast to wade.

While we did not fish when we visited here, we saw many large trout or salmon in the stream connecting Lower Jo-Mary and Pemadumcook lakes. The several osprey we saw here provided further evidence of the superb fishing.

Several attractive islands dot the northeast corner of Lower Jo-Mary, but none had campsites that we could find. (The western end of Lower Jo-Mary contains the best campsite on these lakes.) Paddling south from these islands into the southeast tip, you will find another access, larger than the Cooper Brook access, into Middle Jo-Mary. You can make a nice, one-day loop trip by paddling into Lower Jo-Mary on Cooper Brook, then returning via this more southern connecting channel.

On Middle Jo-Mary, just below the connecting creek, sits a classic old private fishing camp: Buckhorn Camps, accessible by boat or float-plane. The small, rustic cabins seem to be out of a different age.

70

Debsconeag Lakes
TI RII WELS and T2 RIO WELS

Maps: Maine Atlas, Maps 42 and 50
USGS Quadrangles, Abol Pond, Rainbow Lake East, and
Nahmakanta Stream—for access from south, Pemadumcook
Lake and Norcross

Area and Maximum Depth: First Debsconeag, 320 acres,
140 feet; Second Debsconeag, 189 acres, 28 feet; Third
Debsconeag, 1,011 acres, 162 feet

Habitat Type: deep lakes with scenic mountains as a backdrop;
marshy areas on Second Debsconeag and Debsconeag
Deadwater

Fish: lake trout, salmon (First Debsconeag), brook trout

Expect to See: loon, bald eagle, beaver, moose, views of Mt.
Katahdin

Take Note: fee to camp; fire permits, Maine Forest Service,
207-827-1800

Getting There

From Millinocket: Go west on Routes 11 and 157 to the T where Route 157 ends and Route 11 goes left, and turn right. Go one block, and turn left, following signs to Baxter State Park. In Spencer Cove (Millinocket Lake on the right and Ambajejus Lake on the left), cut across to the parallel Golden Road. From the Golden Road Checkpoint (no longer active), go 2.9 miles (2.9 miles), and take a shallow left onto an unimproved road (Omaha Beach painted on a concrete post; be careful not to take the sharper left). Go 2.9 miles (5.8 miles), staying left (straight) at the fork near the end, to the Omaha Beach access on Debsconeag Deadwater. The access road, at times, can be in very rough shape.

By Portage: Paddle from Spencer Cove on Ambajejus Lake southwest into Pemadumcook Lake (large lake prone to heavy wind and waves). Cross Pemadumcook to the western end to a portage of about a mile to Third Debsconeag's southern tip (about 10 miles from Spencer Cove). A modification: Paddle through Turkey Tail, Middle Jo-Mary, and Lower Jo-Mary lakes, then

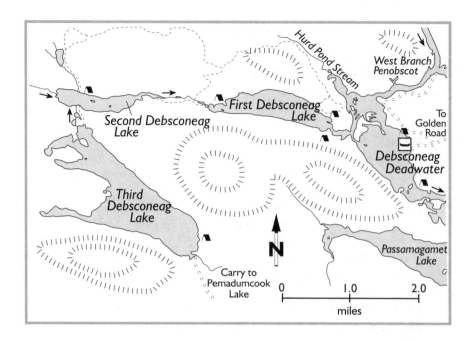

run 50 yards of whitewater into Pemadumcook, putting you closer to Pemadumcook's western end.

Wild, remote, pristine, and magical, the Debsconeag lakes represent the essence of the Maine Woods. Fortunately, through the foresight of Great Northern Paper, which had kept this area unharvested and non-motorized for more than 70 years, and The Nature Conservancy, the 41,000-acre Debsconeag wilderness now protects all of this area from development. Paddling here on a quiet morning or listening to the wail of the ever-present loons from one of the rustic campsites, you can imagine what much of this country once must have been like.

Rushing brooks and portage paths connect several lakes; depending on your energy level and time, you can stay on just one lake or carry through to the others. The more adventuresome can arrange a dropoff and paddle an extended one-way trip through these lakes and on to Pemadumcook and either Ambajejus or the Jo-Mary lakes.

Debsconeag Deadwater

The access delivers you to Omaha Beach on Debsconeag Deadwater. Loons may greet your arrival, as does Mt. Katahdin to the north, which stands sentinel over many lakes in this region. Along the shore you will see northern white cedar, jack pine, red maple, paper birch, balsam fir, red spruce, and a few hemlock. The unusual swampy island area at the northern end provides nesting habitat for wood ducks and keeps the many resident beavers happy.

The north end of Debsconeag Deadwater narrows to a swampy channel where Hurd Pond Stream enters. We saw a bald eagle searching for its next meal here. Campsites on the Deadwater: Omaha Beach, with its wonderful, white-sand swimming beach; northeastern end where the Penobscot flows in; and at the inlet from First Debsconeag.

First Debsconeag Lake

Debsconeag Deadwater and First Debsconeag Lake connect through an open, readily paddleable channel. The fair current in the spring subsides later in the season. Stronger current flows along the narrows between the island and the southwest shore—where water from the Penobscot River circles around the island. You will find great campsites on both sides of the channel here.

Paddling along the southern shore of First Debsconeag, you will get a spectacular view of Mt. Katahdin—when not enshrouded in

Omaha Beach at Debsconeag Deadwater with Mt. Katahdin, still snow-covered in late May, in the background.

clouds. Because of the view, one could easily miss the granite boulders waiting to scrape boat bottoms and the freshwater mussels that populate the clean, sandy bottom. From the north shore, marked by a small sign, a trail leads to some ice caves.

Oddly, our favorite thing about Debsconeag lakes is not the water at all but the surrounding banks and woodland, with their carpets of mosses, club mosses, lichens, ferns, and wildflowers. Trailing arbutus, wintergreen, and creeping snowberry (all diminutive members of the heath family) grow thickly in some areas. Dense cushions of moss and polypody fern drape over many of the boulders here.

Second Debsconeag Lake

For a great way to see the woods, portage into Second Debsconeag. Even if you do not want to carry your boat, walk the easy 0.75-mile trail anyway. The first part runs parallel to the connecting creek, with a wooden bridge crossing the creek, where you can dangle your feet over the edge and watch the rushing cataract. Even with the 30-foot elevation rise, the portage remains generally flat and remarkably dry— even when some pockets of snow remain, as we found in mid-May. We got a good view of a ruffed grouse on the walk. With gear, the portage should take about 25 minutes.

A quiet cove on Second Debsconeag Lake. A passenger waits patiently.

Paddling close to shore on Second Lake—much rockier than First, especially on the west end—you will almost certainly scrape bottom once or twice, but the rounded granite boulders should not do much damage. A couple of islands and a nice campsite sit along the west shore, roughly opposite the inlet brook. In boggy areas, look for the reddish leaves of pitcher plants. Because you can get into Second Lake only by portaging or float plane, you should not see any motorboats here.

Third Debsconeag Lake

You can portage from Second into Third Lake via a trail that starts about a hundred yards east of the inlet brook on the south shore. This trail, both harder to find and steeper in places than the trail connecting First and Second lakes, runs for only half the length. A side trail leads down to one of two small ponds between the lakes. The portage should take 15 minutes one way.

Third Debsconeag Lake seems just as wild as Second, but much larger. Keep an eye out for common terns. We believe they nest on large granite boulders protruding from the water near the north end. In Minister Cove we saw lots of beaver activity as well as seemingly ever-present loons and common mergansers.

Look for the reddish leaves of pitcher plants (Saracenia purpurea) *in the boggy areas of Second Debsconeag Lake.*

The Maine Woods

In most people's minds, the Maine Woods (or North Woods) conjures up thoughts of huge tracts of relatively undeveloped forestland in western and northern Maine. Who can resist the allure of its mountain chains, clear blue ponds and lakes, thousands of miles of streams and rivers, and abundant wildlife? The Appalachian Trail runs through it; the Allagash, St. John, Kennebec, and Penobscot drain it; and Maine preserves some of its finest treasures, such as Katahdin and Baxter State Park, within its borders.

On a broader regional scale, the Maine Woods forms the largest component of the Northern Forest, which spans the northern tier of New York, Vermont, New Hampshire, and Maine, encompassing more than 26 million acres. This largest expanse of forestland in the eastern U.S. includes deep woods and provides a home to a rich variety of wildlife. It boasts an abundance of moose, deer, black bear, otter, loon, osprey, and bald eagle. Less common but also present are bobcat, fisher, martin, and even the threatened Canadian Lynx—the only population in the eastern United States. More than 230 species of birds nest here or migrate through the area. And it provides the best paddling east of Minnesota.

In the late 1980s, paper companies and timber investment companies started selling lands throughout the region, some to development companies, and conservation organizations took note. They identified the region as "The Northern Forest" and began efforts to protect it. In Maine in particular, timberland has changed hands at an alarming rate, and the marketing of these parcels usually touts development potential. Between 1998 and 2003, 5.5 million acres of Maine timberland—more than a quarter of the state's land area—changed hands. Hundreds of millions of dollars will be required in the coming few years in Maine to meet the most urgent conservation needs.

However, the cooperation among environmentalists and sportsmen, politicians from opposite poles, and diverse organizations with widely differing priorities gives us hope that, by the time a third edition of this guide comes out, we will have many successes to report. Already, the Appalachian Mountain Club, The Nature Conservancy, a host of other conservation organizations, the State of Maine, outdoor clubs, and local communities have worked together to protect key swaths of land. In December 2003, the Northern Forest Alliance and the Northern Forest Center reported that, in the decade ending in 2002, outright land purchases and conservation easements permanently protected 1.05 million acres of Maine Woods.

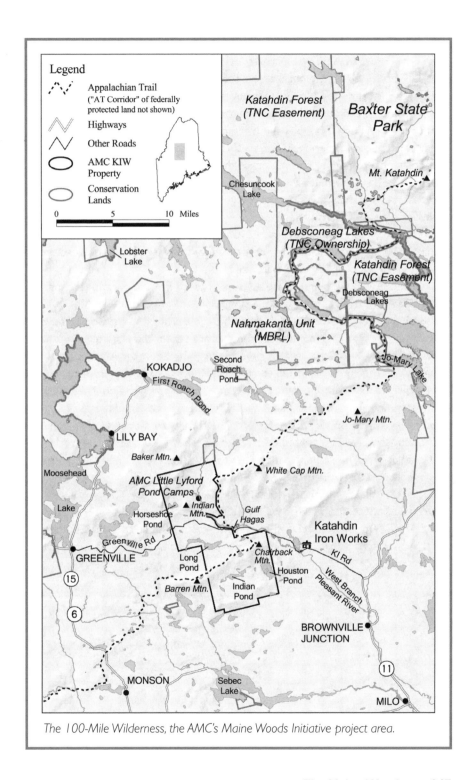

The 100-Mile Wilderness, the AMC's Maine Woods Initiative project area.

Recently, the AMC has increased its commitment to the Maine Woods. In December 2003, it embarked on the largest conservation effort in its 127-year history: the Maine Woods Initiative. The Initiative seeks to address the ecological and economic needs of the Maine Woods region by supporting local forest products jobs and traditional recreation, creating new multi-day backcountry experiences for visitors, and attracting new nature-based tourism to the region. The region of the Maine Woods identified for this project is the "100-Mile Wilderness," a roadless corridor stretching from Monson to Katahdin that contains a segment of the Appalachian Trail as well as Gulf Hagas, a magnificent gorge known as the "Grand Canyon of Maine," a National Natural Landmark. The AMC's investment will make paddling, hiking, skiing, and snowshoeing available to visitors, while reducing overuse on some portions of the Appalachian Trail.

In the initiative's first phase, AMC purchased from International Paper a 37,000-acre tract known as the Katahdin Iron Works Tract. The AMC will draw on its long history in Maine and New Hampshire in developing new trails and a range of accommodations that are scaled appropriately for the natural resources of the area. At time of this publication, the AMC is developing a management plan to determine which portions of the property will be managed for natural resource protection, recreation, certified sustainable forestry, and multiple use. The AMC purchase ensures that these 37,000 acres—rich with opportunities for paddling, hiking, cross-country skiing, and snowshoeing—will be protected and remain open to the public for recreational use. For more information about the Maine Woods Initiative, go to www.outdoors.org/mwi.

(100-Mile Wilderness Map credits: Cartography by Cathy Poppenweimer. Conservation land data provided by the Maine Office of GIS, and the AMC. Data on lakes, rivers, and highways provided by the U.S. Geological Survey. Appalachian Trail information developed by the Appalachian Trail Conference.)

71

Upper and Lower Togue Ponds and Abol Pond

T2 R9 WELS

Maps: Maine Atlas, Maps 50 and 51
USGS Quadrangles, Abol Pond and Trout Mountain

Area and Maximum Depth: Upper Togue Pond, 294 acres, 34 feet; Lower Togue Pond, 384 acres, 53 feet; Abol Pond, 70 acres, 34 feet

Habitat Type: small ponds with spectacular views; some marshy areas

Fish: Upper Togue, chain pickerel; Lower Togue, salmon, white, and yellow perch, chain pickerel; Abol Pond, brook trout

Baxter State Park: www.baxterstateparkauthority.com, 207-723-5140; camping reservations required

Expect to See: loon, beaver, views of Mt. Katahdin

Take Note: 10-HP limit; some development, including scout camps on Lower Togue and Abol ponds

---

GETTING THERE

Togue Ponds: From Millinocket, go west on Routes 11 and 157 to the T where Route 157 ends and Route 11 goes left, and turn right. Go one block, and turn left, following signs to Baxter State Park. Go 15.3 miles (15.3 miles), and turn right toward the Togue Pond Gate. Go 1.5 miles (16.8 miles) to the Togue Pond picnic area and access.

Abol Pond: Continue past Togue ponds to the Togue Pond Gate (fee required). Go northwest on Perimeter Road for 2.9 miles (2.9 miles), turn left, and go 0.4 mile (3.3 miles) to the Abol Beach Picnic Area and access.

Togue Ponds

It just does not get much more beautiful than the view of Mt. Katahdin from Togue ponds. Located just six miles to the north, Baxter Peak rises 4,670 feet from pond level. In the spring (ice-out typically in early May),

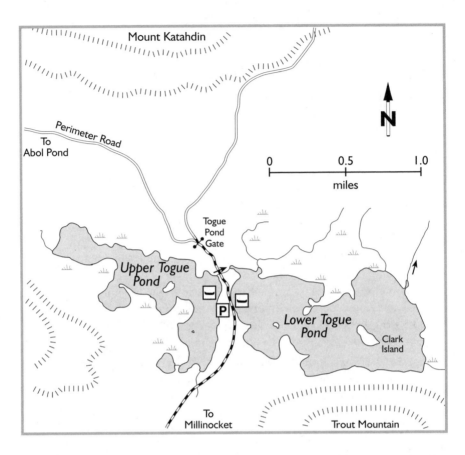

the dramatic snow-capped peak dominates the landscape, just as the Rockies do in the West.

Of the two ponds, Upper Togue (west side of the road), a little more remote, also sports a more varied shoreline. Red pine dominates here—notice the reddish bark, long needles in bundles of two, and small cones—but you will also find white pine (five needles per bundle), jack pine (very short needles with two per bundle), some northern white cedar along the shore, a few red spruce and balsam fir, red maple, and paper birch. Various low, bushy shrubs of the heath family—blueberry, sheep laurel, leatherleaf, bog rosemary, and Labrador tea—grow thickly along the shoreline, mixed in with bracken fern, alder, and a wide range of mosses and lichens. In coves and along Lower Togue's northern shore, look for pitcher plants growing on sphagnum hummocks.

Natural tannins color the water reddish brown. The sandy bottom harbors freshwater mussels, which stick partway out of the sand, filtering out microscopic algae and other prey. We saw several pairs of loons here, a broad-winged hawk, and lots of warblers (including yellow-rumped warbler and yellowthroat) and other songbirds at the far western inlet on Upper Togue. We also saw a half-dozen painted turtles at the inlet.

Beaver abound, as evidenced by several lodges and lots of stumps. The residents of a very active lodge in Upper Togue's cove that extends farthest south had cut over a hillside, with aspen and birch trees strewn as if part of a logging operation. In the boggy inlet into Lower Togue we watched a mink scurry along the shore looking for its next meal. If you catch a glimpse of one, wait around and chances are pretty good it will come out of hiding to take another peak at you.

Abol Pond

While in this area, you might also want to paddle Abol Pond, a narrow pond that runs along Perimeter Road just in from the Togue Pond gate. Abol Pond has a nice sand beach and picnic area and offers a pleasant few hours of paddling. The shallow pond is thick with vegetation: waterlilies, bur-reed, and lots of submerged plants. In a few boggy areas, you can find pitcher plants, cranberry, sphagnum, tamarack, and other northern fen species. We saw a deer and a pair of loons with chick while paddling here on an August afternoon.

Lower Togue Pond provides spectacular views of Mt. Katahdin throughout the paddling season.

72

Lobster Lake
Lobster Twp

> **MAPS:** Maine Atlas, Map 49
> USGS Quadrangles, Lobster Mountain, Penobscot Farm, and Big Spencer Mountain
> **AREA AND MAXIMUM DEPTH:** 3,475 acres, 106 feet
> **HABITAT TYPE:** deep lake with marshy coves and sand beaches
> **FISH:** salmon, lake trout, brook trout, white perch, yellow perch
> **EXPECT TO SEE:** loon, common tern, ducks, moose
> **TAKE NOTE:** fill up with gas in Millinocket or Greenville; no personal watercraft; camping and entrance fees required (North Maine Woods, www.northmainewoods.org); established campsites do not require fire permits; camping only in designated sites, first-come basis; geology, www.state.me.us/doc/nrimc/mgs/sites-1998/oct98.htm

GETTING THERE

From Millinocket, go west on Routes 11 and 157 to the T where Route 157 ends and Route 11 goes left, and turn right. Go one block, and turn left, following signs to Baxter State Park. In Spencer Cove (Millinocket Lake on the right and Ambajejus Lake on the left), cut across to the parallel Golden Road. From the Golden Road Checkpoint (no longer active), go 42.9 miles (42.9 miles), through the Caribou Checkpoint (open 24 hours; pay fees), and turn left at the Lobster Lake/Northeast Carry sign. Go 3.4 miles (46.3 miles), cross over the Lobster Stream bridge, and park on the left.

From Greenville, go north on Main Street/Lily Bay Road, staying on the main road to Kokadjo and the Sias Hill Checkpoint (no longer active). From the checkpoint, go 9.5 miles (9.5 miles), and turn left onto the Golden Road. Go 15.0 miles, through the Caribou Checkpoint (open 24 hours; pay fees), and continue as above.

Lobster Lake, shaped like the two parts of a lobster claw, is certainly one of the finest paddling and camping lakes in Maine. To reach the

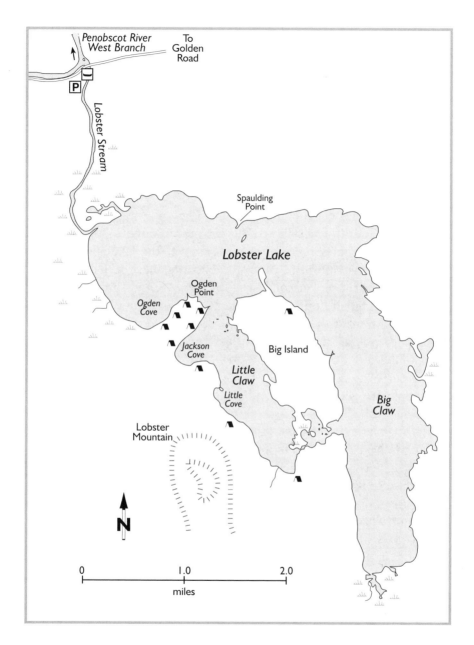

lake, paddle up Lobster Stream from the confluence of Lobster Stream and the Penobscot River West Branch. The 2-mile paddle traverses a wide, deep stream with barely perceptible current. In fact, the stream actually changes direction depending on the volume of water coming down the West Branch. At high flow in the spring, Lobster Stream can reverse direction and serve as an inlet into Lobster Lake. The marshy shoreline, dense with alder, sweetgale, and other water-tolerant plants, provides a home for beaver and moose.

After paddling up Lobster Stream and entering the lake, head left (north) where several coves extend into the marsh. We came upon a moose here along with a family of common goldeneye.

Several well-maintained campsites—complete with picnic tables, fire rings, sites for at least a half-dozen tents, and superb sandy beaches for swimming—lie across the way in Ogden Cove. Because shallow water extends quite a way out, young children love this spot. Three separate campsites occupy Ogden Point (Ogden North, Ogden Point, and Ogden South), each with room for multiple tents. All sites have sandy swimming beaches and great views over the lake and across to Big Island. Three other fine campsites occur farther south along Little Claw's western shore: Jackson Cove, Little Cove, and Little Claw.

Around Ogden Point from Ogden Cove, you enter Little Claw. In windy conditions, this section feels more protected. Rounding Ogden Point and looking down into Little Claw almost takes your breath away. Gulls and terns nest on the small, protruding, rocky islands, and jagged cliffs extend down into the clear blue water, interspersed here and there with sandy coves. Wind-sculpted cedars and pines perch precariously on the high overlooks, ferns and mosses festoon the rocks, all nestled beneath picturesque mountains. In our paddling throughout Maine, we have not seen a more scenic spot.

Particularly attractive Big Island separates Big Claw and Little Claw. The 2,000-acre island includes tall cliffs, sandy beaches, and protected marshy coves. Quoting from the Maine Geological Survey: "Along the shores of this beautiful lake . . . is some of the most spectacular geology found anywhere in the state. In outcrop after outcrop, the shore of the lake reveals a complex geological story that begins with deep-sea sediments, is punctuated by several periods of igneous activity and folding, and ends with shallow marine sediment that is profusely fossiliferous."

Thick groves of protected old-growth red pine (only 1 percent remains in Maine) and some huge hemlocks grow on the island's higher sections. Northern white cedar, white pine, and the unusual jack pine grow along the shore. A rare tree in Maine, jack pine grows in profusion here, including some unusually large specimens. The very short needles (3/4" to 1-1/2") twist at the base and grow in bundles of two.

The cones take two years to grow and, until mature, remain oddly twisted. After maturing, they may stay on the tree for more than a dozen years. Fires help open the cones and disperse seeds.

At the south end of Big Island you can paddle through a narrow channel into Big Claw. Lined with sedges and thinly sprinkled with yellow pondlily, fragrant waterlily, and bur-reed, the marshy channel provides rich habitat for moose and numerous bird species. Paddling here in late July, the sound of songbirds filled the air, and we saw several wood ducks in the vegetation along the shore.

The Big Claw portion of Lobster Lake has much less variation than Little Claw. At 3.5 miles in length and as much as a mile across, Big Claw can also get pretty rough in windy conditions. At the lake's southern tip, a wonderful marshy area begs to be explored. Rounding a point of land into this marshy cove during an evening paddle, three moose greeted us: a cow with calf and a yearling cow. Grasses, sedges, bulrushes, and the aromatic sweet flag *(Acorus americanus)* grow in profusion here.

In 1981, the state acquired from Great Northern Paper a permanent conservation easement to the shoreline of Lobster Lake, extending back 500 feet from the high-water line. The easement protects the shoreline from development and timber harvesting.

Cow and calf moose browse for water plants at the south tip of Lobster Lake.

~73~

Canada Falls Lake
Alder Brook Twp, Pittston Academy Grant,
and Soldiertown Twp

Maps: Maine Atlas, Map 48
   USGS Quadrangles, Canada Falls Lake and Tomhegan Pond
Area and Maximum Depth: 2,627 acres, 24 feet
Habitat Type: large, shallow lake
Fish: brook trout
Expect to See: loon, osprey, moose, scenic views
Take Note: camping and entrance fees required; fire permits,
   Maine Forest Service, 207-827-1800

Getting There

From Rockwood, go west on Routes 6 and 15, and turn right 0.1 mile after the gas station, crossing Moose River. Go 0.1 mile (0.2 mile) to the T, turn right onto 20 Mile Road, and go 16.9 miles (17.1 miles) to the 20 Mile Checkpoint (follow signs to Seboomook Wilderness Campground). After the checkpoint, take the left fork (do not follow Seboomook signs). Go 3.5 miles (20.6 miles), turning right at the yield sign, staying on the main road, followed by a left turn at the stop sign. Go 0.7 mile (21.3 miles), turn left at the sign for Canada Falls Lake, and go 2.5 miles (23.8 miles) to the access on the left.

Don't be shocked when you arrive at the Canada Falls Lake access. The relatively large campground fills with campers, dogs, children, beer cans, and noise in the middle of the season. We could not wait to get out onto the much more peaceful lake. When we paddled here on a weekend at the end of July, with only light breezes rippling the surface, we saw one other boat up close on the water, trolling at idle speed down the long outlet channel. Fishermen seem to like Canada Falls Lake for the same reason that signs warn away the high-speed boating crowd. A gazillion submerged and not-so-submerged stumps provide plenty of hiding space for fish and make speedboating dangerous.

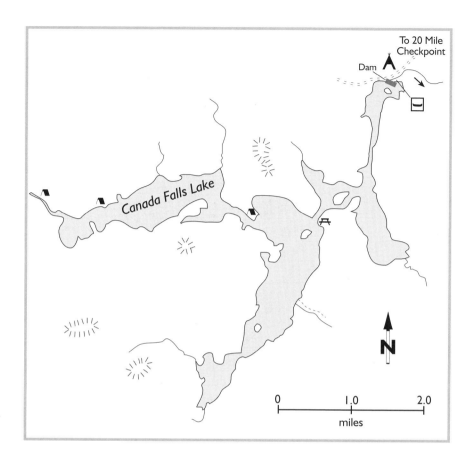

A jumble of roots, stumps, and downed timber covers the shore in many places, which detracts a bit from the dark-hued rows of pointed fir and spruce receding back into the many-layered hillsides. Entering the main lake, one is immediately taken with the beauty of three saw-toothed peaks off in the distance. You will find hearing the enchanting calls of loons from a remote campsite as the sun sets over distant peaks far preferable to the barking of dogs at the campground.

We watched in solitude as an osprey wheeled about doing aerial acrobatics in search of a meal. It seemed as if some invisible hook held one wingtip fixed as it pivoted in the sky for a better look, eventually flying off to a quieter cove with improved visibility into the water below. Ring-billed gull, white-throated sparrow, cormorant, black duck, loon, great blue heron, and many other birds announced their presence. A female merganser with a raft of young in tow fled before us, ducking under the safety of some downed timber.

Osprey

The northern coniferous forest dominates the shoreline and hill-sides surrounding Canada Falls Lake, but spruce, pine, and fir have not totally squeezed out the deciduous species, as we saw many small red maple and paper birch, along with some quite large yellow birch. In places, beaver had stripped some of the deciduous trees of their bark. As we came around through the marshy area behind the big island at the end of the outlet channel, we surprised a deer that had come down for a drink.

Although we found few marshy areas to explore, we very much enjoyed our paddle on Canada Falls Lake, with its long arms and lots of nooks and crannies to explore. We recommend spending more than one day exploring fully the extensive shoreline of this wonderful place.

Northern Maine

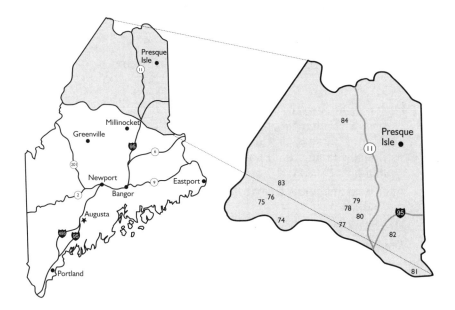

This remote region offers solitude and wildness to the intrepid paddler. The Northern Region encompasses 200,000-acre Baxter State Park, home to Katahdin, Maine's tallest peak at 5,267 feet. Aroostook County, so large and remote it is known simply as "The County," comprises most of the Northern Region. The largest county east of the Mississippi, it covers more land than Connecticut and Rhode Island combined. The County contains 2,000 lakes, rivers, and streams, including the spectacular Allagash Wilderness Waterway, a 92-mile-long corridor of state-protected waterways winding through the northern Maine Woods. Featured trips include the Penobscot River West Branch and Chesuncook Lake (Trip 74), where Thoreau made an historic journey; remote Allagash Lake (Trip 83), devilishly difficult to reach but loaded with wildlife; and Sawtelle Deadwater (Trip 80), just north of Baxter State Park, where we have seen moose on every trip.

74

Chesuncook Lake and West Branch Penobscot River
Chesuncook Twp, T2 R12 WELS, and 6 more

Maps: Maine Atlas, Maps 49 and 50
USGS Quadrangles, Caribou Lake North, Caribou Lake South, Chesuncook, Cuxabexis Lake, Harrington Lake, Longley Pond, Mud Pond, Penobscot Farm, Ragmuff Stream, Rainbow Lake West

Area and Maximum Depth: 26,200 acres, 150 feet; river length, 20 miles

Habitat Type: huge, scenic lake

Fish: landlocked salmon, brook trout, lake trout, white perch, yellow perch

Chesuncook Lake House: www.chesuncooklakehouse.com

Expect to See: loon, osprey, moose

Take Note: fill up with gas in Millinocket; frequent hazardous paddling conditions; do not take novice paddlers here; camping and entrance fees required (North Maine Woods, www.northmainewoods.org); camping only in designated sites; no fire permits required; little development on Chesuncook, more on Ripogenus and Caribou lakes along the Golden Road

---

GETTING THERE

West Branch Penobscot River: From Millinocket, go west on Routes 11 and 157 to the T where Route 157 ends and Route 11 goes left, and turn right. Go one block, and turn left, following signs to Baxter State Park. In Spencer Cove (Millinocket Lake on the right and Ambajejus Lake on the left), cut across to the parallel Golden Road. From the Golden Road Checkpoint (no longer active), go 42.9 miles (42.9 miles), through the Caribou Checkpoint (open 24 hours; pay fees), and turn left at the Lobster Lake/Northeast Carry sign. Go 3.4 miles (46.3 miles), cross over the Lobster Stream bridge, and park on the left.

Ripogenus Lake: From the Golden Road, just past Ripogenus Dam, turn right at the Allagash Gateway Campground sign (about 33 miles from Millinocket), and launch from the campground (fee) or the public access.

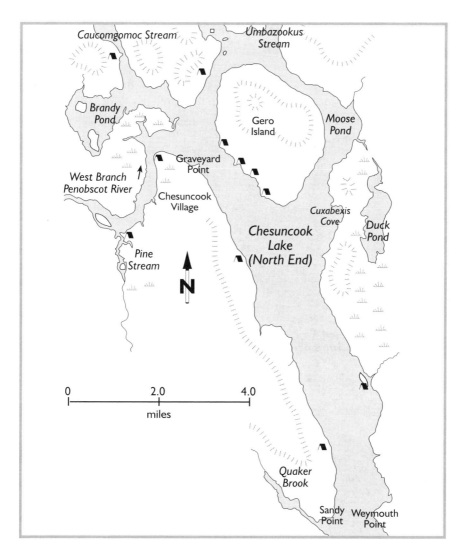

In many ways, Chesuncook Lake—Maine's third largest, after Sebago and Moosehead—and Penobscot River West Branch that feeds it represent the quintessence of northern Maine. Huge, wild, and beautiful, Chesuncook stretches for 20 miles; though only 1 to 3 miles wide, even modest winds can generate very rough conditions.

Chesuncook, an Abenaki word, means "place of the principal outlet" or "place where many streams empty in." Construction of dams between 1840 and 1920 turned broad, grassy meadows, where a number of shallow streams converged, into a huge lake. When Henry David

Thoreau paddled here in 1853 and 1857, a small lake existed, but with completion of the Chesuncook dam in 1904, the rising lake eliminated some West Branch and Pine Stream rapids and portions of many streams.

The larger Ripogenus Dam, built in 1920 to control the West Branch level for the transport of pulp mill logs—a practice banned in 1972—raised the water level enough that Ripogenus and Caribou lakes merged with Chesuncook. The largest privately owned dam in the United States, Ripogenous Dam's concrete structure stretches for 795

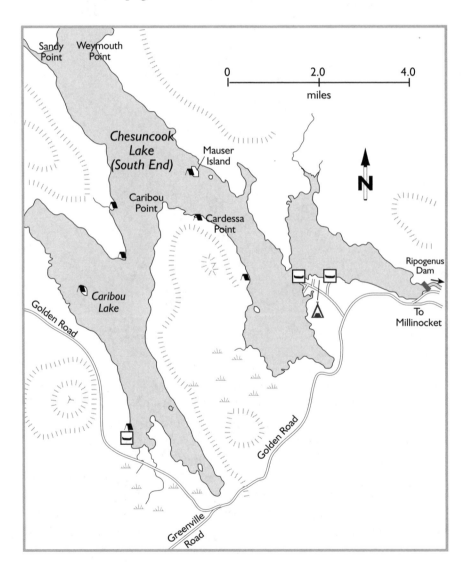

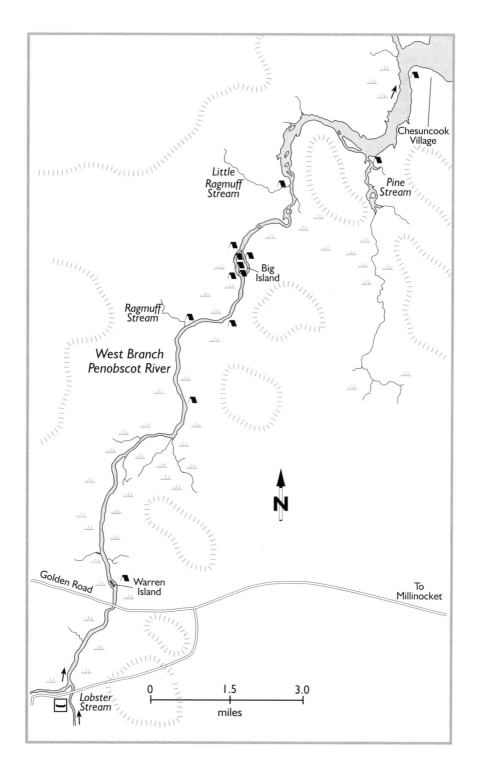

Little
Ragmuff
Stream

Chesuncook
Village

Pine
Stream

Big
Island

Ragmuff
Stream

West Branch
Penobscot River

N

Golden Road

Warren
Island

To
Millinocket

0   1.5   3.0

miles

Lobster
Stream

feet in length and 83 feet in height. In the early 1950s, the owners retrofit the dam with 37-megawatt hydropower turbines.

A wonderful trip extends from the Lobster Lake outlet stream along the Penobscot West Branch and into Chesuncook Lake. From the Lobster Stream access (see Lobster Lake, Trip 72), you paddle nearly 20 miles to Chesuncook Village on the lake. This West Branch section flows gently, with only a few stretches of quickwater, especially between Big Island and Little Ragmuff Stream.

Watch for moose along the river's winding course. We saw four during an early October trip, one a huge bull whose broad antlers reflected early morning light as we rounded a river bend. We also saw white-tailed deer, merganser, osprey, Canada jay, migrating snow geese, loons, and kingfisher.

Balsam fir, spruce, northern white cedar, and white pine grow along the West Branch's heavily wooded shores, with alders and other shrubby vegetation closer to the water. You can explore several West Branch inlets on the way down to Chesuncook. More than a dozen campsites perch along the riverbanks between Lobster Stream and Chesuncook. Putting in late in the day, we camped at Warren Island just below the Golden Road—a place where Thoreau camped and now sometimes called Thoreau Island. Another half-dozen campsites occur on and near Big Island, about 10 miles from the Lobster Stream access.

As you round the river's final bend, buildings of Chesuncook Village (accessible only by boat or float plane) appear on the right. The village offers a number of lodging options, including the Chesuncook Lake House. The lake here does not look huge because Gero Island—more than 3,000 acres of Maine Public Reserve land with four beautiful campsites—obscures your view. The area north of Gero Island offers many hours of exploration, as well as connections to Caucomogomoc Lake (Trip 77) and Umbazooksus Lake. About a dozen other campsites occur on both sides of the lake, along the inlet streams to the north, and on Mouser Island in the south.

The northwest-southeast orientation of Chesuncook Lake generates very rough water, as winds tend to blow from the northwest or southeast. We fought strong winds for hours as we slowly made our way down the lake's eastern shore. Waves lapped over the bow even in modest winds; another boater told us that he's seen four-foot waves here. We prefer to use sea kayaks with spray skirts here, rather than open canoes.

75

Loon Lake, Big Hurd Pond, and Little Hurd Pond
T6 R15 WELS

MAPS: Maine Atlas, Maps 49 and 55
USGS Quadrangles, Caucomgomoc East, Caucomgomoc
West, and Ragmuff Stream

AREA AND MAXIMUM DEPTH: Loon Lake, 1,140 acres, 45 feet;
Big Hurd Pond, 250 acres, 27 feet; Little Hurd Pond, 180
acres

HABITAT TYPE: shallow ponds with marshy coves

FISH: brook trout, white perch, yellow perch

PINEGREE FOREST PARTNERSHIP: www.newenglandforestry.org/
projects/Pingree.asp; Pingree family and New England
Forestry Foundation developed a 762,000-acre conservation
easement that includes protection for the west shore of Loon
Lake and Big Hurd Pond

EXPECT TO SEE: loon, osprey, bald eagle, common tern, moose,
white-tailed deer

TAKE NOTE: fill up with gas in Millinocket; no personal watercraft;
fire permits required, Maine Forest Service, 207-435-7963

GETTING THERE

From Millinocket, go west on Routes 11 and 157 to the T where Route 157 ends and Route 11 goes left, and turn right. Go one block, and turn left, following signs to Baxter State Park. In Spencer Cove (Millinocket Lake on the right and Ambajejus Lake on the left), cut across to the parallel Golden Road. From the Golden Road Checkpoint (no longer active), go 45.1 miles (45.1 miles), through the Caribou Checkpoint (open 24 hours; pay fees), and turn right onto Ragmuff Road. Go 18.2 miles (63.3 miles), staying on the main road, following signs to the Caucomgomoc checkpoint, and turn left into the Loon Lake access and dam.

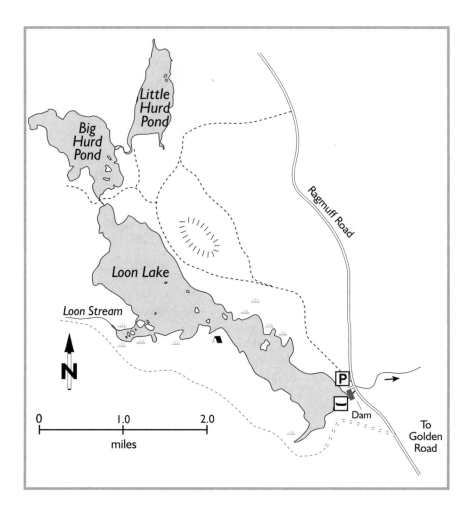

Loon Lake

We set out on Loon Lake on a calm July evening, with scarcely a ripple on the water's surface, the only sound the steady dip of paddles and the plaintive cry of loons on this aptly named lake. We left behind thoughts of the long drive on bumpy logging roads through clear-cuts and third- or fourth-generation spruce/fir regrowth. Few people visit Loon Lake; most pass by on their way to more famous paddling destinations.

Unlike nearby Allagash River and Allagash Lake, this wonderful place lies off the beaten path yet remains readily accessible by vehicle. Loon Lake offers about 10 miles of shoreline to explore, plus a paddleable section of the Loon Stream inlet. Big Hurd Pond provides another 3.5 miles, plus islands.

A young paddler takes a turn in the solo canoe on Loon Lake.

Loon Lake and Big Hurd Pond have quite varied shorelines, with coves to explore, marshy areas providing great bird habitat, rock outcrops draped in moss and ferns, and majestic white pines overlooking the water. Though we could not find the nest, we saw an adult bald eagle and several immatures. We lost count of osprey and loons.

Loon Stream inlet—shallow, marshy, and dotted with islands—has abundant wildlife and remains our favorite section. Floating vegetation crowds the channel, and we saw nesting ring-necked ducks here. You can paddle some distance up the inlet stream, at least at high-water levels.

Big and Little Hurd Ponds

With high-water levels—the case when we visited in mid-July—you can paddle easily from Loon Lake into Big Hurd Pond. The Loon Lake level can drop considerably, though, making access into Big Hurd more difficult. Even at high water, watch out for rocks in the connecting channel.

Big Hurd Pond, small compared with Loon Lake, has a protected feel to it. When we paddled in from Loon Lake as the sun dipped down over the western hills, the place seemed magical. Near the access from Loon Lake, several islands crop up, along with a few more near the pond's center. Mostly solid rock, the islands' huge granite boulders reach down into the water in places. Look for thick carpets of moss and lichen and copious blueberries in season.

To get from Big Hurd into Little Hurd Pond, paddle up a shallow stream, then carry your boat about a hundred feet over a rocky area and small ledge. In the early morning we saw four deer (three were bucks) and a moose. An unusual sight, two of the deer and the moose browsed close together along the Little Hurd Pond outlet—they would have fit into one camera frame. Common terns continually skimmed the pond's surface during our paddle here.

Though we saw lots of wildlife at Little Hurd, paddling here is not enjoyable. Extremely shallow—with few places deeper than a foot—the lake has a bottom of thick organic ooze. Currents created by paddling agitate the bottom, leaving a trail of thousands of tiny bubbles of marsh gas. Even a family of common goldeneye swimming along left a bubble trail. Little Hurd probably does not have too many centuries of life left before filling in and getting taken over by encroaching tamaracks and bog vegetation.

76

Caucomgomoc Lake and Rowe, Round, Daggett, and Poland Ponds

T6 R14 WELS, T6 R15 WELS, T7 R14 WELS, and T7 R15 WELS

MAPS: Maine Atlas, Maps 49 and 55
   USGS Quadrangles, Caucomgomoc Lake West, Caucomgomoc Lake East, and Allagash Lake

AREA AND MAXIMUM DEPTH: Caucomgomoc Lake, 5,081 acres, 79 feet; Round Pond, 375 acres, 17 feet; Daggett Pond, 461 acres, 20 feet; Poland Pond, 490 acres, 34 feet; Rowe Pond, 250 acres

HABITAT TYPE: shallow lake, ponds, and connecting streams with miles of shoreline

FISH: salmon, lake trout, brook trout, white perch (Caucomgomoc); brook trout, white perch, yellow perch (ponds)

LOON LODGE: www.loonlodgemaine.com, 207-745-8168

PINEGREE FOREST PARTNERSHIP: www.newenglandforestry.org/ projects/Pingree.asp; Pingree family and New England Forestry Foundation developed a 762,000-acre conservation easement that includes protection for the northeast shore of Caucomgomoc Lake, east shore of Rowe Pond, and all of Round, Daggett, and Poland ponds

EXPECT TO SEE: loon, osprey, bald eagle, moose, otter, white-tailed deer

TAKE NOTE: fill up with gas in Millinocket; paddle smaller ponds when winds blow on Caucomgomoc; no personal watercraft; fire permits, Maine Forest Service, 207-435-7963

GETTING THERE

Caucomgomoc Lake: From Millinocket, go west on Routes 11 and 157 to the T where Route 157 ends and Route 11 goes left, and turn right. Go one block, and turn left, following signs to Baxter State Park. In Spencer Cove (Millinocket Lake on the right and Ambajejus Lake on the left), cut across to the parallel Golden Road. From the Golden Road Checkpoint (no longer

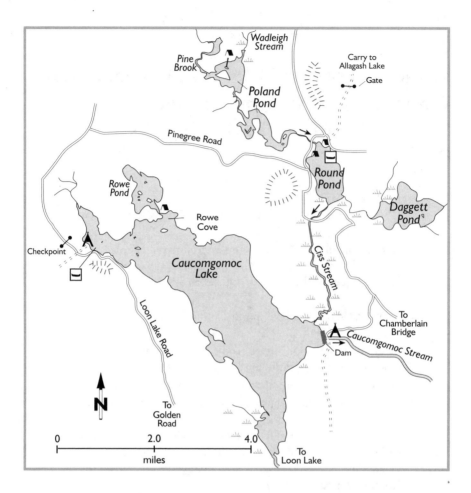

active), go 45.1 miles (45.1 miles), through the Caribou Checkpoint (open 24 hours; pay fees), and turn right onto Ragmuff Road. Go 25.6 miles (70.7 miles), staying on the main road, following signs (if still in place) to the old Caucomgomoc Checkpoint, and turn right into the access and campsite, 0.2 mile before the checkpoint.

Round Pond: From the Caucomgomoc Checkpoint, go 4.7 miles (75.6 miles), and turn right onto Pinegree Road. Go 7.5 miles (83.1 miles), and turn left. Go 1.6 miles (84.7 miles) to the access on the right.

These bodies of water lie in the heart of northern Maine canoe country. While more famous for the Allagash Wilderness Waterway, this area also offers superb lake and pond paddling. Caucomgomoc Lake provides a good starting point, but with its northwest-southeast orientation, it often suffers from strong winds and rough water.

The west end of Caucomgomoc, where the lake seems less large, and the east end, where one can travel up into Round, Daggett, and Poland ponds, appeal most to the quietwater paddler. The more adventuresome can reach Caucomgomoc by paddling or poling downstream (north) from Loon Lake for 4 miles or can use Caucomgomoc as an Allagash Lake access (see sections on those lakes). We put in on Caucomgomoc and spent several wonderful days exploring this area. We started out paddling the northwest inlet and the shoreline over to Rowe Pond, staying our first night at the Rowe Cove campsite.

Caucomgomoc Lake has a wild and highly varied shoreline. In the northwestern tip's narrow inlet channel, we spotted an otter, and we watched another for about a half hour between Rowe Cove and Caucomgomoc Dam. We saw lots of loons, several bald eagles, osprey, moose, and deer along here. Gorgeous islands, including Henry's Island, which sports a small campsite, dot the surface of Rowe Pond. During an early morning paddle, we heard a group of coyotes howling off in the woods.

Ciss Stream and Round Pond

Ciss Stream enters the lake just northwest of Caucomgomoc Dam. With adequate water levels, Ciss Stream provides very enjoyable paddling up into Round, Daggett, and Poland ponds. The barely perceptible current will not impede your progress as the wide stream wends its way through a broad, flooded valley, strewn with sun-whitened stumps and fallen trees. We watched osprey fish along here with their characteristic hovering manner, spooked a few ducks, and then watched a huge bull moose at close range near the Round Pond entrance.

Loon Lodge perches on the northeast shore of Round Pond. This very nice and relatively new sporting camp offers various levels of accommodations, as well as boat-ferrying service partway into Allagash Lake (see section on Allagash Lake). Being the only sporting camp in this part of Maine makes it ideal for paddlers preferring more luxurious accommodations.

Daggett Pond

Round Pond provides access into two very nice ponds. At Round Pond's southeast end you can paddle Little Ciss Stream east into

A family-sized canoe, with lots of space for people and gear, offers a comfortable paddle on Caucomgomoc Lake.

Daggett Pond. Watch quietly for moose, deer, and otter as you round this gentle stream's many bends. Daggett Pond, 1.5 miles long and rich with wildlife, offers about five miles of beautiful, highly varied shoreline to explore. We watched three moose along the marshy shore at the pond's northwest end.

Firm ground comes right down to the water on the more wooded eastern half of the pond. On the point of land extending into the pond along the northeastern shore sits Fort Daggett—not a fort at all, but an elegant summer camp built back in the early 1900s and rarely used today.

Poland Pond

Poland Pond, to the northwest of Round Pond, differs markedly from Daggett Pond but also provides a great day trip. You have to do a bit of upstream poling or pulling your boat through a few hundred yards of quickwater to get there. For wading and lining your boat upstream, be sure to wear water shoes or a pair of old sneakers to help negotiate the rocky, slippery bottom. At the remains of an old dam, carry your boat about 30 feet up over a small rise to get into the pond. Going back downstream, with high enough water, you should be able to paddle the modest rapids below the carry.

Because the dam failed, dropping the water level, a band of younger vegetation grows along the shore, providing superb deer forage. We counted six deer —including two large bucks—as we paddled on the pond one mid-July day. Tamarack and other northern fen species grow along the pond's boggy sections.

A narrow channel at its mid-point divides long, narrow, highly convoluted Poland Pond. You may find downed logs blocking Pine Brook, which flows into the pond's northwest tip, but with a little work you might be able to get through and explore farther north. At the pond's northeast tip, you can explore the Wadleigh Stream inlet.

Drift logs add a playful diversion to a day's paddle on Poland Pond.

The smaller island at Poland Pond's north end also has a very nice campsite, from which you can walk over to a huge rock face and look out over the pond—often at deer or moose browsing on shoreline vegetation. The campsite has a small beach; campfires here require a permit from the Maine Forest Service.

77

South Branch Ponds

T5 R9 WELS

MAPS: Maine Atlas, Map 51
   USGS Quadrangle, Wassataquoik Lake

AREA AND MAXIMUM DEPTH: Upper South Branch Pond, 84
   acres, 76 feet; Lower South Branch Pond, 93 acres, 60 feet

HABITAT TYPE: small, deep, oligotrophic ponds in a spectacular
   setting

FISH: brook trout

BAXTER STATE PARK: www.baxterstateparkauthority.com,
   207-723-5140; camping reservations required

GEOLOGY: www.state.me.us/doc/nrimc/mgs/sites-2000/may00.htm

EXPECT TO SEE: loon, forested hillsides and beautiful mountains

TAKE NOTE: no motors; canoes for rent; this popular area
   includes a campground and gets a lot of traffic; illegal to
   remove fossils (or anything else) from the park

GETTING THERE

From I-95, Exit 58, go left (west) on Route 158, which turns into Route 11 north, to Patten. Turn left on Route 159, which turns into Grand Lake Road at Shin Pond. From Shin Pond, go 16.4 miles (16.4 miles) to the park gate (fee). From the gate, go 7.1 miles (23.5 miles) on the Perimeter Road, turn left at the South Branch ponds sign, and go 2.2 miles (25.7 miles) to the Lower South Branch Pond access.

Spectacular. Awesome. Superlatives barely convey the beauty of these ponds and surrounding mountains. The ponds perch in an alpine valley about a thousand feet above sea level, and the surrounding mountain peaks rise another 2,500 feet, much of that rise in exposed rock faces.

   The shorelines of the South Branch ponds—each less than a mile in length and among the smallest bodies of water in this guide—lack variation, and the extremely oligotrophic, crystal clear waters are nearly devoid of life. In the right light, you can see down more than 20

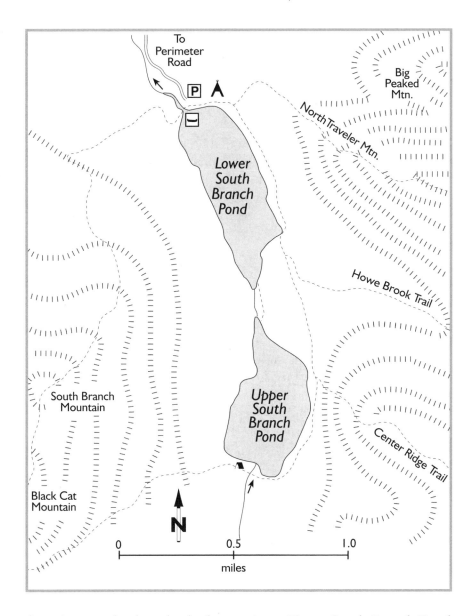

To
Perimeter
Road

Big
Peaked
Mtn.

North Traveler Mtn.

Lower
South
Branch
Pond

Howe Brook Trail

South Branch
Mountain

Upper
South
Branch
Pond

Center Ridge Trail

Black Cat
Mountain

N

0   0.5   1.0

miles

feet. Apparently, though, the loon pair on Upper South Branch Pond can find enough fish, and the freshwater mussels we saw here can find enough microscopic life.

At the southeastern tip of Lower South Branch Pond, you can portage into Upper South Branch Pond over a fairly flat, several-hundred-yard trail. Jagged, sheer cliffs of Baxter's Katahdin granite extend down into the water, making Upper Pond even more spectacular than Lower Pond. Steep, dramatic ridges of Traveler Mountain lie to the east. The charcoal-gray rhyolite on these ridges differs geologically from the pinkish Katahdin granite, which cooled very slowly deep underground, forming large crystals. Traveler Mountain rhyolite—lava from a volcanic eruption—solidified into finer-grained crystals about 400 million years ago.

The fossiliferous rock that you find here represents another interesting geologic feature of the South Branch ponds. Look along the shoreline for pieces of sandstone or shale embedded with fossils of small brachiopods, marine animals superficially resembling clams. Glaciers carried these fossil-bearing rocks here, one of the few places in Maine where one can find fossils.

Hardwoods dominate the vegetation around South Branch ponds, including paper birch, red maple, sugar maple, and beech. A few white pine, red pine, spruce, and fir scatter amid the hardwoods. In the understory you will see the large-leafed striped maple and beaked hazelnut (which produces an edible filbertlike nut). Logging began here in the mid-1800s, first for white pine, then spruce, and finally pulpwood. The last logging ended in 1965, when the remaining logging rights ran out, according to the deeds negotiated by Percival Baxter when he acquired the land. Governor Baxter gave to the state of Maine 200,000 acres of land acquired over a 45-year period—one of the most impressive private land-protection efforts ever. We should all be thankful to Governor Baxter for his farsighted vision in preserving the beauty of this area.

From the campground, enjoy the spectacular hikes in this part of Baxter. The North Traveler Mountain Trail provides dramatic views down into the South Branch ponds. The Howe Brook Trail leads to a spectacular cascading waterfall on the side of Traveler Mountain. You can also backpack south along Notch Trail to Russell Pond and remote Wassataquoik Lake, which provides the most remote paddling in the park (has rare blueback trout; canoes available for rent on an honor system).

~ 78 ~

Grand Lake Matagamon
Trout Brook Twp and T6 R8 WELS

MAPS: Maine Atlas, Maps 51 and 57
USGS Quadrangles, Frost Pond and Trout Brook Mountain
AREA AND MAXIMUM DEPTH: 4,165 acres, 95 feet
HABITAT TYPE: large, deep lake
FISH: salmon, lake trout, yellow perch
BAXTER STATE PARK: www.baxterstateparkauthority.com,
207-723-5140; camping reservations required
EXPECT TO SEE: loon, osprey, moose, white-tailed deer
TAKE NOTE: wind can make paddling hazardous; no fire permits
required at designated sites; camping fees

GETTING THERE

From I-95, Exit 58, go left (west) on Route 158, which turns into Route 11 to Patten. Turn left on Route 159, which turns into Grand Lake Road at Shin Pond. From Shin Pond, go 16.3 miles to the access on the right, just before the Baxter State Park gate.

About half of Grand Lake Matagamon lies within Baxter State Park boundaries. The park allows motors here and on Webster Lake, but protects them from development. With 6.5 square miles of water, coupled with its remoteness, Grand Lake Matagamon provides a large measure of solitude and will take two or more days to explore fully.

The park maintains five campsites on the lake; distances to the campsites: Togue Ledge, 2.5 miles; Boody Brook, 4.7 miles; Second Lake, 4.9 miles; Pine Point, 6.1 miles; Northwest Cove, 7.1 miles.

Grand Lake Matagamon has changed from the time Thoreau paddled it in the mid-1800s. Much of it remains wild, but the downed timber he had to negotiate drowned long ago with higher lake levels produced by a new concrete dam. An obstacle course of exposed and barely submerged stumps remains in shallower areas, but you can now reach most of the lake by boat.

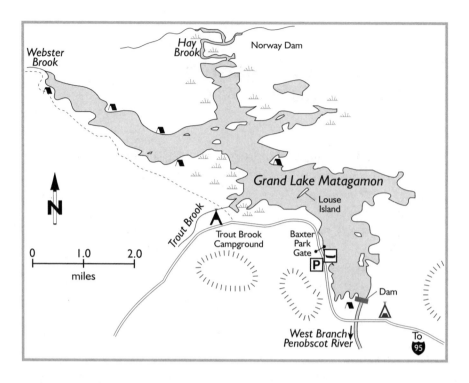

When Thoreau stopped on Louse Island, where he ate fried moose, he found all three species of pine, and those three species remain today. Besides the widely distributed red and white pines, you can find fair numbers of rare jack pines on Louse, as well as on other islands and along the shore. Maine represents the southern extension of the range of jack pine, which grows almost to the Arctic Circle, the farthest north of any pine species. It can be distinguished from other pines by its short, 1- to 1.5-inch-long needles. Note the persistent thin, curved cones from 1 to 3 inches long, often with two cones growing on opposite sides of a branch. The seeds from these cones are important wildlife food.

As you paddle out from the access, go left around the first island to view a thick stand of jack pine, along with paper birch and quaking aspen. Besides breaking up the view, dozens of islands provide scenic spots for picnics, swimming, or just lounging around—bugs permitting.

Continuing around to the left, a series of coves appears, one of them connecting to Trout Brook, which leads up to Trout Brook Farm Campground in Baxter Park. When the wind is up on the main lake, one could put in at the campground and paddle down Trout Brook to the lake, through an extensive marshy area. When we paddled here, a pair of osprey nested at the lake inlet. More marshlands, seldom visited by boaters, appear just south and north of the inlet. Look for moose in the early morning and evening in this largest expanse of marsh on the lake. The marsh and alder swamps of the sinewy north inlet, which is

Spruce Grouse

called Norway Dam, provide another good area for moose. Also, we saw many white-tailed deer along the shore in the middle of the day.

Balsam firs, topped with pointed spires, occur with great frequency in the Trout Brook area. Note the beautiful dark-purple cones, two to four inches long, pointing upward from the branches. An important browse plant for moose and white-tailed deer, the dense balsam foliage also provides refuge for spruce grouse and many smaller birds as well. We watched flocks of cedar waxwings darting from the alders and firs to catch insects out over Trout Brook, with its absolutely crystal-clear water.

Several flickers have chipped out holes in the dead trees of the marshland, inadvertently providing homes for numerous cavity-nesting birds, such as wood duck, common and hooded mergansers, chickadee, nuthatch, wren, tree swallow, bluebird, and kestrel. Matagamon offers hours—even days—of bird-watching and wildlife viewing.

Forested islands and boulders appropriate for picnicking, swimming, and sunning appear in profusion. Wildlife abounds, and solitude awaits those who would explore the marshy coves and inlets. For an exciting and varied vacation, combine paddling here with hiking the extensive trails of Baxter State Park.

The Loon
Voice of the Northern Wilderness

No animal better symbolizes wilderness than the common loon, *Gavia immer*, whose haunting cry resonates through the night air on Maine's larger lakes. The bird seems almost mystical, with its distinctive black-and-white plumage, daggerlike bill, and piercing red eyes. But like our remaining open space, the loon is threatened over much of its range. We who share its waters bear the responsibility for protecting this wonderful bird.

A large diving bird that lives almost its entire life in the water, the loon visits land only to mate and to lay eggs. Loons have a very difficult time on land because their legs, positioned quite far back on their bodies to aid them in swimming, prevent them from walking.

The loon has adapted remarkably well to water. Unlike most birds, it has solid bones, enabling it to dive to great depths. It also has internal air sacs that control how high it floats. By compressing this sac, a loon can submerge gradually, with barely a ripple, or swim with just its head above water.

Its heavy body and rearward legs make takeoff difficult. A loon may require a quarter mile of open water to build up enough speed to lift off, and it may have to circle a small lake several times to build enough altitude to clear nearby hills or mountains. When migrating, a loon flies rapidly—up to 90 miles per hour—but cannot soar.

Loons generally mate for life and can live for 20 to 30 years. The female lays two eggs in early May, and both male and female—indistinguishable to the casual observer—take turns incubating the oblong, moss-green eggs. Because loons cannot walk on land, they always build their nests very close to shore—where a paddler can scare birds away and a motorboat wake can flood the nest with cold water. Loons most often nest on islands to hide the eggs from predators, such as raccoons and skunks. On some lakes, floating platforms constructed to improve nesting success rise and fall with water level, reducing the likelihood of flooding or stranding a nest.

Loon chicks hatch covered in black down and usually enter the water a day after hatching. Young chicks often ride on a parent's back to conserve heat and to avoid predators. They grow quickly on a diet of small fish and crustaceans; by two weeks of age, they reach half the adult size and can dive to relatively deep lake bottoms, covering more than 30 yards underwater. Loon chicks remain totally dependent on their parents, however, for about 8 weeks and do not fly until 10 to 12 weeks of age. After leaving the nest, loons follow their elders to saltwater wintering areas and do not return to land for three or four years—until they reach breeding age.

On the threatened or endangered list in most other Northeastern states, loons remain plentiful in Maine. Slow but steady growth over many years seems to have plateaued recently at an estimated population of 4,500, and as development encroaches on lakes—destroying loon nesting habitat —and recreational use increases, loons become increasingly at risk.

Besides encroachment by humans and nest predation by raccoons, loons suffer mortality in many other ways. According to the Tufts University Wildlife Veterinary Clinic, chicks die primarily from collisions with personal watercraft and motorboats, and adults die primarily from ingestion of lead sinkers and jigs. As with other diving waterfowl, ingestion of lead sinkers and shotgun pellets poisons loons. The New Hampshire legislature took the forward-looking step of banning lead sinkers and jigs effective January 1, 2000. Maine followed on January 1, 2002. We also need a total ban on lead shotgun pellets in wetland areas. Maine loons also bear the highest mercury levels in the United States; most of that mercury emanates from older, coal-fired power plants in the Midwest that the current administration has exempted from modern pollution controls.

Because paddlers can easily disturb loons when nesting, watch for warning displays during the nesting season, early May through mid-July. If a nest fails, loons may try up to two more times, though the later a chick hatches, the lower its chance of survival. Keep away from loons and nest sites to help ensure their survival.

Loons have lived in this area longer than any other bird—an estimated 60 million years. For more information on how to protect the loon, visit the website of the Maine Audubon Society, which has conducted loon counts since 1983 (www.maineaudubon.org/conserve/loon/index.shtml).

Scraggly Lake (Northern)
T7 R8 WELS

MAPS: Maine Atlas, Map 57
   USGS Quadrangles, Hay Lake and Trout Brook Mountain
AREA AND MAXIMUM DEPTH: 842 acres, 70 feet
HABITAT TYPE: clear deep lake with forested hillsides
FISH: salmon, brook trout, lake trout, yellow perch
EXPECT TO SEE: loon, moose
TAKE NOTE: no personal watercraft; official campsites do not
   require fire permits

GETTING THERE

From I-95, Exit 58, go left (west) on Route 158, which turns into Route 11 to Patten. Turn left on Route 159, which turns into Grand Lake Road at Shin Pond. From Shin Pond, go 6.8 miles (6.8 miles), and turn right at the Scraggly Lake Management Area sign. Go 10.1 miles (16.9 miles), following signs for Scraggly Lake, to the access and campground.

Scraggly Lake lies just northeast of Baxter State Park, entirely within 10,000 acres owned by the Maine Bureau of Public Lands, which manages not only for timber but also for wildlife, important plant communities including several tracts of old-growth forest, and recreational opportunities.

By almost any standards, Scraggly Lake, with its crystal-clear water and highly varied shoreline, is a treasure. The deep coves and long, sinewy inlet to the southwest provide more than twelve miles of shoreline to explore, along with dozens of islands. In late spring and early summer, however, be careful especially near islands so as not to disturb nesting loons.

On the lake's west arm, you can paddle up Mitchell Brook for about a mile, including both forks. The quiet, meandering channel with barely perceptible current flows through a northern bog ecosystem, replete

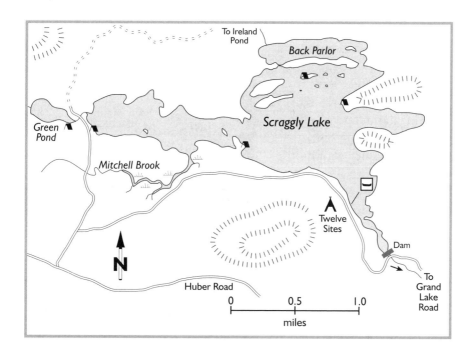

with pitcher plants, sundews, sphagnum, leatherleaf, cranberry, bog rosemary, and the feathery light-green tamarack—the first tree to take hold as a mat of sphagnum and bog vegetation extends into a body of water. When we explored here just after sunrise in August, the first rays of mist-filtered sunlight illuminated thousands of dew-covered spider-webs on the low bog vegetation, giving the place a magical, jewel-like appearance.

On the northern shore of Scraggly's western arm, we watched a mink for several minutes as it peered out at us from the protective cover of a fallen tree. Keep an eye out for mink along the shoreline of ponds, where they hunt for food—fish, chipmunks, frogs, and such. If you catch a glimpse of one, stick around for a few minutes; curiosity will likely cause it to pop back up for another look at you.

Numerous rocky islands contribute to the beauty of the lake's northern section. At one point, you can walk several yards over a nar-row spit of land into the long east-west arm at the north end. Or at the northeast end, you can paddle into the deep cove. Note the lone, ancient, old-growth white pine on a point of land that extends into the lake. If you get out of your boat, you will see that this last remnant of the stately white-pine forest that once dominated the land was almost cut down many decades ago—perhaps more than a century—and that the wedge cut has gradually grown over. With a trunk more than 3 feet in diameter, the tree could be 500 years old.

We saw plenty of moose sign, but no moose, though we did see several white-tailed deer browsing along the shore and chest-deep munching on pipewort—an aquatic plant that sends long, narrow stems and buttonlike flowers above the water's surface. We also saw great blue heron, black duck, wood duck, common merganser, pileated woodpecker, and quite a few loons.

Daybreak on Scraggly Lake

The pebbly shoreline and sandy bottom—except in boggy areas—support lots of freshwater mussels. White pine, hemlock, cedar, red spruce, balsam fir, white and yellow birch, white ash, and sugar maple populate the shoreline. An 80-acre section of old-growth hemlock forest (the largest such remnant forest in the state), with trees up to 400 years old, occurs about a mile west of the lake in the Scraggly Lake Management Unit.

Two significant stands of mixed-age woodland comprising 137 acres grow north of the lake, around Ireland Pond. Though not truly old growth because some cutting has occurred there, many large individual old-growth trees of various species occur here, including red spruce, hemlock, balsam fir, white pine, sugar maple, and yellow birch. Though Huber Road provides gated access to Ireland Pond, the adventurous could take a day trip, hiking from Scraggly Lake into this scenic 35-acre pond.

～ 80 ～

Sawtelle Deadwater
T6 R7 WELS

Maps: Maine Atlas, Maps 51 and 57
   USGS Quadrangle, Hay Lake

Area and Maximum Depth: 218 acres, 30 feet

Habitat Type: long, narrow, marshy channel through extensive
   wetland

Fish: yellow perch

Expect to See: wood duck, ring-necked duck, kingfisher, great
   blue heron, osprey, moose, beaver, otter

Take Note: fire permits, Maine Forest Service, 207-435-7963;
   camping at the Seboeis River campsite 0.7 mile before reaching Scraggly Lake turnoff

---

GETTING THERE

From I-95, Exit 58, go left (west) on Route 158, which turns into Route 11 to Patten. Turn left on Route 159, which turns into Grand Lake Road at Shin Pond. From Shin Pond, go 6.8 miles (6.8 miles), and turn right at the Scraggly Lake Management Area sign. Go 1.8 miles (8.6 miles) to the access on the left.

A dam built years ago to power a sawmill created Sawtelle Deadwater. With the mill's removal in 1955, wildlife biologist Francis Dunn of the Department of Inland Fisheries and Wildlife urged the state to manage the area as waterfowl habitat. The purchase, completed in 1985, created the Francis D. Dunn Wildlife Management Unit. You will see nesting boxes for wood ducks and hooded mergansers, and you may find some wild rice that the department planted. We saw many ducks each time we visited.

   The winding marshy channel of Sawtelle Deadwater provides one of the best spots to see moose throughout the summer until late August. Paddling here in early August we counted six, some on shore, others wading in the water and muck. We also have seen otter, muskrat, and beaver.

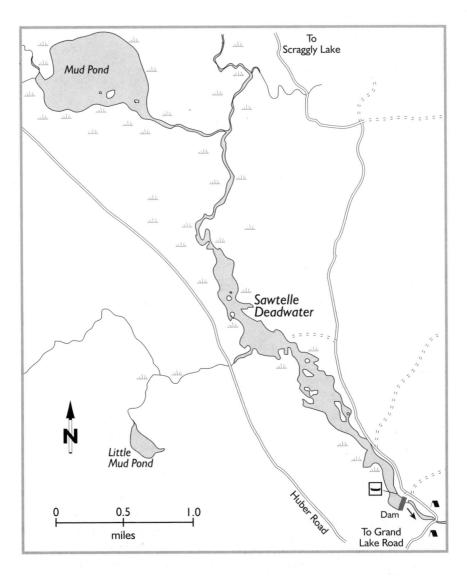

You may also see an unusual invertebrate of the phylum Bryozoa. These colonial bryozoa, *Pectinatella*, grow more commonly farther south—we have seen them in only a few Maine ponds. Look for globular masses attached to submerged sticks or rocks. The individual units (called zooids) appear as small bumps on the mass, and the colony looks like a jellied pineapple. Each zooid's ciliated tentacles filter out microscopic food particles; these tentacles retract at lightning speed into the protective ectocyst. Colonies can grow to the size of a watermelon by summer's end. *Pectinatella* grows only in relatively pure water. Look amid the rocks in the outlet below the dam for colonies; we also saw a smaller number upstream on submerged logs.

Lush growths of alder, cattail, pickerelweed, bulrushes, arrowhead, sweetgale, water celery, fragrant waterlily, yellow pondlily, water shield, pondweed, and bladderwort populate the area. Farther away from the water, common tree species include northern white cedar, tamarack, white pine, paper birch, bigtooth aspen, red maple, balsam fir, and red spruce. On the right side as you paddle upstream, look for a sizable grove of red pine. One time that we paddled here, we had to portage over a small beaver dam on the stream.

Look for kingfishers diving into the water after 2- to 3-inch fish, of which they consume many each day. Mature females sport a rust-colored band on the chest; males and immature females do not. We also saw numerous great blue herons and several osprey.

Grassy islands populate the wide southern section of Sawtelle Deadwater. Some you can paddle around; others lead to dead ends—at least by midsummer. As you paddle north, the deadwater narrows gradually to a channel 20 to 30 feet wide. Eventually you will reach the remains of an old bridge, and several hundred yards past that the channel divides. We did not paddle very far up the right fork, but if you take the left fork, you can paddle about two-thirds of a mile up to Mud Pond.

We might have chosen to call it Muck Pond. Your paddle can easily penetrate a foot or two into the organic ooze at the bottom of this wide, shallow pond. We saw a moose cow and calf browsing along the western shore, and if you spend any time at all here, you should see deer enjoying the copious vegetation.

81

Crooked Brook Flowage
Danforth

Maps: Maine Atlas, Map 45
    USGS Quadrangles, Brookton, Danforth, and Stetson
    Mountain

Area and Maximum Depth: 1,645 acres, 20 feet

Habitat Type: shallow, marshy pond

Fish: smallmouth bass, white perch, chain pickerel

Expect to See: ducks, beaver in the evening

Take Note: wind from the north or south can cause treacherous
    conditions; fire permits, Maine Forest Service, 207-827-1800

Getting There

From Danforth, turn off Route 1 onto Route 169. Cross the railroad track, go
0.3 mile, and turn left. Take another immediate left into the Danforth Town
Park and access.

Paddling out from the access maintained by the town of Danforth, you
will see numerous exposed stumps and rocks on the upper part of
Crooked Brook Flowage. This long and narrow section also funnels
wind. When the wind blows strongly out of the north or south, this
area can have deep swells and whitecaps.

Several unobtrusive houses perch along the bluff above the western shore near the lake's north end. They soon disappear from view,
and evidence of human presence abates until you get to the far end of
the southeast arm. Deciduous trees predominate here, with occasional
hemlocks and pines thrown in. Aspen, paper birch, red maple, and
alder grow throughout.

The two southern arms provide lots of coves to explore, many
with inlet streams. The shallow coves grow thick with cattails and other
marsh vegetation. Islands dot the surface of the southeast arm. We
saw dozens of feeding ducks behind the large alder-covered island in

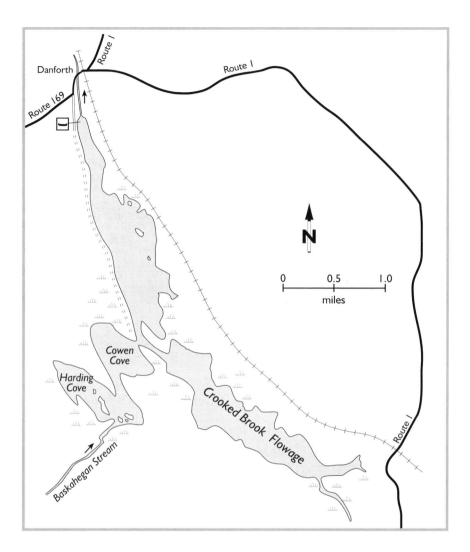

Harding Cove's huge marsh. You can paddle back up Baskahegan Stream about a hundred yards, until you run into a series of riffles cascading down into the flowage. The clear-cut alders make us wonder if the resident beavers are in training for paper-company careers.

82

Mattawamkeag Lake
Island Falls and T4 R3 WELS

> **Maps:** Maine Atlas, Map 52
>   USGS Quadrangles, Mattawamkeag Lake and Oakfield
> **Area and Maximum Depth:** 3,330 acres, 47 feet; river length,
>   4 miles
> **Habitat Type:** winding river and large, shallow, scenic lake with
>   islands
> **Fish:** white perch, smallmouth bass, chain pickerel
> **Expect to See:** loon, bald eagle, osprey, beaver
> **Take Note:** development on Upper Mattawamkeag Lake; fire
>   permits, Maine Forest Service, 207-435-7963

Getting There

Mattawamkeag River: From I-95, Exit 59, go east on Route 159, and turn right onto Route 2 west. Go 0.6 mile (0.6 mile), turn left onto Merriman Road, and go 1.6 miles (2.2 miles) to the access on the left (last road section in poor shape).

Upper Mattawamkeag Lake: From I-95, Exit 59, go east on Route 159, and turn left onto Route 2 east. Go 1.8 miles to the access on the right.

In addition to paddling Mattawamkeag Lake, one can also paddle the very scenic, fairly wide Mattawamkeag River. Except for a few fishermen, the river sees little boat traffic and is an excellent choice when the wind blows. Because of meanders, the wind has few lengthy straight sections to build up waves. When we paddled here one August afternoon and evening, three-foot swells greeted us out on the lake, while the river could only dish up a few ripples. In the lazy, late-summer current, the slightest breeze blew us back upstream.

From the Mattawamkeag River access, you wind around eastward toward the lake. Occasional weedy fields interrupt the wooded shoreline, and boulders line the shore in places, some protruding out into the river. Although the banks sport high tree diversity, silver maple grows

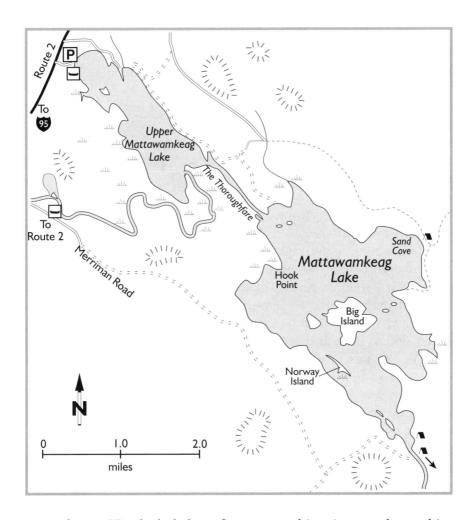

in profusion. Hemlock, balsam fir, spruce, white pine, northern white cedar, sugar maple, yellow birch, and many other species also grow along the fertile riverbank. Several potential campsites lurk under the dense canopy of large hemlock and other conifers.

Major game trails lead down to the water's edge, a white-tailed buck snorted at us from the dense undergrowth, and numerous beaver slapped the water with their tails as we paddled back to the access at sunset. In addition to flocks of cedar waxwings, several great blue herons, and a few osprey, we came very close to a mature bald eagle before it flew from its aerie. Rounding a bend, just past an alder swamp, we surprised an American bittern standing in some grass, and it exploded into the air with a squawk.

As you paddle out onto Upper Mattawamkeag Lake, emerging from an extensive stand of rushes, note the tiered fields on the distant hillside. After clearing the river mouth, paddle around to the right about a mile down through The Thoroughfare to Mattawamkeag Lake. Look carefully around the channel edges at what look like cattails for an occasional patch of sweet flag, with its three-inch-long dense flower spikes growing out of the stem's center. You can distinguish these leaves by their off-center midvein and spicy aroma. Horsetail, yellow pondlily, pickerelweed, and other aquatic plants crowd the edges of this shallow channel.

As you clear the channel, the forested Bug Islands appear, with emergent rocks all around, making this end of the lake quite scenic. Paddling out into the middle and looking back, you can see Mt. Katahdin off in the distance on a clear day. Compared with Upper Lake, little development crowds the shores of Mattawamkeag. Teddy Roosevelt stayed at the cottages on Hook Point. Primarily deciduous trees cover the heavily forested shoreline, but spruce, balsam fir, and other conifers grow farther back.

We saw lots of osprey on Mattawamkeag, along with four bald eagles—two adults and two immatures. They usually nest on Norway Island. Because of the abundant wildlife, the beautiful surroundings, and the views of the mountains in Baxter State Park, the state has protected much of the southern portion of the lake, including more than 7 miles of lakeshore and 126 acres on Big Island, home to a rare stand of old-growth timber.

～ 83 ～

Allagash Lake and Johnson Pond
T8 R14 WELS and T7 R14 WELS

MAPS: Maine Atlas, Map 55
    USGS Quadrangles, Allagash Lake and Tramway

AREA AND MAXIMUM DEPTH: 4,260 acres, 89 feet

HABITAT TYPE: clear, sand-bottomed lake

FISH: brook trout, lake trout

LOON LODGE: www.loonlodgemaine.com, 207-745-8168

PINEGREE FOREST PARTNERSHIP:
    www.newenglandforestry.org/projects/Pingree.asp; Pingree
    family and New England Forestry Foundation developed a
    762,000-acre conservation easement that includes protection
    for all of Johnson Lake and remaining shore of Allagash Lake
    not owned by the state

EXPECT TO SEE: moose, loon, bald eagle, osprey

TAKE NOTE: fill up with gas in Millinocket; entry streams low
    except in spring; no motors; camping only at authorized sites;
    no fire permits required

GETTING THERE

Getting to Allagash Lake is difficult. Follow directions under Caucomgomoc Lake to Round Pond. Use the *Maine Atlas.* We prefer the access at the Allagash Lake Ranger Station.

Allagash Lake Ranger Station: Approaching Round Pond coming from the Caucomgomoc Lake access (see Trip 76), cross the bridge over the Poland Pond outlet stream, go 0.3 mile to the right, and turn left to the Allagash Lake Ranger Station. Go about 2.5 miles to the end, and portage the last mile to the Ranger Station and the access. Loon Lake Lodge will ferry you in for a fee.

Johnson Pond: From Round Pond, after crossing the inlet, immediately turn left, and go north for about 5.7 miles to the Johnson Pond access. Paddle down the outlet and Allagash Stream; the outlet requires portages over beaver dams, and you may have to walk through shallow water.

Allagash Stream: Continue beyond Johnson Pond for about another 1.6 miles, and turn right. Go about 1.8 miles to the access where Allagash Stream nears the road. Paddle downstream to the lake. The road may be bad. The water may be low; the return trip, upstream, will be difficult.

Allagash Lake remains at the top of our list, one of our very favorite Maine lakes. While large and subject to heavy winds, the lake's geometry

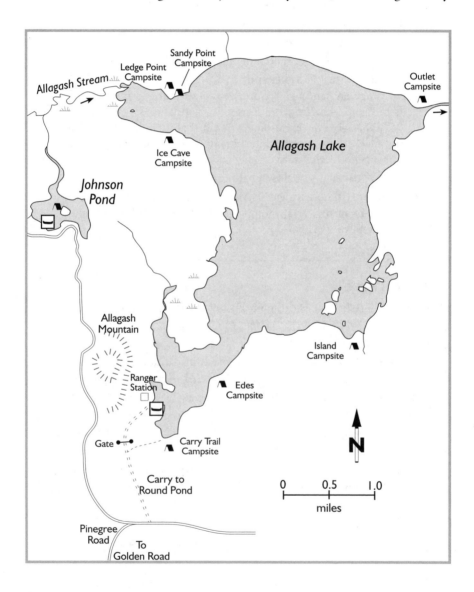

prevents waves from building up as much as on other large lakes in the region. And wind does not affect the large number of protected areas on the lake.

The lake nestles beneath Allagash and Poland mountains with deep, wild forest all around. Moss-covered rocks line the shores of marshy inlets. You will not hear motors or automobiles or even see float planes landing here, being the only Maine lake that excludes all motors, even electric.

Most people travel to this region to paddle the Allagash Wilderness Waterway, created by the state in 1966, and they usually stick to the far better known waters—Allagash River and the string of connected lakes—Chamberlain, Eagle, and Churchill—that some 10,000 paddlers travel each year. Far fewer take the side trip up Allagash Stream to Allagash Lake. Canoes may use up to 10-HP motors on most of the Allagash Wilderness Waterway, but not on Allagash Lake.

When we visited, we spent most of our time in the southern end, protected from the wind, which seems almost ever-present in northern Maine. Two permitted campsites occur at the south end: Carry Trail and Edes. Large groups traveling through Allagash Lake from Round Pond and Caucomgomoc use the Carry Trail Campsite pretty heavily. For small groups, we prefer Edes, with its sandy beach, nice fire ring, and several flat tenting sites.

The cove extending from the south end up to the northwest is simply fantastic. On an early morning paddle we watched deer browse along a grassy section of shoreline, and we surprised a young moose eating pond vegetation as we entered the small pond at the cove's north end. Along the way, take a close-up look at classic northern bog vegetation: tamarack, sphagnum, pitcher plant, sundew, cranberry, swamp rose, sheep laurel, leatherleaf, sweetgale, and—perhaps our favorite—the delicate rose pogonia orchid. We watched several families of common goldeneye along here, studied the graceful, ternlike flight of Bonaparte's gulls, saw osprey and a broad-winged hawk, and watched loons from enough distance to avoid disturbing them.

Farther north, mosses and polypody cover the granite boulders separating sections of thickly wooded shoreline. The clean water and generally sandy bottom support numerous freshwater mussels that filter out microscopic food particles. The many little coves and inlets provide lots of opportunity to look for deer, moose, otter, mink, and other mammals that call this home.

Common terns nest on a few rocky islands, and we saw three gull species: ring-billed, herring, and Bonaparte's gulls, the last an uncommon summer resident in New England.

As the shoreline curves west, you will reach the Ice Cave Campsite. A short hike up the hill takes you to several fascinating ice caves that can be quite refreshing on a hot, humid day. Bring a flashlight, and prepare to get a little muddy as you squeeze down into the cold granite caves, where ice lasts well into the summer.

Also explore the numerous islands, with one campsite, in the southeast corner. Not on a route into or out of the lake, this campsite sees fewer visitors. Campsites at the north end, near the lake's inlet and outlet, receive the heaviest use. Quite a few groups come through Allagash Lake as part of extended trips north on the Allagash River. During three days here, we saw an Outward Bound group and a large group from a wilderness-experience camp.

Johnson Pond

If you want to do some more extended exploring, take a trip up Allagash Stream and a side stream to Johnson Pond. This fairly wide, deep section of Allagash Stream entering at the northeast tip flows slowly, though you will encounter a few riffles. Watch for a narrow stream coming in from the left about 1.5 miles from the lake. You can make your way up this tiny stream, though you have to pull your boat up over several beaver dams and literally pull yourself through thick alder swamps in places.

After the last barrier, the stream opens up gradually into Johnson Pond. Initially, a grassy marsh surrounds this narrow section, but it widens out into a simply gorgeous pond about two-thirds of a mile across with a large island in the center. A sizable campsite exists on the island, with several separate campsites. Several outfitters store boats on the island for clients arriving by float plane, to outfit them for an Allagash River trip. When we visited here in 1994, merlins nested in a tree on the island. More common in northern Canada, these small, rare falcons look somewhat like small peregrine falcons.

Deboullie, Pushineer, Gardner, and Togue Ponds
T15 R9 WELS

MAPS: Maine Atlas, Map 63
USGS Quadrangles, Deboullie Pond and Gardner Pond

AREA AND MAXIMUM DEPTH: Deboullie Pond, 266 acres, 92 feet;
Pushineer Pond, 55 acres, 52 feet; Gardner Pond, 288 acres,
120 feet; Togue Pond, 388 acres, 85 feet

HABITAT TYPE: small, deep ponds

FISH: brook trout and blueback trout; salmon and lake trout in
Togue Pond

OUTFITTING: Pelletier's Campground, RR 1, Box 9, St. Francis,
ME 04774; 207-398-3208

RED RIVER CAMP: canoe rentals, accommodations, www.redriver
camps.com, 207-435-6000

EXPECT TO SEE: loon, osprey, bald eagle, raven, moose, beaver

TAKE NOTE: camping and use fees; no personal watercraft on
Deboullie Pond; fire permits, 207-435-7963

GETTING THERE

A high-clearance vehicle is recommended, though we traveled here in a VW
Rabbit and forded the stream into Pushineer Pond at low water.

From portage, heading north turn left off Route 11 past Dean's Motel,
and go about 1 mile. Turn left onto Paper Company Road, and go to the Fish
River Checkpoint (pay fees). Turn right onto Hewes Brook Road, and follow
the Red River Camps signs, about 26 miles to Pushineer Pond. Road conditions will vary, so a vehicle with some clearance is recommend

From Fort Kent, from the junction of Routes 11 and 161, go west on
Route 161 for 22.0 miles (22.0 miles), and turn left just past the Cross Rock
Inn. Go 0.4 mile (22.4 miles) to the St. Francis Checkpoint (pay fees). Go 7.0
miles (29.4 miles), turn left, following signs to Red River Camps and Public
Reserve Lands, and go 8.5 miles (37.9 miles) to the Togue Pond access on the
right. Go another 3.4 miles (41.3 miles) to the Pushineer Pond access.

Tucked away in the northern reaches of the Pine Tree State—and a long drive from southern Maine—this cluster of small but beautiful, deep ponds provides opportunity for a wonderful north Maine woods experience.

Deboullie, Gardner, and Togue ponds, along with about a dozen smaller ponds, nestle among steep mountainsides in a 20,000-acre section of Maine Public Reserve Lands. Because of the steepness, some significant patches of old-growth forest remain. Though timber harvesting in the reserve occurs on a limited basis, clear-cuts are reserved for habitat improvement.

Like most public reserve land in Maine, the state acquired Deboullie Management Unit primarily through land swaps with private landowners. When Maine divided its land into hundreds of six-mile-square townships and auctioned them off during the eighteenth and nineteenth centuries, each township retained a small portion of widely scattered land in public ownership. Beginning in the 1970s, the state consolidated many small parcels through swaps with private landowners. The state now has about 500,000 acres of public reserve lands in 29 units, ranging in size from 500 to 43,000 acres.

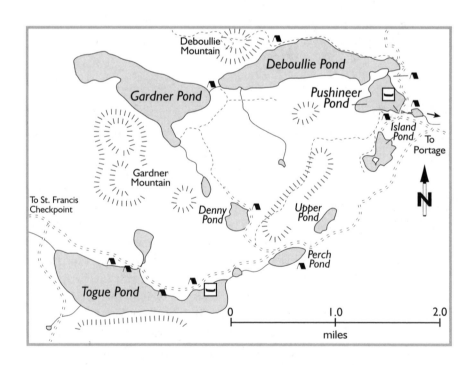

Deboullie and Pushineer Ponds

Put in on Pushineer Pond at the eastern end. A short section of stream connects Pushineer and Deboullie ponds, with a slight elevation rise into Deboullie. We paddled right through the two slight riffles from Pushineer, but beaver sometimes dam this stream.

In French, *deboullie* means "rock slide," and one can easily see the appropriateness of the name as you scan the pond. A large talus slope creeps down along the north shore, and several exposed cliffs look out over the pond. The cliffs and talus slopes here provide habitat for a number of rare plant species.

Deep woods surround Deboullie and Pushineer ponds; the shorelines grow thick with spruce, fir, birch, and red maple. Farther from shore yellow birch and sugar maple mix with conifers. Along the shore, look for mountain ash (in the rose family), whose flower clusters provide a nice spot of white during June, and whose bright orange-red berries add variety to early autumn colors. A dense band of alder crowds the shore, making disembarking difficult. The shore itself contains sharp chunks of granite. Use care paddling here, as these rocks can put deep scratches in your boat.

A wonderful, though steep, hike traverses from Deboullie Pond to the top of Deboullie Mountain and a fire lookout tower, which affords spectacular views of the north woods. The trail starts about two-thirds of the way up the pond's north shore—keep an eye out for a campsite and small stream that enters the pond here. The trail climbs about 800 feet in 0.6 mile, taking about a half hour. You can also reach this trail from the campsite area at Deboullie Pond's east end.

Deboullie, Pushineer, and Gardner ponds have native populations of threatened blueback trout (a char, in the same genus as brook and lake trout). Blueback char *(Salvelinus alpinus oquassa)*, found in only ten bodies of water in Maine, descend from anadromous, or sea-run, arctic char that became isolated from the sea during the most recent glaciation.

Gardner Pond

From the campsite on Deboullie's far-west tip, an easy portage trail leads into Gardner Pond. If Deboullie is beautiful, Gardner is spectacular, wild, and dramatic, with tall, jagged, basalt cliffs and large patches of scree. When we paddled here, ravens called from hidden cliff aeries below Gardner Mountain. A 42-acre patch of old-growth spruce-fir forest lies

The top of Deboullie Mountain offers a superb view of Deboullie and Pushineer ponds (right), and Black Pond (left).

between Gardner Mountain peak and the pond. (Deboullie Management Unit has five patches of old-growth spruce-fir forest totaling 153 acres.)

We watched an osprey dive for a fish and a bald eagle soar over Gardner Mountain. You can explore a few yards up the small inlet creek at the western end of Gardner Pond. Look here for the tiny sundew plant, whose sticky hairs trap small insects (see page 88 for more on carnivorous plants).

Togue Pond

Less visually striking and somewhat less remote than Deboullie and Gardner ponds, Togue Pond lies south of Gardner and closer by road to Route 161. Unlike Deboullie and Gardner, the state stocks Togue Pond with salmon to improve recreational fishing, and you will see motorboats here.

The shoreline of Togue Pond differs significantly from that of Deboullie and Gardner ponds. Northern white cedars, more prevalent here, extend right down to the water's edge, in contrast with the alder that dominates the shoreline of the more northern ponds.

Appendix:
Leave No Trace

The Appalachian Mountain Club (AMC) is a national educational partner of Leave No Trace, a nonprofit organization dedicated to promoting and inspiring responsible outdoor recreation through education, research, and partnerships.
The Leave No Trace program seeks to develop wildland ethics—ways in which people think and act in the outdoors to minimize their impacts on the areas they visit and to protect our natural resources for future enjoyment. Leave No Trace unites four federal land management agencies—the U.S. Forest Service, National Park Service, Bureau of Land Management, and U.S. Fish and Wildlife Service–with manufacturers, outdoor retailers, user groups, educators, orgnizations such as the AMC and the National Outdoor Leadership School (NOLS), and individuals.

The Leave No Trace ethic is guided by these principles:
- Plan ahead and prepare
- Travel and camp on durable surfaces
- Dispose of waste properly
- Leave what you find
- Minimize campfire impacts
- Respect wildlife
- Be considerate of other visitors

The AMC has joined NOLS–a recognized leader in wilderness education and a founding partner of Leave No Trace–as a national provider of the Leave No Trace Mater Educator course. The AMC offers this five-day course, designed especially for outdoor professionals and land managers, as well as a shorter two-day Leave No Trace Trainer course, at locations throughout the Northeast.

For Leave No Trace information and materials, contact:
Leave No Trace Center for Outdoor Ethics,
P.O. Box 997, Boulder, CO 80306
Toll Free: 800-332-4100, or locally, 303-442-8222;
Fax: 303-442-8217; www.LNT.org

Index to Bodies of Water

Get Out & Get Active with the AMC

With the AMC, you can participate in a wide variety of outdoor activities, connect with new people, and help to protect the natural world you love. Join us and each year you'll receive 10 issues of our member magazine, *AMC Outdoors*, which will keep you informed of environmental issues and outdoor recreation opportunities—including hiking, paddling, biking, and snowshoeing—across the Appalachian region. You'll also enjoy discounts on AMC skills workshops, lodging, and books. You can also join our Conservation Action Network (CAN) and help increase public influence on critical conservation issues *today* at www.outdoors.org/conservation/can.

AMC Outdoor Adventures

Develop your outdoor skills and knowledge through AMC Outdoor Adventures and Workshops! Learn to rock climb, snowshoe, or navigate by map and compass. From beginner backpacking and family canoeing to dogsledding and guided winter camping trips, you'll find something for any age or interest at spectacular locations throughout the Appalachian region, including the Maine Woods, White Mountains, Adirondacks, Catskills, and the Delaware Water Gap. For a full listing and to make your reservations, go to www.outdoors.org and click on Education.

AMC Books & Maps: Explore the Possibilities

AMC's hiking, biking, and paddling guides lead you to the most spectacular destinations in the Appalachian region. We're also your definitive source for how-to guides, trail maps, and adventure books. AMC Books: Explore the Possibilities at www.outdoors.org/publications.

AMC Destinations: Be Our Guest

From the North Woods of Maine to the White Mountains to the Delaware Water Gap, the AMC offers a wide variety of accommodations, from full-service lodges to backcountry huts, shelters, and campsites. Experience outdoor adventure at its best as our guest. Get trip suggestions, check lodging availability, and make reservations through our website, www.outdoors.org.

Contact Us Today

Appalachian Mountain Club
5 Joy Street
Boston, MA 02108
www.outdoors.org

AMC Book Updates

AMC Books strives to keep our guidebooks as up-to-date as possible to help you plan safe and enjoyable adventures. If after publishing a book we learn that trails are relocated or route or contact information has changed, we will post the updated information online. Before you hit the trail, check for updates at www.outdoors.org/publications/books/updates.

While hiking or paddling, if you notice discrepancies with the trail description or map, or if you find any other errors in the book, please let us know by submitting them to amcbookupdates@outdoors.org. We will verify all submissions and post key updates each month.

AMC Books is dedicated to being a recognized leader in outdoor publishing. Thank you for your participation.

AMC Books & Maps
5 Joy Street
Boston, MA 02108

About the Authors

ALEX WILSON is a writer living in Dummerston, Vermont. He is an avid paddler and has coauthored three other guides in this AMC Quiet Water series with John Hayes, covering all New England states and New York. He is president of BuildingGreen, Inc., the Brattleboro, Vermont-based publisher of Environmental Building News and other publications about green building. He is a widely published freelance writer for such magazines as Fine Homebuilding, Architecture, Landscape Architecture, the Journal of Light Construction, Solar Today, and Popular Science, and he has written several books on green building topics topics. He serves on the boards of the U.S. Green Building Council, the Conservation & Research Foundation, and the Vermont Chapter of The Nature Conservancy.

JOHN HAYES is a former professor of biochemistry and environmental science at Marlboro College in Marlboro, Vermont. He has paddled in Minnesota's Boundary Waters Canoe Area, in Georgia's Okefenokee Swamp, and in Florida's Everglades, as well as throughout the Northeast. John has written for *National Geographic Traveler* and has edited numerous solar energy conference proceedings. He was book review editor of the *Passive Solar Journal* and served as vice chair of the American Solar Energy Society. When not in the classroom, he often leads natural history field trips to Central America, Southwest deserts, the Rockies, the Everglades, Borneo, and Africa.

Notes

Notes

Notes

Notes